The Yaal Players
Memories of Old Jaffna

The Yaal Players
Memories of Old Jaffna

Vimala Ganeshananthan

Kumaran Book House
Colombo – Chennai

The Yaal Players
by Vimala Ganeshananthan ©

First published and printed by
Kumaran Book House and Kumaran Press Private Limited
No. 39, 36th Lane, Colombo 6, Tel.: 113097608, 112364550, Email: kumbhlk@gmail.com
Publication No.: 548
ISBN 978-955-659-3624
First Edition 2013
Reprint 2013

Online publishing and printing by
CreateSpace
This Edition 2014
ISBN 978-149-603-9477

In memory of Emily Gnanam - my mother

Preface

The idea and the motivation to write this book came to me when I read my mother's non-chronological accounts of her early life in Jaffna and later in Trincomalee. She had written these episodes in a few exercise books. It was written in her beautiful flowing hand and that writing could have been taught and nurtured only by the English missionary teacher of her school. These recollections were of her life in the early twentieth century. Her memories of her childhood and of her siblings were vividly recalled. So too the mundane, everyday life in her village was written of, but mostly spoken of. Though a greater part of her life was in the east, she would drift back to her life in Jaffna and the memories it held for her. The memory of her grandfather stood large in her life and less so her school and the places she visited with her family. She was a voracious reader and there was hardly a time when a book was absent in her hand or left face down on a nearby table. She perused the daily English newspaper from cover to cover and became savvy in her knowledge of the politics of Ceylon and its impact on the north and east. No less was her knowledge of world events. She was able to read even at the age of ninety-three. She had perfect eyesight and hearing. Whatever she read about she was keen to impart to us and to anyone who was willing to listen, even to her domestic help who was indifferent to her enthusiasm. My mother wrote so legibly and in old-fashioned good English. No colloquial terms were ever used by her. Her family members were always referred to as father, mother, sister, brother and other English terms of family. Her spelling of words was impeccable. She would boast that "spelling" was a separate examination paper within the main English paper of the Senior Cambridge examination. Her writings, however, had no

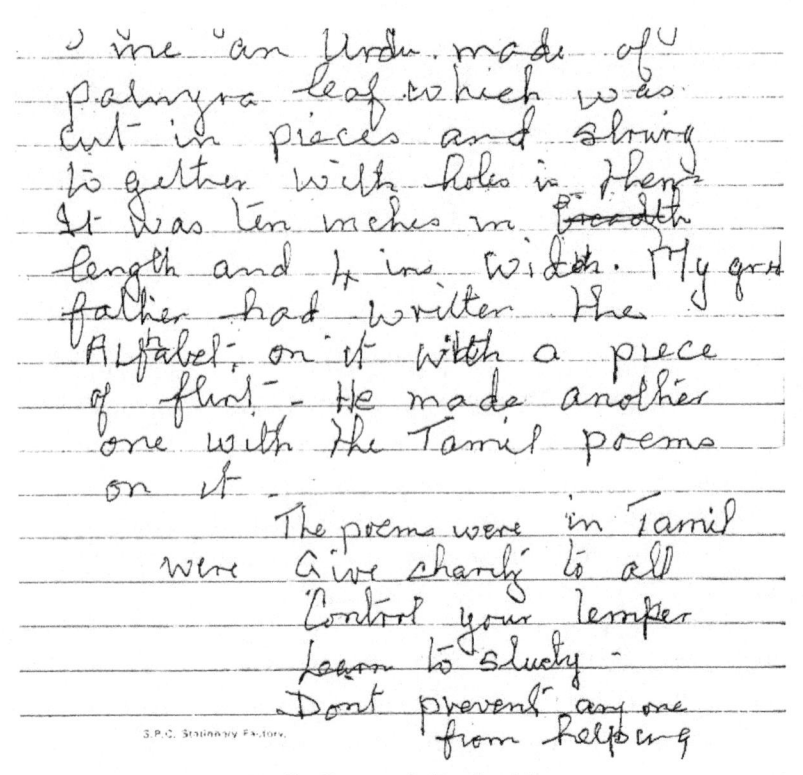

Emily Gnanam's handwriting

chronological order. This had a charm of its own and I have left them like that. Events in her village could be followed by the British era, a day in a sibling's life followed by the rule of the Dutch and an incident in her mother's life juxtaposed with the Portuguese period in the north. The last chapter contained Christian hymns that were recalled from memory. Dementia set in when she was ninety-four years old. She had visual hallucinations of her predeceased siblings and only spoke of them. She died after a short illness.

I am grateful to her for imparting her love of reading to her family. She would recommend or give books of her choice to be read by us. However, she had set ideas regarding the reading of books. She disapproved of reading *Wuthering Heights* during the Christmas season or *Forever Amber* when we were in our teenage years. She would not permit us to go to the local cinema on Sunday.

I have kept her written narrative and her spoken recollections as the nucleus of this book. To keep the same narrative style of my mother, the greater part of this book researched by me, is also written in the first person narrative as if my mother had written the story. The historical and political facts that were relevant to the north and the east before and during her lifetime were verified from innumerable books on Ceylon history. A detailed history of the north and east has not been written in any single book on the general history of Ceylon. This book has tried to give a sense of history, places visited and glimpses of the social life of the northeast.

Acknowledgement

I was fortunate to have known Christine Wilson, the well-known author of many books especially of Ceylon. She was one of the senior supervisors of the 'Wadiya Group,' a group of aspiring writers in English, of which I am a member. The members met with many supervisors once a month and read their works. I thank all the members for their critical and encouraging comments on my writing.

On my frequent visits to Christine, who was then in poor health, she would insist that I read my unrelated articles and then remarked that I should write a novel for which I felt I had no talent. When I read extracts of my mother's writings of her life and events in the North East, Christine turned to me and said, "There's your book." Her enthusiasm made me peruse my mother's writing and I began this book. Whatever I wrote, I read to her but it was not for long. Her demise was a loss of a friend and mentor.

Brenda Jayasinghe, a friend of mine, became my next mentor and critic of my work. She was a retired English Honours teacher. She was a typical pedagogue. She read my work with a red pen in her hand, crossed my 't's and minded my 'p's and 'q's. I was reduced to a schoolgirl doing my assignments. She was a great source of encouragement, with her insistence that I write a chapter a week. She enjoyed reading about Jaffna, as she had been a frequent visitor to the north. I had almost finished writing when she succumbed to a sudden brief illness and never recovered. It was not only a loss of a dear friend but a regret and a disappointment that she did not see the completed book.

I thank Ganesh my husband for his quiet encouragement, for his comments and for giving relevant books on Ceylon and the North East, whenever he came by them.

This book may have taken many more months to see print if not for Rupa Simithraaratchy, a close friend of mine of many years. She typed my quite illegible writing on her computer and she was a wizard at it. There can be no end of my appreciation of her as she typed, retyped and typed again, without a murmur.

I thank the assistant librarians of the reference sections of the Colombo Public Library and the Royal Asiatic Society for helping me with the relevant books on the history of Ceylon, with special reference to the North East, by many authors and which covered many eras.

A special thank you to Sandamali Wijeyanayake, the assistant librarian of the Royal Asiatic Society library, who ever so willingly placed on the reading table, almost every history book that even had a line on the history of the North East. In addition, she also gave me books containing photographs of old Ceylon. She would do this over many days and even over quite a few months. Her help was immeasurable.

I thank Mr. D.G. Newton for lending me the past numbers of the *Jaffna College* magazines.

I thank Platé Ltd. for copies of some photographs and Studio Times for a copy of a photograph of Swami Rock.

Wikipedia, the free encyclopaedia was a great source of information of the American Mission.

I thank Judy Pasqualge for editing this book and helping me with its title.

I am grateful and thankful to Kumaran Book House and their patience with me, in publishing this book

I thank my friends and relatives who prodded me on to finish this book.

Vimala Ganeshananthan

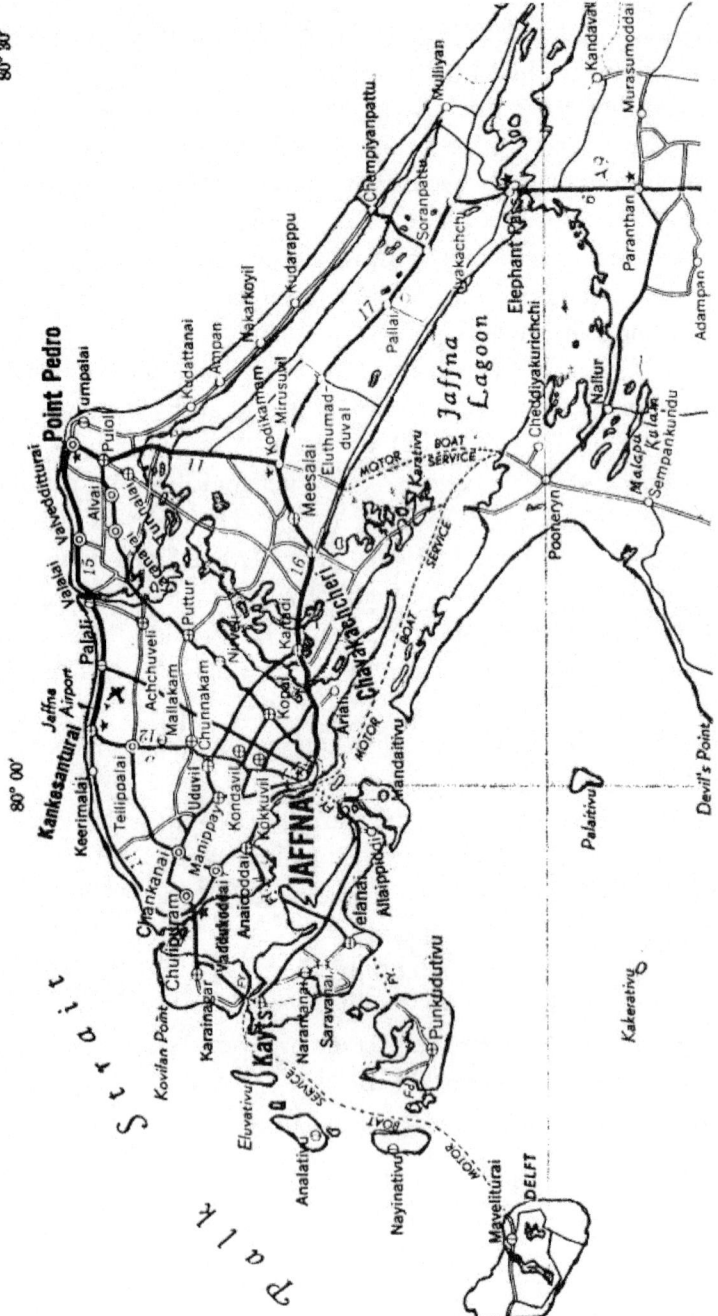

Map of the Jaffna Peninsula

Grandfather in his generosity was also a godfather to us. We were still living in Karainagar. My father, having been a teacher at the American Mission School on one of the islands around Jaffna, left for Malaya to follow better prospects of jobs and remuneration. His brothers were already there and encouraged him to come over. Grandfather had built us a house in that large compound. Houses built for his sons and their immediate family members were also in that compound.

We needed a separate house of our own as there were seven of us children, mother and my maternal grandmother. Grandfather took over the running of the house, ready with advice and finances. He was large as life to me. I trailed in his footsteps whenever I could. My grandaunts had left home after marriage, each taking with her a handsome cash dowry instead of land or house. Land was not given as they would be staying with the in-laws, who would have given a portion of their land to the sons.

It was 1907, I was four years old and grandfather spoke about the American Mission School in our village that I would soon be going to. He described it to me, to get me interested in it. The school was two hundred yards distant from us and had the usual two rectangular buildings of schools. The one for the younger children was of brick, mud and cadjan thatched roof. There were half walls with two gaps that served as entrances. The floor was earthen with fine white seasand strewn generously over it. At one corner stood three or four rows of desks and tables, for those who had graduated to Standard Three. I was quite excited about going there.

He prepared my school materials months before I started schooling. He made me two *erdus*, palmyrah frond strips with writing on them. He also bought me a slate and pencil. I watched him prepare the *erdus*. He cut the palmyrah fronds into strips, ten inches long and four inches wide. He took two of these, cleaned them smooth, and then strung them together with a string passed through holes made on one side. He took a steel flint and carved out the first twelve basic letters of the Tamil alphabet on one strip.

On the other he wrote extracts of Tamil poems. I remember them even today as he made me memorize them months before school.

"Give charity to all."

"Control your tongue."

"Learn to study."

"Don't prevent anyone from helping you."

I looked forward to school as I, the fifth of a family of seven, was left much to myself and walked with grandfather or even aimlessly alone in that large land of ours where everything we needed was grown. I was excited as the first day of school dawned. Grandfather dressed me for school. When I look back, I feel embarrassed at what I wore that morning. A white material with a green border was wrapped round my waist and it swept my ankles. That was all! I had nothing above it! My feet were bare too. Years later when I questioned my mother as to why she didn't dress me better she said nonchalantly, "What difference did it make? Your four-year-old cousin Kumar and you were the same above the waist." It was worse when an aunt remarked that Meena came topless but in a sari, the end of which was thrown over her bosom and then tucked at her waist in front, to work in the garden. She was of a *Nalavar* caste, low in society; she had to come like that because of her caste. I was more horrified that I went to school topless.

Holding my grandfather's very large hand and armed with the two *erdus*, the slate and its pencil, I walked confidently to school. I must have been two feet tall but felt taller and straighter than a palmyrah. The *erdus* were not needed. I wondered whether he wanted to impress the teacher with them. There was no modern belief that a parent or grandparent should stay near the school for reassurance of the child. Grandfather patted my head and let go of my hand. I strode into school with the others of my age group, almost all topless, ready to get hold of the throat of the academic world but found myself submissively sitting on the sand.

The bell rang. The female teacher came in, modestly dressed in a light blue sari, close necked blouse, midriff and bosom hidden. She greeted us with a soft "Vannakam." The greeting was shouted back at her. This greeting meant the start of lessons. Learning was by rote. It started with the alphabet. The teacher vocalized one letter and we shouted it back to her. I could have shouted all the letters at her, so well was I prepared by my grandfather. So it went on, letters and numbers shouted and all the children shouting them back at her. The attention on her was so concentrated, we didn't hear the shouts of the other classes separated from us by an imaginary line!

I always wondered whether the letters were pushed into the brain by sheer volume of noise or by the teacher looking intently at the opening and closing of so many mouths, satisfied that all was understood well.

To my great disappointment the slate was not used for the first few weeks. We practiced drawing the letters and numbers on the beautiful white sea sand that was heaped in front of us. We had no idea of time. School ended when the teacher said "Vannakam" again. Armed again with *erdus* and slate I had to trek back the two hundred yards home. It was blazing hot, the sun shimmered in front and burnt our soles. We rushed from one shady tree to the next, cooling our heels five minutes under each tree. I got back hot, tired and with burning feet. I was grateful for the clay pot of water and tumbler near the gate of our home. The metal tumbler had a beaked nose. It was difficult at my age to use this type of tumbler as the water had to be poured into the mouth from the beak-nosed end. It was taboo to put the lips on the rim of the tumbler. I held it up and poured the water, most of it out than in my mouth. I went in with my cloth soaked and my hair and chest wet. To draw attention away from the mess, I told grandfather that nobody had asked for the *erdus* though I waved them around wanting someone to be curious about it. Nobody had been. However, I hugged grandfather for making them to make me feel important. I always regretted that I didn't preserve them, though they were so common at that time. A few years later when I knew about the topless local women that denoted their caste, I whispered to grandfather and asked him whether I was born low in my family.

I hardly saw my older siblings at school. Their classrooms were in a different building. They had the privilege of desks, chairs or long tables and benches. I met them at lunch when they came in later than I, looking important and full of knowledge. My eldest sister Chellam was very petite, pretty and light skinned. The younger sister was not so pretty but vivacious. She had a mind of her own. Nesam was fearless too. She would make wonderful repartees in any argument against any one of us. Some of these were mere wind and words. She was very much like my father who had a fantastic vocabulary and was very vociferous. He could be harsh in speech too. She found in him a formidable foe in an argument.

Nesam was in a middle grade and the school had its annual sports-meet. One of the events of the meet was the 'Needle and Thread' race. Believe it or not, Nesam partnered a boy for this race! The year was 1910, when this was unheard of. I am sure that even if there was a girl available for that race, she would still have been bold enough to partner a boy. She and her partner won the race! The news of this was relayed by a sneak of a neighbour to my father, who was back from Malaya on his yearly holiday. A happy and smiling sister came home. I feared for her. Father was ready with a leather strap in his hand. She may have run off if only she had seen him earlier. He got hold of her and gave her five lashes on her back. I cried in fear and in empathy with her, but not a tear did she shed. Mother stopped him beating her further.

She walked to the back of the house and met a grandaunt in grandfather's home, who must have rubbed her buttocks with oil! I didn't see her that night but to my amazement I saw her on the top of the roof the next morning, replacing some broken tiles and my mother standing below, pleading with her to get down and let Ramu do that job! She gave the impression that racing with a male and climbing the roof like a male were common occurrences in the village! When my father was getting his bags ready to go back to Malaya, he told my sister that if she ever did anything unexpected again, he would give her in marriage to a low-caste boy! Nesam, I presumed, would not care a hoot if he did so!

It was a couple of years later that I asked my grandfather the reason for the variations of skin colour among us siblings, the two older ones having a light coloured skin like grandfather's. He smiled, but now when I think of it, he might have smirked. He then told me that I should know some history. "Our earliest light skinned invaders were the Portuguese. Before they arrived in 1505, there were Portuguese missionaries who had already converted the coastline Hindu fisher folk to Roman Catholicism. In 1501 there were four main kingdoms in Ceylon – Kotte, Sitawake, the smaller Raigam and Jaffna. The king of Kotte, Bhuvenekabahu, invited the Portuguese to help him fight the Arab traders who were getting the better of the spice trade, and also to protect him from the two southern kingdoms. The wind and the wave brought the Portuguese, but the cinnamon trade planted them firmly here.

Jaffna had no spices. Puviraja Pandaram was the king of Jaffna, who also ruled Mannar as well as the islands, oversaw the Vanni, and his economy flourished with the pearl fisheries from Mantota to Kalpitiya, and its trade from Mannar to Tuticorin. There was also a wonderful elephant trade. Elephants were brought from the south and the Vanni through Elephant Pass to Jaffna, and then they were sent abroad via Urukuthurai, later called Kayts. Each elephant was taxed, with more being paid for a tusker. Jaffna was strategically placed on the trade route to South India, especially along the Malabar Coast. The Malabar pirates and their Jaffna counterparts became rich by pirating and claiming sunken ships with their contents. The harbour for the pirates was Nedunthurai, now Delft.

The Portuguese eyed the pearl trade of Mannar. The romance between the king of Kotte and the Portuguese was on the wane, the king wanting to get rid of them. A name remembered in Jaffna was Viceroy Bragnea, who tried to conquer Jaffna in 1520. He was aware that mercenary soldiers were arriving in Kotte via Jaffna. This was at the request of the king of Jaffna to the Zamorin of Tanjore. There was an urgency for the Portuguese to conquer Jaffna. The viceroy and his forces conquered Mannar, but were beaten back by Jaffna, again thanks to the Zamorin of Tanjore. The king survived, but to maintain peace he had to pay tribute to the Portuguese who ruled from Mannar. Taxes on elephant went on as before, the king very cunningly taxing the Portuguese for every elephant that went through mainland Jaffna. The king was furious too at the conversion of his Hindu subjects to Roman Catholicism, whether forced or otherwise, and killed quite a number of the converts. The pearl trade flourished under the Portuguese but the pearl fishery was getting exhausted.

General Mendonca was another name remembered in Jaffna. The ruler of Jaffna was killed by Mendonca in battle. The administration of Jaffna was always in the hands of the Vellala mudilayars, adigars and thalaivars. The adigars were the officials who collected the revenue. The same type of administration of the former days was continued under the Portuguese. The Portuguese set up a puppet king, Ethiramanasingham, a nominal Christian. He covertly helped the king of Kotte by allowing passage again to the South Indian soldiers sent by Tanjore. He too cunningly taxed the Portuguese on each elephant going through Jaffna to Kayts.

With the death of Ethiramanasingham, Chandrasekeram alias Sangili usurped the throne over his nephew, the rightful heir, and also over a Catholic mudaliyar whom the Portuguese preferred. He made the same mistakes as his predecessor, killing the converts. In 1543 Alfred de Sousa with a large force landed in Nedunthurai, and which was named Ilha Das Vacas, the Isle of Cows, by the Portuguese. It was a strategic place from which to wage battle. Sangili survived by bribing the Portuguese with gold coins and money. Money was first used in Jaffna instead of gold and barter. Cash was in *Cakran*, *Rees* and *Zerafins*. Sangili had made an alliance with Veediya Bandara, king of Kotte. He made the alliance stronger by sending two of his daughters to marry into the royal family.

During the rule of the Portuguese their title 'Dom' was the rage in Jaffna. Vellalas and others who were not honoured by the title bought it. Sangili managed to rule, but again foolishly killed six hundred to seven hundred Christian converts in Mannar. This was in 1544. From then on the Portuguese were determined to get rid of him. Sangili with the help of the Telugu warriors fought the Portuguese, but when defeat was inevitable, Sangili burnt his palace, took refuge in the Nallur temple and starved the Portuguese within the Jaffna Fort, but it was to no avail. Finally he fled to Elephant Pass and became vassal to the Portuguese paying his dues in money and elephants. In fact, tuskers were specified and insisted on. He promised to convert to Roman Catholicism. Finally General Oliviera Noronho fought Sangili and his mercenaries and defeated him. Sangili tried to escape to India with his family, cash and jewels, but he was intercepted and killed. Money and jewels were the rewards given to Noronho's soldiers. By now the Dutch had taken the eastern coast and were a threat to the Portuguese. The Portuguese sent the younger members of Sangili's family to religious monastic orders in India, to ensure that no member of the younger generation would claim the Jaffna throne. To prevent the mudaliyars, who were once powerful with the local ruler, becoming turncoats and inciting the troops to revolt, the Portuguese were settled in Jaffna, with a gift of land.

The king of Kotte laid claim to Jaffna citing marital alliance. A Christian monarch was recommended and Dom Jaco, nephew of Bhuvenekabahu who fled to Goa after conversion, was thought of, but this was not to be as Dom Jaco died there. A Brahmin claimed the throne promising to be converted, but Oliviera Noronha became the overall ruler of Jaffna. In 1560, fifty years after the arrival of the Portuguese in Ceylon, many of them lived within the Tamil community. An officer and his soldiers were sent to our village. They had come to Jaffna with no wives or family. In time, a few light and dark-skinned members appeared in the village. In a few years' time skins became lighter, then light, and dark members of families appeared in the village depending on the combination of blood of dark and light partners. That was the reason why two of your siblings are dusky and the others light skinned," remarked my grandfather, patting my head in sympathy.

Emily Gnanam would suddenly stir from her catnap in the armchair and ask what day it was and which year it was. She asked the same questions almost daily. Really, it had no relevance to her. She had forgotten yesterday and what she had eaten a few hours ago. "Did I have lunch?" was a constant query. Dementia was setting in. She was ninety-four years old.

When times of alertness set in, large structures like fences and palmyrah trees in her village compound became dominant in her memory. "You should have seen the fence around grandfather's *valavu*, the compound. The house, the paddy field, the vegetable plots and the fruit trees were enclosed by this fence." The fence was almost sacred to a householder and made sacrosanct. Though everyone desired more land, it cannot be ill-gotten by shifting fences. If trespass was suspected there would be a war of words and then physical body blows, irrespective of family relationships.

Grandfather, she said, had a live fence round his property of a few acres. The fence was always green and pretty. It was made by planting the young saplings of the local Tulip and Glyceridia plants along and within the boundary of the property. They were planted

A Live Fence

very close to each other and when they put out leafy branches the fence looked so very pretty. They were then laced together tightly with ropes. Like other fences in the village they became goat, cow, chicken, dog and peek-proof but this fence never proved to be one-hundred percent peek-proof. Each and every villager knew the lives, loves and scandals of their neighbours. If the branches were deftly pulled apart we had a good view and heard their conversation and gossip easily. When the branches grew over six feet tall, they were clipped and fed to the goats. Most householders had at least a couple of goats with their kids at any given time. No vegetation was ever wasted in a dusty, dry and arid land. This type of fence was the most economical. Dried plants and old ones were pulled out and replaced by the ever-present young Tulip and Glyceridia plants.

Of all the trees within this long rectangular fence, grandfather was most fond of the clump of palmyrah trees, no more than fifteen of them, in a corner of the garden. He took greater pains, however, over the small plots of paddy and the vegetable garden. The palmyrah needed no care. Actually it's a weed palm with fanlike fronds, commonly called the fan palm and grew anywhere, even on cracks in concrete stones. However, it was called the father of Jaffna and coconut its mother. "The palmyrah is the heavenly tree," so said uncle Sivam. It provided food, drink, fencing, fertilizer, medicine and timber. The Brahmins called it the 'devil's tree' because of its toddy. However, uncle Sivam relished the elixir that came from it – the fermented toddy. The longer the fermentation, the greater the potency. Grandfather would rent a few trees to the toddy tapper of the *Nalavar* caste. I saw him mostly from the months of January to July, the right time to tap the palmyrah blooms. These blooms would only be seen after twenty years of growth, when the tree was at its tallest.

I must have been about seven years of age. It must have been a Saturday or a holiday. I saw the toddy tapper come in. The *verti*, the cloth that would normally be at ankle length, was abruptly raised, the front portion taken behind between the legs and tucked at the back to convert it to a respectable loin cloth. He wore a breastplate of leather as the trunk of the palmyrah was so rough and his ankles were held together by a circlet of palmyrah fibres covered again with leather. His life depended on this circlet. He would have four to six prepared clay pots, tied round his waist. He went up using the buttresses formed by the bases of fallen fronds. They gave a good foothold. They stuck out at regular intervals and were so convenient for him. I would watch fascinated as he embraced the trunk and raised his feet and put them on two buttresses above and then stood up on them. He embraced the trunk one step higher, repeated the whole procedure and went up higher and higher. I would get giddy looking up to see him getting smaller in size and then he disappeared into the crown of fronds. He had disappeared to bruise the young blooms of the inflorescence held within the spathes. He descended the tree without the pots. I was relieved that he got down safe. He repeated this whole process on the trees that he rented out from grandfather. He climbed each tree individually as no ropes could be tied between trees as in the case of tapping coconut trees. The palmyrah is not cultivated at regular intervals and the stems were too rough. The tapping of trees was done over several days. The first tree was climbed up again after three to four days, quite early in the morning. This time he carried a larger pot or a gallon container.

There was great anticipation within the household when the elixir was brought down. All were ready with scroll or cone-like cups made of tender palmyrah fronds, the *pila*. The first draw of the pot was the sweet toddy, which was enjoyed more by the females than the males. It was poured into these leafy cups and sipped long with great relish. The share of toddy and rent was paid promptly by the tapper to grandfather. Most of the toddy given to grandfather was left to ferment to be drunk later as an alcoholic beverage, by the males and a sprinkling of women too, before the midday meal. It was soporific after the meal. There was a saying in our village, "The children drink milk, the men toddy and the women nothing." This was not quite true as the women too enjoyed the sweet toddy and even the fermented drink.

Most of the toddy was sold by the tapper to the tavern. Many members of many castes rubbed shoulders in the tavern which seemed to have levelled the caste barrier for a short period of time.

It made all equal in their bonhomie or belligerence. The higher caste would excuse it as not bad, permissible and temporary. Everything was explained and excused. Such was the power of the palmyrah toddy. Caste was re-established with sobriety.

When I was in my early teens our family acquired relatives from the mainland, even up to the village between Inuvil and Tellippalai. There was a paucity of Christians in Karainagar. The American Mission had spread its wings to build a church, its oldest, and a school attached to it, at Tellippalai. There then began a small community of Christians. When a spouse was acquired in that village a larger number of relatives too came into the family. Maniks, a short version of Manikalingam, was one such acquired relative. It was always the best of times for Maniks. He was the youngest in his family, pampered and spoilt by his widowed mother. His older brothers had attended the mission school Union College and got certificates equal to the Senior Cambridge. With these in hand, they obtained the middle grade clerical jobs in the Malayan Railways run by the British who were at that time the colonizers of most of the Southeast Asian countries. The brothers sent money regularly to the mother and, in fact, the 'Money Order' economy flourished in Jaffna as there were many from Jaffna abroad.

Maniks left school early with no paper qualification, not even the equivalent of the Junior Certificate. From late teens to manhood he looked for respectable jobs, relying on his impeccable caste. Caste was just not enough for jobs. He enjoyed loafing in the village and came back home for his meals. He refused manual work, as the latter was for the low-caste people, he told his mother. He took a great liking for the sweet toddy that was brought down from the palmyrah trees in his garden. He saw members of the caste of toddy tappers climb down with agility, bringing down the pots of toddy. They gave him his share of the toddy and rent for the trees. From drinking 'sweet' toddy to the 'fermented' was a short step, and then a shorter step to the tavern where it was plentiful. It was easy to go from one tot to many. The more Maniks drank, the closer he rubbed shoulders with all castes and the more generous was the sharing of tots and 'bites' between them. Tavern and the market made a temporary memory loss of castes! Maniks usually came home late afternoon, had his generous portion of lunch, burped the gas of toddy, stretched himself on a colourful mat in the open verandah and snored away the rest of the alcoholic breaths which were blown off by the breeze of the palmyrah fronds. When sober, which was very rare, he would be charming, related anecdotes, tales and jokes picked off the tavern. He had a way with people and they would listen and enjoy his company. He was also generous with the little money he had.

His brother on holiday to his village saw Maniks' dissipation. He persuaded him to start a book store. The rent was paid, books stacked, and Maniks sat behind the desk and an assistant sold the books. He did well. But Maniks had no idea of business and no inkling of cost, sale and profit. He boasted of his profit but drank away the cost, sale and profit of his business. The store could not be renewed. His mother persuaded her son abroad to send money again. With advice, pity and generosity the money was sent again. The book shop recommenced. He could have lived happily ever after except that he again drank away the cost, sale and profit. Pity and money stopped coming. At dusk, when he was relatively sober, he would visit a few relatives, but his visit would only end when the ballast train from KKS to Jaffna tooted and passed his village at ten at night. He had so much to say! Marriage was tried, but it did not cure the alcoholism. His wife and son soon went back to her village. He would have gone the way of all alcoholic flesh, but his name was not forgotten due to one incident. By this time he went from dizzy and delightful self to a drunk, garrulous, disorderly and then onto a disgusting self, when villagers and family too avoided him. If they saw him drunk and almost falling into a haystack by the side of a lane they quickly crossed to the other side of it as if Maniks had become a low caste man to be avoided.

Once coming home drunk and late at night, he fell into the deep well in his garden. There was a splash and a cry for help. The members of the family and relatives living in the same *valavu* rushed to the well, and in the light of the hurricane lanterns found Maniks immersed in the water, and clinging to a cemented buttress jutting from the wall of the well. His mother arrived, absolutely fed up with him. A huge strong basket woven from palmyrah fronds that could hold twenty gallons of water was brought from the well sweep of a larger well and was tied to the rope of the pulley of the well and let down the well where Maniks was. Maniks, now sober, climbed into it. While pulling him up, the rope broke and he fell again with a greater splash. His mother, at her wit's end, screamed, "Do not pull up this Saturn-born alcoholic son of mine. Let him drown in the well."

Stronger rope was tied to the basket and Maniks came out, the water displaced from the container soaking him. It seemed to pour out of him. He was sober, but not wiser.

What made this tale of the incident live long after him was his own narration of the incident. "It was moonlight and I came home a little drunk. Even then I could close my eyes and walk from the gate to my house. For my ill-luck the moon suddenly hid behind clouds and darkness fell. I kept walking and tripped over the small bund of the well. I felt myself going down. As I was going down I said to myself, 'O Ho, the well,' and then I fell with a splash. I could hear the fuss made by the family when they pulled me out. By the way, I fell twice because my cousins had no sense to see or feel the tattered condition of the rope! If not for the moon hiding behind clouds, I would have gone home straight from gate to door."

The incident was repeatedly recalled by many with great glee, as the well was at an angle of forty-five degrees and a distance of fifty feet from the gate. He simply didn't go straight from gate to door! The nieces and nephews and later the grandnieces and grandnephews remembered him as the "O Ho, the well uncle Maniks." The tale is related even now, and will be for many years.

I see in my memories the large house in the *valavu*, the compound. The largest house in Karainagar was the one built by my paternal great-grandfather Pillai, a shortened form of a long name I presume? He was considered one of the richest villagers in the village. My great-grandfather being the only son inherited the entire twenty acres of land.

Grandfather was the eldest of four boys and a younger sister. The sister after her marriage moved to her in-laws home and took with her the customary cash and jewels, the cash to help build a home in her in-law's land. Grandfather's house was twenty yards away from our house, which was also built by him. Our house was of modest proportions though of the same design.

In my younger days in the village, I would spend more time in his house, enjoying his company. Grandmother, Manonmani, and a widowed niece Kamalam were the others there.

My grandmother had a tanned complexion and was slim and tall. She was an introvert, in absolute contrast to my grandfather who was very talkative and demonstrative in his affection.

Grandmother and her niece Kamalam ran the household efficiently and quietly. I would give my mother a dozen excuses to visit grandfather a dozen times a day. I would use the rear entrance as other family members often did, when visiting grandfather or other uncles and aunts in the same compound. I would climb and tread the long but shallow four steps to reach the rear door which was kept open during the greater part of the day. The door of heavy satin wood was very high, two panelled and opened it seemed to space, air and breeze. The front door seen straight across from the rear one was invariably closed by a stout cross bar. Thieves were few, but the dust was plentiful, and would sweep through the tall doors, to be layered on the concrete floors. At first glance the whole of the interior would look like an elevated rectangle of smooth cemented floor only. As I walked further in I would see a central rectangular-shaped drop, the courtyard from this floor to the sandy ground. The cemented part was twelve feet by four feet wide on the sides and a little less in breadth at the front and at the rear. The doors were at the front and rear. It was great fun to sit at the edge of the floor and dangle my legs over the courtyard. The courtyard was covered with fine sea sand that covered the brown earth beneath it. We as children would go down into the courtyard, feel the sand with our feet and pour it through our fingers. It looked like white sugar. White sugar was first seen by us when it was brought by my maternal grandmother on her return from Malaya. She had five sons working there! Usually we used brown sugar or local jaggery to sweeten our hot drinks.

The courtyard was open to the sky, and the breeze poured in and swirled in the open spaces around it. The roof was high and a ceiling was unheard of. Compared to this spacious central section, the rooms small and insignificant opened on to the elevated cemented portions which surrounded the central courtyard. They appeared like patios to the rooms. The door opening into each room was narrow, not too high and two panelled. It opened into a small room with windows also of two panels. The room had a bed, a wooden box to keep fresh clothes in and a long wooden strip of wood with hooks, secured to a wall, to hang the used clothes. It seemed ascetic. There were six such rooms, four on the sides and two that opened on to the rear end of the courtyard.

Invariably, in each room a collection of palmyrah leaf woven mats, each rolled on itself, stood in a corner of the room. Sometimes a table was found in the room, but most often not. The house was termed '*Naatchara*' House, which meant it had four portions. Families were large and rooms were never in excess. Invariably two to three of the same-sex siblings occupied one room. Curtains for doors and windows were never hung as they interfered with the flow of air and breeze, which was welcomed in the hot weather that became only hotter. Looking back, what struck me most was the paucity of furniture in that large cemented place. There were only the essentials – a square table and four chairs made of satinwood, heavy and squat, a few straight-backed rattan-covered chairs and of course the easy chair on which grandfather would loll when he was not in the garden. The rattan of that chair was replaced more often than that of the others.

One room at the back was always kept closed. Much later I was told the secret of that room. Any post-pubertal female who was considered unclean by the occurrence of her menstrual period was isolated in that room. Aunt Kamalam who had similarly used a room like this said she was not only considered unclean but temporarily low caste too, which meant that the kitchen and well were taboo to her. There was only a table with a plain wooden chair, a bed, a clay jug of water, an aluminium tumbler with a beaked rim and a few personal clothes. All these articles had to be washed at the end of the unclean period which was about four days. She would then be taken to the well and water poured on her by another relative. Till then, food and water were brought to that room and handed to her at the door. When she finally left it for her bath, the room was washed. The linen and clothes were washed by the washerman of the '*Kudimai*', the lower householder caste. Incense was lavishly strewn on burning coals, held in long-handled brass bowls so as to drive out all uncleanliness and probably the mosquitoes. This practice took many decades to be discarded. Even my cousins followed it.

When I was going on to my eighth year of age, my mother and her mother were excitedly talking, holding a letter from abroad. My grandmother was a lucky sister of five brothers. They, after their education in Jaffna Central, obtained a certificate, the FA – that is First in Arts, which made them eligible to read a degree usually at the university in the Madras Presidency or less frequently in the University of Calcutta. These colleges had a steady stream of ambitious young men coming from Jaffna. My uncles had not the means to go to a university. Instead they found the readily available, well-paid clerical jobs in the British railway and the postal departments in Malaya very tempting. One by one they left Jaffna for Malaya. Transport was by bullock cart, a journey of three weeks to the harbour in Colombo, and then by modest cargo cum passenger steamer to Malaya. They told me that they had never met any southerner or stepped on the roads of Colombo. The journey was from Jaffna to the steamer. The uncles abroad bought a large house in the heart of Jaffna town. It was on Second Cross Street. The naming of roads was so unimaginative. First to Fifth Cross streets joined two parallel roads, one being the Main Street. The names of roads denoted the places they led to. There was the KKS road, the Point Pedro road, the Kandy road, the Nallur road, the Manipay roads, and so on. There was also the Temple road, leading to the temple or Kachcheri road leading to the kachcheri! There was no road celebrating any colonizer then, nor any change of names thereafter. A few buildings in Christian schools alone were named after the missionaries. So prosaic and practical was the northerner who thought convenience more important than illustrious names.

The house that uncle Nalli and his brothers bought in Jaffna was old, beautiful and had been designed by the Dutch. We were offered the use of this house so that my mother could educate us in an English-language school, Vembadi, which was within walking distance of the house. The uncles abroad thought we should become sophisticated and English speaking instead of languishing in our village. We were thrilled by the news but I was sad too as it meant leaving our home and more so leaving grandfather in Karainagar. I was like grandfather's shadow, that blended with his, at noon and it would be hard to be without his constant presence. All this exciting news was in the letter that my mother held.

This news saw us travelling by boat to the mainland, then by buggy cart to Jaffna town passing Vaddukodai with its large school buildings of Jaffna College. I was intrigued as to why the house was titled 'Dutch.' It was large and airy with such thick walls. Every door and window looked large. After a cursory look over of the house we turned back home. Getting back seemed longer as the day was hotter. The sea on the return journey sparkled too with the heat.

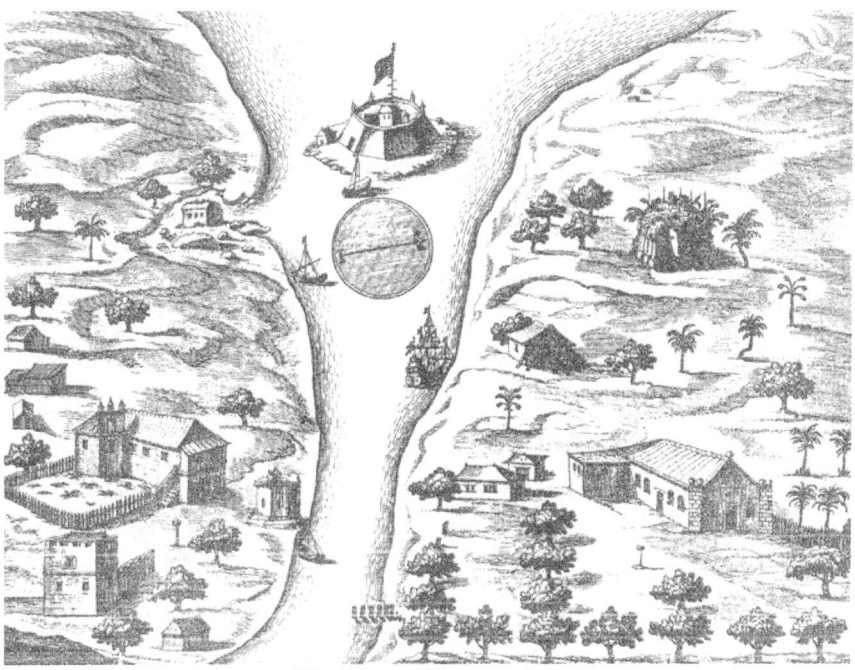

The Fort of Hammenhiel

When I questioned grandfather about the Dutchness of the house, he broke forth into history again. I would shift from one leg to another but my impatience didn't deter him at all. He told me that the Dutch took Batticaloa in 1632 led by General de Veert. Rajasinghe II who ruled in Kandy wanted to get rid of the Portuguese, so he invited the Dutch East India Company in 1631.

The Portuguese too were waning in power and out of favour with the king. The Nayakkar dynasty ruled in Kandy. The king now controlled the cinnamon trade. The Dutch took Trinco after three years. They had no clue as to what was available in the east. They thought it was cinnamon! The king seemed to have chosen between two evils and replaced one foreigner with another. The Dutch seemed a lesser evil. The popular adage was green pepper exchanged for ginger. In spite of agreements and covenants, the Dutch aimed at controlling lands that produced spices. Colombo was captured from the Portuguese but in no way was it given back to the king. They stole more land and pretended that they protected them for the king. The Dutch bartered the east for land in the south as the king wanted access to the sea for trade. That was why when Robert Knox arrived in Kottiyar Bay, he was arrested by the Kandyans and taken to the king in Kandy.

In 1656 only Mannar and Jaffna were under the Portuguese. The Dutch took their time. They had to be sure of their lands in the south as their relationship with the king had soured. The Dutch finally came with a large armada under Admiral Van Goens. They took the fort at Mannar and marched overland through the Vanni, crossed Pooneryn lagoon and landed at Chavakacheri. They marched to Navatkuli and then marched west for two hours to reach Jaffna. It was 1658. The Portuguese put up resistance for three months and finally surrendered. The Dutch found Jaffna placid in spite of the resistance put up by the Roman Catholics, with Indian Roman Catholics helping them. They expelled the Portuguese in 1658. The Dutch had made a detour by land to avoid Fort Cays and incarcerated the Portuguese and the local people who joined them within the fort in Jaffna. They starved them till they surrendered.

The Dutch had to capture the fort of Cays that was situated on a sandbank at the mouth of the water between Karativu and Velanai – Kayts, to prevent any Portuguese coming from the South. They captured the fort and named it Hammenheil as it looked like the heel of a hock of bacon. I don't think the Jaffna native knew neither pig, nor bacon nor pork as these were taboo for the Hindus and the names meant nothing to them.

The Dutch soon changed the names of places especially the islands. Oorothurai changed to Kayts and Nedunthivu to Delft, and a part of Karainagar to Leydon. Only the name Delft survived. They changed the whole façade of Jaffna including houses. The Portuguese houses had narrow columns and arches, and the narrower verandah of the house was referred to as the 'Solar.' The smaller but high-roofed Portuguese design of few rooms became many rooms. Each room became lofty, airy and had walls of greater thickness. "You are going to live in one of those now – a Dutch house," so said my grandfather.

Ruins of Portuguese houses in Atchuvely, Jaffna

The courtyard of grandfather's house opened to the sky. The smooth cemented portions surrounding the courtyard were interrupted by pillars reaching to the beams of the roof. The pillars were of teak, square in shape and had designs cut into them. The pillars at our home were of concrete and the very tall pillars found in the old houses of Karainagar were made of palmyrah wood, smoothed and painted.

The house itself was built of coral stones plastered with mud and mortar and appeared like concrete. The courtyard was screened off on top by wire netting to keep out the ubiquitous crows. This courtyard was the heart of the home. The female relatives of every home in that compound would find excuses and dropped in to see grandmother, especially at midmorning, to have a chat. They brought their vegetables to be cooked by them for that day and the rice to be gleaned. They sat on the cemented platform and I would be mesmerized at the speed in which leaves were detached from the stems while they chatted. The leaves were cut finely by an outwardly curved knife fixed to a two-foot horizontal low bench designed to be sat on. The female aunts, cousins or even grandmother's niece would sit demurely sideways with their legs stretched out and covered modestly by their saris. A similar device was used to scrape the coconut but using a finely serrated steel knife attached to a similar bench. Scrapers and cutters fixed to a table were a thing of the distant future!

Much gossip was exchanged while they cut and chopped the vegetables. Their gossip was sharp and unkind if it was about the number of proposals brought to a not so pretty girl or of the puberty ceremonies of another female carried out on an inauspicious day. An hour or two was dawdled away chopping, scraping and gossiping. Then suddenly, they rushed back to their small, smoky kitchens built at the rear of their homes.

In contrast to her house, grandmother's kitchen was small, dark and smoky. Cooking in the kitchen was considered a very temporary sojourn and the females just put up with it. A cemented raised platform with stones placed in triangles was the fireplace.

There was space above it but there was no chimney. During cooking, smoke swirled around the kitchen and was only taken away by the breeze blowing through a small window and the door. The smoke billowed in the kitchen if two or three fireplaces were used at the same time. Firewood was used economically with coconut shells initiating the fire. Every kitchen had on its' work table the steel scrapers and cutters. With constant bending, stretching and lifting things off the floor with bent knees, the women had straight attractive backs. It was rare to see a fat aunt in the family. Only the old inactive ones became fat.

In the midst of the kitchen gloom there would be a glimmer and shine coming from brass utensils. They would be on a table, stacked one inside the other, a set of them coming in different sizes. The chopped vegetables were strewn on winnowing fans which were made of woven and decorated palmyrah leaves or on brass platters. They were then taken out and washed in large brass bowls. It was taboo to wash fish and meat in these bowls. The gleaned rice would first be winnowed in a brass winnowing fan to blow off the finer grit, and washed in a brass shallow bowl with ridges to trap the smaller stones and dirt. My grandmother or Aunt Kamalam would swirl the bowl around to trap the stones and do it three times to perfection. Rice was cooked in a clay pot reserved for cooking rice. Another clay pot with water was always on a fireplace and was a ready source of drinking water. Whether boiled or not, the water was always brackish. Soap took an age to lather and much water was needed to wash it off. Meat was cooked outside the kitchen and the utensils used for the cooking were stacked on a wooden rack also outside the kitchen.

All households had stacks of these brass utensils. They needed much effort to keep them glowing. Every so often, tamarind, salt and powdered brick would be briskly rubbed on them, left aside for an hour and then washed thoroughly. Once food was cooked the kitchen was left spotlessly clean. At meal time, rice and curries were placed in appropriate-sized brass bowls, stacked and carried through the rear door of the house after crossing the rear verandah. If footwear was worn, which was rare, it was always left on the verandah. Grandfather's brass plate and tumbler were on the table, all ready and bright for the meal. Many others would eat their meals off banana leaves. Each leaf was cut to rectangular plate-size pieces, washed thoroughly and waved over the embers of a fire to make them lie flat on the table. There was less work when banana leaves were used. Once a meal was over the leaves would be fed to the cattle in the stall. Aunt Kamalam was the hands and feet of my grandparents. She was a young widow. The small community was not harsh on her and she was not expected to shave her head, nor be covered in a white sari from head to foot. However, she never wore bright or even dark sober colours. Her saris were always of pastel shades or white with blue or green borders. These dull colours were considered inauspicious for celebratory ceremonies. She would go with the others to the temple but no flowers adorned her hair and no red '*pottu*' on her forehead or on the hairline.

At any celebratory event like puberty and weddings she would be missing. I would look for her and find her far from the noise and bustle, getting the needed things ready for others to use. She had lost the position of standing behind the bride or circumbulating the brass tray which held the three lit wicks the, '*alathi*', a ceremonial ritual performed in front of the bridegroom or couple. I would see her, when everything was over, help to clear the things used and she did it so pleasantly and quietly.

My maternal grandmother lived with us as long as I could remember, for grandfather was long dead after many years of teaching in schools scattered within the islands of Jaffna.

Our house, built by my paternal grandfather and gifted to my father, was within the land of my grandfather's vast property. The other sons also had a plot of land each with a house. All those living in those homes were within hearing distance of each other and probably quarrelling distance too but without facing any adversary. Our home had a similar design to grandfather's but was smaller. With Christian missionaries making the occasional visit to our village, they would suggest curtains for doors and windows. These looked elegant but certainly cut off not only the light but the breeze most welcomed within the house. Grandmother's name was Jane Augusta, a name which made us smile indulgently at her when we grew older. When we were younger and first heard that name, our jaws dropped in awe as it reminded us of Rome and Caesar! She was very proud of her name, though it didn't quite match with names like Manonmani and Kamalam our kith next door.

Harriet Wadsworth Lathrop Winslow

My great grandfather was a catechist in the parish where his family was one of the earliest converts to Christianity. He was proud to give her such a name. The name, she told me proudly, was that of an American Missionary who taught at Uduvil Girls School. She would also, with greater pride, announce that she went to the first English girls' school, not only in Jaffna, but in Southeast Asia, founded by Harriet Wadsworth Winslow in 1835. As in the older sister school, Jaffna College, the curriculum included the basic subjects as well as astronomy, Tamil literature, a bit of Sanskrit and philosophy. When she completed the Junior Cambridge examination at the age of seventeen or eighteen, she was fit to be a teacher.

Uduvil Girls School

She said her uniform was simple, a cloth wrapped round the waist and a blouse or jacket to cover the bosom. When older she wore a sari. Unlike her family, the girls of the lower castes had to be coaxed to attend school in cloth and blouse too and not in cloth and bare bosoms as had been their tradition. These girls' schooling was erratic. They attended school for a short period to receive the gift of two cloths per year. They had no desire to learn. "The general opinion of the males in their families was if they know anything more than the way to market, to cook rice and sweep the compound, they would be less valuable as wives", wrote the principal of Uduvil. After her schooling, it was marriage for my grandmother, an arranged one. Her marriage, arranged within her village situated between Inuvil and Tellippalai, was a topic of conversation for many years.

The catechist father had a single plot of land that could be given as dowry. Catechists were never rich! He had six daughters. The eldest, my grandmother, was given the only plot of land. Something seen or tangible must be given as dowry in an arranged marriage. Grandmother was tall, attractive, dusky and had a brilliant smile. But that was not enough for a proposed marriage. So she, being the eldest, was given the land. When her younger sibling was to be married there was no house nor land and very little cash to give her. It was a disgrace to get a girl married after an arranged proposal without a dowry. It would be even more difficult to initiate a proposal.

Marriage proposals came for her younger sister. There was consternation! The dowry? Grandmother invited her sisters to Inuvil, the paternal grandfather's house. She connived with the sisters and agreed that she would write the ownership of that single precious bit of land to the younger one who in turn must write to the next female sibling and so on, till the last sibling owned it. This was a generous gesture to save face. Ultimately, the youngest got that plot of land. She married a young man, Amaran of the same village and a house was built on it. "All's well that ends well," but I often wondered whether the brothers-in-law took it in their stride or whether they knew they were in possession of an imaginary plot of land.

My grandmother was remembered for decades for her very Christian generosity. Christian fervour was most seen in the first and second generations of converts. With her education at Uduvil, grandmother was qualified to be a teacher. Grandfather who was also a teacher was keen that the girl he married must be a teacher. They started their rotation of teaching in the islands of Velanai, Kayts and Delft, where the American Mission had elementary schools. In the mainland schools all girls covered their bosoms with jackets above the cloths they wore but this could not be insisted on with the lower castes. They arrived to start school, topless. My grandmother, with the help of another teacher, would sew blouses for the girls from material bought by the mission. It was an easy task, for every girl in every village was trained to be a seamstress. In spite of all this, the girls would spend a couple of hours or so in school in between morning and afternoon tasks at home.

The headmaster and teachers played the role of counsellors in these island schools. The parents would bring them their problems. They would request that the teachers chastise the children with corporal punishment for wrongdoing at home, shirking their own responsibilities. The female teachers would be requested to teach their daughters cooking and sewing. They would also seek their assistance with marriage proposals as the school had contact with many families. After marriage the villagers would come for advice on baby care. The villagers looked up to the school staff with awe and respect.

Grandmother related to me the incident of a storm and squall in the sea around the island, which damaged a large number of houses. The school was the refuge, and the villagers were there for almost a week till they rebuilt their homes. They were fed and looked after by the American Mission that did not lack financial resources. My grandparents were transferred in rotation to Velanai, Delft and Nedunthivu islands. They raised five boys and two girls. Finally they asked for a transfer to the mainland to send their boys to Central College, a Methodist Mission school, and their girls to Uduvil, grandmother's former school of happy memories. From her generation onwards education was an industry in Jaffna and the academic goal for a girl was the Senior Cambridge examination. Books and learning were gifts to the Tamils from antiquity.

Grandfather, in his ramblings of days gone by, would beam with pride as he recalled the educational advantages he gave his sons. My father was the eldest of his five sons. Grandfather had his education in the vernacular only in the village school founded by the American Mission. My father Vedanayagam, who had his elementary education in the English school of the American Mission of the village, was bright enough and, more so, rich enough to be sent to the English school at Vaddukodai. This was the premier school and the pride of the American Mission. First referred to as Batticota Seminary and Boarding School – Batticota, an anglicized version of Vaddukodai - it had been founded in 1823. The Methodist and Anglican missions had a head start in founding schools and building churches but they didn't spread their wings to the northwest of the peninsula or the islands in the northern waters. Their schools were in Jaffna town, its suburbs and villages.

Though American trade predated the work of the missions in Ceylon, Jaffna was not a recipient of this trade. The missionaries, Rev. Samuel Newell and his wife were sent by the American Mission Board in New England. New England had a community of ardent Protestants probably the descendants of the Mayflower entourage. The Boston Brahmins who lived in New England were very rich and considered very snobbish too. The latter trait was written about in a famous limerick that said, "The Lovells spoke only to the Cabots and the Cabots spoke only to God". Snobbish or not, their generosity in cash sailed over the seas to reach the far flung American Mission in Jaffna. It helped to build the schools and later the dispensary.

Rev. Samuel Newell

When Rev. Newell arrived in Colombo, Briton - its ruler, was not pleased as it was at war with the United States in Upper Canada.

The Newells were sent away, but Rev. Newell returned alone in 1813, having lost his wife and daughter. Then he was asked by the governor to start the American Mission as there was a paucity of Protestant missionaries. In 1816 Rev. Newell travelled to Jaffna and set up the American Mission and its first church, which replaced the Dutch one, in Tellippalai, a conservative village.

Tellipallai American Mission Church

Five other missionaries followed Rev. Newell but they were not a welcome lot in Colombo. Governor Brownrigg diplomatically sent them all to the arid north. Their coming was like a monsoon downpour in the warmest and wrong month of the year! Jaffna blessed the British for sending the Americans north, and was in turn blessed by the coming of the Americans.

The Americans were not in search of spices like their foreign predecessors. Their search was for souls. They set out to win them by the Bible and bilingual education. They came to Jaffna when night meant lanterns and a journey meant bullock carts.

My father, who physically looked like my grandfather, was so unlike him in his speech and moods. He was taciturn and spoke

Batticota Seminary

when he was in a garrulous mood. When in such a mood he gave great details of his schooling. "Thankfully the Batticota seminary was right beside the road that went towards Jaffna. Karainagar was a boat journey away. Twenty minutes of rowing by the boatman and one stepped onto this road and within a few minutes' walk there stood the school of new buildings and paths. Vaddukodai was a maze of lanes and neat small houses within fences or walls. Some houses abutted on the school buildings. The lanes meandered round the school. Small shops selling every type of merchandise jostled with the houses for space. Sometimes stepping out from a door of the school, it was only a step further to the door of a home, so close were they," he recalled.

"There was much rapport and bonhomie between village and school from its very inception. Nothing happened in school which was not known by the villagers and no village activities of any kind that were not known to the school.

One of those five missionaries, Rev. Warren, was very keen on educating the students in both Tamil and English. He started bilingual schools in the west of Jaffna and in the islands. Their goal was 'social reform, elimination of poverty and better lives for all.' The village saw the American Mission give their utmost and best to the schools. Rev. Poor, the best known of those first five missionaries, founded the Batticota Seminary in 1823."

My grandfather would then interrupt my father's flow of reminiscences with, "Thank God for the paddy fields and the money left to me. I was able to pay the school fees of all my sons. Actually, Batticota Seminary started as a non-fee levying school but couldn't afford to do so after a while." The greater number of parents were not able to pay the fees. There were many bright students too in the feeder schools of the mission in the villages.

The American Mission made a great gesture by allowing parents who couldn't afford the school fees to mortgage their lands to the mission. The student's tuition was then free. The lands were to be redeemed by paying the school fees owed, when the young men got employment. Time was not stipulated, but the villagers' conscience made them pay promptly. They could not have hoped for more as so many of their sons had the great opportunity of education while their parents were allowed to live on the mortgaged land and till it.

The school in Vaddukodai was in the midst of lush green paddy fields, tall sturdy palmyrah, coconut palms and satin wood trees. The mahogany and flamboyant trees stood sentinel to small ponds. Colour was spread by the numerous and perennial hibiscus blooms. The Christian culture of the village had been brushed with the overlapping paints of Portuguese, Dutch and British rule.

The ancient Portuguese Roman Catholic church became a Calvinist one of the Dutch, by the removal of statues, elaborate altar and structural religious decorations. This became the American Mission church and its ceiling was embellished with pine wood from New England. What the mission could not do for years as social reform was to make a dent in the caste system.

The school was a boarding school, with a few day scholars. The boarding had only Vellala caste students. The day students were a mixture of the Vellala and lower castes. The latter, willingly or not, took their place to study seated on the ground and which they did in the church too. Father spent eight years in Batticota seminary. He would rattle off the medley of subjects that were taught there. Applied science, math, English, Tamil, Sanskrit, astronomy, music, art, theology, philosophy, a smattering of medical science and electricity – the latter was discovered only ten years earlier. The

The Church at Vaddukodai

missionaries were keen that the students must know Tamil language and literature thoroughly. The final qualifying exam, when the student was seventeen, was the F.A., the First in Arts, which qualified a student to enter a university in India. The much recommended one was Madras University. There was great pride and rejoicing when the first student of Batticota Seminary to graduate was Charles Winslow Thamotherampillai.

By 1848 the American Mission had 105 Tamil schools and 16 English schools. Most of them were patronized by a majority of Hindus.

While the seminary marched on, the females were not forgotten. In 1816 only three females could read and write. Harriet Winslow made her appearance and without wasting time founded the girls' school at Uduvil, which was the first girls' school in Asia, and in 1824 she founded the Udupitty Girls' boarding school which again was the first girls' boarding school in Asia. Harriet Winslow did not have it easy. She met much opposition from the men. Females were considered the property of their husbands and their primary role was to be housewives and bear children. To entice the girls and their parents, they were offered gifts and a promise to give money for their dowries. In addition, they were given clothes for school wear.

The school started in a small way, but there was no turning back. The village of Uduvil ultimately had three schools: the mission station school, village school, and Uduvil boarding school.

Sir Emmerson Tennant, the Secretary in the British government, visited the schools in Jaffna and the Batticota Seminary. He was astonished at the knowledge exhibited by the students and ranked Batticota with any European university.

Sir Emmerson Tennant

For all this march towards education, the winning of souls lagged behind. Of the ninety-six boarders only eleven were Christian. The American Board in New England thought that too much prominence was given to Science and English, and little time to biblical instruction. The seminary seemed to be a stepping stone for employment. The seminary then wanted to admit only Christians and it was closed for a short time. The alumni and the village were shocked and upset at the turn of events and rallied round the school with financial help and other support. It was opened again in 1867. The seminary was renamed Jaffna College.

Conversions, however, still went on and the converts in Vaddukodai took the names of missionaries or of their teachers, whom they admired at their baptisms. There sprang up the Williams, Hensmans, Danforths, Mills, Taylors, Cloughs, Hooles, etc., among the Tamils. There was an instance where baptism was compulsory to sit the F.A., a foolish move that was revised later. There was no hesitation or compunction in a few Hindus to convert. After the exam or later, they cunningly or wisely reverted to their Hindu names. Those having had a Christian surname denoting families of the same status, caste and village were reluctant to let go of it. Their American or biblical names were hyphenated to their Hindu or Tamil names. Thus popped up bizarre combinations like Jeremiah Balasingham or Clough Subramaniam or even Spencer Rajendram - all devout Hindus!

I was happy that father retained his original Hindu name after conversion. Grandfather would have died of anger and shame as he was a prominent member in the committee of the village temple and took his religion seriously. Ironically, typical Hindu and pure Tamil names have been retained in the Christian families such as the Casinaders, Subramaniams, Velummyilum, Sethukavalars or the different *Thambies* and *Aiyas* that ended their names. They added biblical or English names as their first names.

Even after leaving school, my father and my uncles kept in touch with the college and the changes there were conveyed to us.

I was twelve years old and attending Vembadi, the Methodist Mission school in Jaffna town. I would walk from our home, on Second Cross Street, to school and back, invariably chattering with my two siblings.

We were too young to realize the effects of the First World War. What affected us were the scarcities of white sugar and all other imported provisions which, if available, were at a higher price. We went back to drinking coffee and tea with palmyrah jaggery. I could manage reading the English newspapers. They were the main source of information for us. Books were borrowed from friends or from the school library and read avidly. My mother could not afford to buy books other than the stipulated school books. Father was in Malaya and the money sent via the post office was hardly sufficient to manage a household of nine, which included my maternal grandmother too. When my younger brother bought and brought home a pound of sugar, it was as usual inside a cone made of newspaper. I had this habit of unwrapping these cones carefully to read that half sheet of newspaper. Unwrapping one such paper cone and flattening it on the table with the sugar still on it I read the news item in dark big headlines, "Emden has fled again!" I read of the German raider of the sea during the First World War. I pushed the sugar around to read more of the paper, till my mother demanded the sugar, which I gladly put into a given container, and continued reading. The sub-headline screamed: "Capt. Muller does it again." Nobody seemed to have made a name like his in the First World War. Outdoing his name was the name of his ship, Emden. Her shape was said to be sleek, and her many boilers needed to be hand fed. She had guns, torpedoes, and a three-hundred-member crew. The name Emden slipped into our vocabulary as the newspapers were full of her. She had made an appearance in the Bay of Bengal in 1913 and destroyed enemy ships along its coast down to the south of Ceylon. The British were horrified at her escapades, but admired her secretly. The colonized cheered the Emden all the way. I read about the German prisoner of the Boer war in the south, who was suspected of helping the Emden. He was taken from a wildlife sanctuary where he worked, to prison!

The Captain of the Emden was not only brave, but chivalrous too, releasing the crews before the warships were sunk. The more publicity the Emden had, the more the destruction and greater the legend. The ship would sail disguised as a British warship with an extra artificial funnel built, in addition to its' usual three, hoodwinking the English ships and sinking them. Instead of sticking to its rampage on the seas, she made the mistake of sailing to the Cocos Island, disguised again as a British warship, to destroy the British communication centre there. The disguise was uncovered and an Australian warship forced the Emden to run aground. The captain surrendered only when he realized that his ship was destroyed beyond repair. He tried to sink his ship, but failed, and then gave himself up. It was reported in the papers that Captain Muller was taken to England as prisoner. Many years later, in 1923, he died of malaria! What an anticlimax!

The long account of the Emden was almost like an obituary of a great personality. She had been named Emden after the city where she was built. Her sister ship, the Dresden, was also built there. Capt. Muller took command of the Emden in 1913 and served in the German fleet. That very year she left the fleet and started an epic and destructive life of her own spreading terror and pandemonium in the first few months of her short life. Her description included the number of coal-powered boiler funnels and all other mechanical details, which I have forgotten as I was not interested in such things. Not only the Emden, but her captain and the three hundred and sixty men of her crew, became famous for their exploits.

The word Emden became a byword in the speech of the people in villages and towns in the north. Every clever and smart student was called Emden. Even a shrewd and sly individual got the title of Emden. The name was only forgotten long after the end of the war.

Armed with all these facts, I looked forward to the weekend visit to Karainagar to impress my grandparents. We started our journey by buggy cart early when it was cool. We went to the end of the road at Vaddukodai and took the boat home. The sun now hot beat down on our heads and up came the umbrellas which too became hot. While in the boat, I imagined my grandfather getting dressed in his clean spotless white *verti*. He wore it in a very individualistic manner by making a pleat in front and then tucked it into his waist in front. No one else did so. His shawl would be wrapped round his waist and most often he would be bare bodied with holy ash on his chest, and a little of it on his forehead. His feet were in strapped Indian chappals. He was broad, tall, strode forth with fellow village cronies trailing him and met still others in a shady lane. He would never forget to take his ebony walking stick with a silver knob on top. He was quite sturdy and didn't need a walking stick as a prop but took it for effect!

When I finally reached home, I found him seated with about a dozen others on the fine sand of a shady lane. I was shocked to hear him talking of the Emden to that crowd. I had forgotten that my brother Seeva had come home from Singapore, where he was a medical student. He had told my grandfather about the exploits of the Emden. I felt deflated but still gave him some more details that he wasn't aware of. The villagers were in awe of what he said. The scene of grandfather and his village friends seated, with him holding forth on any and every topic that was read by him, or relayed to him, is still sharp in my memory.

We were living in Jaffna town, occupying our granduncles' house. They were still in Malaya and their visits to Jaffna were infrequent. My older sisters, younger sister and I were in our teens, rearing to see places and villages of the peninsula where relatives lived. These villages were too far from Karainagar for us to have visited them earlier.

We wrote to our rich uncle Sinna that we were keen to see him and his family at Inuvil, a village on the KKS road. Prompt was his reply. Every Jaffna man was proud of what he produced from that stubborn earth that was his. Uncle Sinna was no exception. He wrote of his tobacco fields, and was keen that we should see them and the mini factory at the back of his house, where cigars were made.

I was fourteen years old. We intended to kill two birds with one stone by visiting a cousin of my mother's who had given birth to a baby in the mission hospital in Inuvil.

We visited uncle Sinna the following Saturday. No visits were done on Sunday, as that day was sacrosanct, and church going was compulsory. We travelled leisurely by buggy cart. Inuvil was a village in the interior and one of the most fertile in the Valigaman West region. Nearing the village we saw with envy how green it was. Jaffna town was so dusty brown, and its few green trees had been pushed out by the concrete houses.

Nearing Inuvil I saw bedraggled brown linear bundles on the fences of the houses we passed. They looked too brown and dirty for clothes. My ignorance of what these untidy bundles were made my older sisters smile and then giggle. I was told they were long tobacco leaves, drying in the sun.

We stepped out of the cart at uncle's gate and the earth we stepped on was actually red like the colour of ground red bricks. Fine red dust swirled around our ankles and feet. There were affectionate greetings and cups of hot sweet milky coffee. Uncle Sinna was impatient to show off his harvested fields, and those that were being harvested. He had about three acres of land to grow tobacco. Much to his annoyance I told him proudly that grandfather's land was bigger. He then boasted that he grew a thousand tobacco plants in a quarter acre of land. He was able to rent some land to the *Koviyars*, a caste living on his land. They, in turn with the males of their families, were helping in the harvesting and manufacture of cigars.

Uncle Sinna was so enthusiastic and went to such details. He told us that the humble *suruttu* became the sophisticated cheroot of the West. Every other sentence of his started with the words 'Actually as a matter of fact' and this amused us no end. Uncle Sinna began again, "Actually as a matter of fact the Portuguese introduced tobacco to the north just after their conquest of it. Tobacco was one of the first cash crops. The price was paid in

Tobacco Fields

cakrans and zerafins, the cash money of the Portuguese. Later onions and chillies too became cash crops. The Portuguese knew that tobacco was good for the disease called Beri-Beri and smoking was a relaxation for the soldiers. The locals tried mixing the tobacco leaf with their betel chew, which made it tastier because of the added nicotine."

Uncle Sinna again, "Actually as a matter of fact there was an exchange of Indian and Jaffna chewing tobacco as preferences of one over the other was always prevalent. Then the Dutch, only eager for more money, taxed the Indian variety so exorbitantly that the price of it became prohibitive. The local tobacco was grown more and then it too was later taxed more!"

After the rainy months of October and November, he had the fields ploughed with hoes, *mammoties*, and the cattle manure was added to the soil. He boasted again, "I had to put four cart loads of manure to every quarter acre of field." He lacked cattle so he had to buy the manure. "Actually as a matter of fact to have cattle, you need straw, for straw you need paddy lands," he said with regret. Then the green manure of the leaves collected in pits over months had been added to the fields. The seeds saved from the last harvest were grown in nurseries. The seedlings were very delicate and needed the shade of woven coconut leaves over them. The seedlings had to be kept moist. When replanting, two seedlings were put in together with three feet of space between the plants.

They were watered by hand, which meant carrying buckets of water from a trough near the well. Watering had to be done in the cool of the evenings. "If a seedling died, another of a pair that survived was planted in the empty space. Nothing was wasted!"

Watering must have been tedious. "Actually as a matter of fact I was thankful for the intermittent rains. The fields needed constant weeding and manuring." Uncle had one well sweep in his garden. My grandfather had three for his paddy fields.

When the plants were ten feet tall and bearing long leaves, topping was done by plucking the leaves from the growing points. Uncle demonstrated even that. It was between the forefinger and thumb.

A couple of weeks later, the plants had been uprooted, leaves cut off and exposed to air in open sheds, which we could see at the back of the house. Pits were also pointed out to us, in which the leaves were later put to ferment. They were taken out, tied in bundles, smoked in special rooms and hung out to dry. Such bundles were those I saw on the fences.

We saw about twenty-five young men and boys seated on mats in a shed, shredding the dried tobacco leaves with crude rough tools. These were rolled and wrapped in a tobacco leaf itself, and made into dark brown, four-inch long and one-and-a-half-inch broad cigars. Hundreds of them lay on the ground. We really smelt them, but it was overpowered by a horrible pungent smell of a liquid. It was the pungent steam of the *koda* broth! The *koda* was a mixture of palmyrah toddy, spices and leftover twigs and stems of tobacco. These were brewed in a large pan.

"Actually as a matter of fact this pan was brought from England. It was expensive. It is sturdily built, will last twenty years and holds sixty gallons of the mixture." Uncle said this with great satisfaction.

We saw the pan that was sitting on a mud plastered furnace, built to use firewood economically. It was impossible to stay near it for long. The strong cigars called 'wet' were those that had been placed in this brew, taken out and dried. The cigars had turned black, broader and smellier. These were then covered with a special tobacco leaf brought from the Eastern Province. The less smelly one was the 'dry' one. Jaffna had no beedi tobacco. It was a good thing too as otherwise it may have meant another tedious tour of beedi tobacco for us. This reminded me of one of those rare trips to the south of Ceylon and to the hills where we were taken on a detailed tour to see the manufacture of tea.

After all this walking and listening, we were so famished that we were thankful for my aunt's lunch of country rice with fried fish, curried chicken, a *piratel* as it was called, vegetables and *millagathanni*, a peppered water.

While walking out to the gate we saw uncle's meticulously kept garden. Roses bloomed in all its colours, in large earthen pots filled with the red earth. They had replaced the humble hibiscus of which we had plenty in our urban environment. While getting into the buggy cart he gave me a bundle of cigars to be given to grandfather. I saw the thousands of cigars he made daily which would have made him really wealthy. I thought, but I did not say, that he could have given a larger bundle of cigars.

We were too tired to visit the newborn baby.

When I lived in Karainagar, and not having reached the age of puberty, it was permitted to move around from *valavu* to *valavu* – compounds separated by fences. After puberty a girl had to be accompanied by a suitable family member. The adjacent compound and the *valavus* even further from ours were owned by relatives. A 'strip' – a portion of land called a *thundu* in Tamil – was occupied by members of a particular caste, either of high or lower-caste villagers. In fact, there was a strip occupied by members of our own extended family right next to the strip of land of another caste. These partitions were seen in almost every village. Everyone was safe to walk around in our village as everyone had some knowledge of his or her neighbour.

I would announce that I was going next door to uncle Kumar's. Uncle Kumar and his family lived next to us and within the common strip of land. My grandmother, who was so specific about relationships, would tell me that uncle Kumar was my *amman*, literally, the mother's brother. Amman or maternal uncle had a great and important part to play in the rituals at puberty and wedding ceremonies. My grandfather called after me and said, "He'll be repeating all the wonders of the palmyrah tree. He will ask you to name all its uses and products. So be prepared for a long visit."

I saw my uncle's long fence that abutted ours and I saw it winding along even before I spotted his house. The fence had been renewed and looked the loveliest fence of the neighbourhood. There was great activity of refencing the whole property. It was a palmyrah frond fence, as he had so many groves of them in his compound. I watched with wonder as my uncle's labourers made this beautiful and artistic fence. The fronds and thick stems of the palms were held erect and lined up with hardly a space between them. They were interwoven and tied with a rope made of horizontal strips of the stems of the fronds without a peek-space between the fronds. The fence looked like a row of slim dancers who held large green fans tinged with yellow.

The fence looked so pretty and new. These 'palmyrah dancers' were seen going on for quite a distance and together made a sturdy barrier. Uncle Kumar had only to spend on his workmen. His compound with his palmyrah groves surrounded his large solid house. The fence he had removed had lasted for two years. I saw

A Palmyrah fence

that white ants had marched through the dried and now discarded old fence. The droopy dishevelled old fronds had been stripped small and there was so much of these strippings on the ground. Some would have gone to feed the cattle and the others dumped in many of the compost pits scattered in his garden.

Uncle Kumar saw me in the lane, hailed me and suddenly disappeared from view. He had actually gone through his gate. I followed, but felt lost in the lane, as I could not locate the gate to his compound. I trudged further forwards a few more yards, but I still could not find the gate. I went back and forth and closely looked at the fence for a gate that he must have used. Finally I found it and felt a fool for not recognizing it. It was like all gates in our village, flush with the fence. It too had been made of palmyrah fronds within a wooden frame and blended with the fence.

I entered the gate and found a huge mound of freshly cut palmyrah fronds. He had harvested an excess of what he needed, almost the leaves of fifty palms, each palm having yielded fifty fronds. He was selling those he didn't need. My mind boggled at the sight of so many palmyrah trees in his compound. Harvest of the palmyrah fronds was done once in two years.

While he was bargaining and selling the excess fronds, others loaded them into long double bullock carts, like the ones my grandfather had. As I expected, he asked me to enumerate the uses of this palm and its products. He forgot that the palmyrah was a sentimental plebeian, a favourite of the north. Everyone knew everything about it. The coconut was a high class 'horse' compared to the palmyrah 'bull.' I had been told that the palmyrah had a hundred and one uses, but it was too much to remember since I was still young. I did remember the edible things that came from it - the jams, cordials, yams and jaggery. He was disappointed that I had missed naming so many other products. He reminded me of the colourful baskets, boxes, winnowing fans, hats, fans and so on.

Uncle was well known for the degree of thrift even in that thrifty community. He would allow only two percent of his palms to be tapped for toddy. His relatives were always left disappointed during the toddy season! He would calculate the money he could make if the untapped blooms were left to become fruits and the fruits' pulps turned to jam and cordials. Most of the yams that came from germinating dried fruits were sold while the rest of the yams were boiled to eat or dried and turned into flour, an essential ingredient of a broth called *kool*. He was wealthy as he sold so much of the produce of the palmyrah trees.

I tentatively asked him for some immature fruits. Very surprisingly he got a bunch of them brought down from the tree. My cousins and I relished scooping out the three 'eyes' in which there was a sweet jelly-like substance called *nongu*. I still remember its taste. In the corners of the compound were mounds of earth, long and rectangular in shape, which reminded me of the fresh burial mounds of the churchyard. Dried palmyrah fruits had been buried in these mounds to germinate and give out a bunch of underground yams that would be dug out later.

Grandfather's compound too had such mounds, but they were fewer. I trailed back home and all I could talk for days was about was that beautiful fence. Everybody agreed that when new, the palmyrah fence outdid a live fence in its loveliness.

I remember the mornings in the village. They stand out in contrast to the dusk when only a few of us were in the compound, unlike the many seen in the morning. In our family the one who pottered around in the garden in the early hours of the morning was my grandfather's brother Suram. He didn't go out to work. He had retired with a pension from his former government clerical post. He made himself useful in some manual work. I saw him coming out with a not so clean *verti*, bare bodied. He wanted to make the water channels free of excess silt, so he took the *mammoty*, a digging tool, to the site. The *verti* was at his ankles, impractical to work in. I saw him flex one leg of his at the knee, then raise his heel and take the edge of the *verti* within reach of his hand. He then lifted, folded the *verti* and tucked it into his waist. Not satisfied with it as he needed more movement, the folded *verti* was raised higher, taken between his legs to the back and tucked in at the waist. The *verti* had been converted into a pair of thick shorts. A sarong was hardly worn by the older generation, but years later I saw my brothers in sarongs worn like it was in Malaya, the sarongs at the waist turned in like a belts, which made them sit more securely. My mother's brothers, four of them in Malaya, sent these colourful sarongs. Even before that, the Arab traders had brought the sarongs from Indonesia to the Malabar Coast and then to the Jaffna peninsula. The Ceylon Moors always wore them in place of the *verti*. Later the sarong became popular because it was like a sewn skirt and was easier to wear than the *verti*.

I have digressed. It was a couple of days before Pongal, the pre harvest festival. Suram turned around, saw me and requested me (I think it was more of an order) to go to his brother-in-law's *valavu* and ask him to send a bundle of tender green coconut leaves to make decorations for Pongal. I set off. I actually walked in a maze of lanes. In fact, every village is a maze of lanes. I walked along one lane and if I didn't know the direction in which to turn, I would have been walking around in squares and rectangles, as fences were of those shapes. Fences were four, five or even six feet high, the latter reflecting the idiosyncrasy of the owner!

Most lanes were covered with soft white sand. That morning was cool and I walked to my uncle's place reminding myself that I should return before the sun made the sand sizzle and scorch my unshod feet. All the villagers too went about barefoot. Errands were done early and people were at their best earlier in the day. Villagers were very early risers. Four thirty was never too early.

The many strips or portions of land within our village duplicated and triplicated the people of the same castes. I was told that there were twenty-four main castes, but subdivisions within a caste had stretched the numbers to one hundred and fifty! Next but one to us were the strips of the *Nalavar* and the *Pallars* castes, the toddy tappers. These two castes also worked as day labourers. There were strips for the *Pararyar* caste too, who were coolies and sweepers, one-time weavers of the past, and then were the drummers at funerals. The lowest of the castes was the washerman to the toddy tappers! My Christian grandmother would tell me that a man of a lowest caste of *Thurumpan*, made a noise while walking by dragging a palmyrah frond which heralded his coming. The high-caste person then moved to the opposite side. I should and would have loved to tell her that she was only a first generation Christian and her grandfather would have done the same. I did wonder why the low caste man accepted rules dictated to him. I was told that the other strips had their own castes – the goldsmith, blacksmith, the extinct silk and cotton weavers who flourished in Portuguese times. The strips could be of carpenters, potters, oil pressers or various subdivisions of the fisher caste. *Pandarams*, the temple cooks and the *Natuvars*, the musicians, were of the middle range castes and had their own strips. Many of the barbers and washermen owed allegiance and some lived on the Vellala compound. Their relationship was like a hereditary right to serve a particular family, who in turn would look after them in times of trouble and distress. Both castes were considered low castes and untouchables, as one washes dirty clothes and the other cuts hair, which is considered dirty, like nails!

The relative I was going to see lived in the Vellala strip of village a little further from home. Communities in the Vellala strip got on well socially and intermarriage was frequent. Vellalas of some strips thought they were superior to other Vellalas on another strip. A common query of where you came from – east, west, north or south – labelled you as a good, or better Vellala. However the Vellalas who lived on different strips referred to each other as *engadaal*, "our people". The barber and washerman had the same question of who was better, even though they were of similar low castes. There were strips of fisher folks, who in turn divided themselves into the higher *Tevars*, the seafarers and the ordinary fisherman. The various strips of different castes had no social interaction.

I manoeuvred the lanes. These lanes were much later the stumbling block for the army. The 'Tiger' rebels knew and negotiated the lanes easily. The army followed them, lost its way, and ran into a blank fence.

I arrived at the Vellala strip where my uncle was and saw groves of coconut standing in his garden. There was a large concrete house, a garden and coconut palms - all of which were fenced in with cadjan. I found workers splitting the coconut fronds and weaving them into continuous sheets. These were tied horizontally and arranged in panels between wooden posts of the fence. The fence was very ordinary looking, in fact quite dull and ugly, compared to the live fence of grandfather's and the newest palmyrah fence of the other uncle. I did not comment on his fence, but asked for green leaves and young coconuts. The coconut tree was elegant compared to the sturdy 'bull' of a palmyrah with its thick girth and height. The coconut got its name from the Portuguese. It came from the name of a species of monkey – macoca. The three eyes of the husked coconut looked like the face of the monkey. Trouble and planning were taken to plant and grow coconut in less fertile soil. Salt and fertilizer were added to help its growth. The palmyrah sprouted anywhere and grew without any attention. The coconut palm died without the assistance of man. That day's labourers at my uncle's compound had stripped the midribs of the coconut fronds for their *ekels* that were used in brooms for sweeping, and they were very efficient. The broom had no long handle, but was only a bundle of *ekels* tied firmly together at one end and splayed at the other. The womenfolk bent over them and swept homes and compounds with such perfection.

Husks were stacked. Uncle Selvam sold them to the coir maker. A toddy tapper was bringing down pots of toddy. There was no anticipation of it as seen in the case of palmyrah toddy, which was sweet. The temple workers were there to collect the cadjan for the temporary structures and sheds needed for the annual festival of the temple. Cadjan was sold as it was used for roofs, walls and fences. However, on counting the products of the coconut tree, they were found to be far fewer than that of the palmyrah, which had a hundred and more uses. Uncle was smug about his coconut trees. "So, you want young leaves from the 'holy tree?" was his opening question of the conversation. Coconut was used for Hindu rituals in homes and temples. They were broken at the commencement of sowing, and again at the harvesting of paddy. Flowers, camphor, plantains and coconut were offered at a *pooja*. The palmyrah fruit never saw the temple! So plebeian and unwelcome it was. However, the palmyrah wood, which was the strongest timber after forty to eighty years of its life, was used in the rafters and reepers to support the orange tiles of the temple!

Grandfather was good at using palmyrah leaves for writing on. Uncle claimed the writing was even better using coconut leaves and a metal stylus. He was keen and showed the letters cut on the *ola*, the palm leaf. The letters were then made clearer by rubbing oil and charcoal over the leaf. I was impatiently waiting to interrupt him to say how good grandfather was with the palmyrah leaf, but never got a chance. I was accompanied back by a labourer carrying a bundle of young coconut leaves and a few coconuts. The hot sand made me walk faster. His parting, mocking words, "The palmyrah fruit? Who offers that unholy fruit to God?" were still ringing in my ears when I reached home. I made up my mind that whatever that uncle said, I would be loyal to grandfather and to the palmyrah, however unholy and plebeian it may be. I was never tired of hearing that unique leathery sound of the wind rushing through the fronds of that tree, nor the mellow sound of the cooing doves who, with the frisky squirrels, were always within the topmost fronds of the palmyrah tree, searching for and then relishing the ripe fruits. Only a tired crow sat on a palm frond of the coconut. Then it streaked away with a beakful of toddy stolen from the pot of it on that tree.

Emily Gnanam remembered Pushpam. Pushpam was ready for marriage. She was one of my many Hindu cousins. The joy of celebration was already in the air. Marriage was almost compulsory in our village. Though our family was one of two converted Christian homes adjacent to Hindu ones, our kinship made all of us participants in every procedure that led to marriage and, believe me, there were so many steps in it. The northerners are traditional and family orientated. Puberty, marriage, and even death, had many ceremonies and rituals. The most colourful and joyously celebrated occasion was a wedding.

It was Jane Austen time for marriages and had been for centuries in our village. Into a proposal of marriage crept pride and more prejudice, sense but little sensibility, proposals and disposals. There was subtlety in gathering information, and this meant an ear to gossip – good, bad or malicious, lots of decorum to find out how pretty the bride was, the cash behind the looks and last not least, how suitable the parents were! Pushpam's marriage was an arranged one like the ninety-nine percent of marriages in Jaffna. She was not given a say in the preparations. An arranged marriage in Jaffna was not of two individuals, but of two suitable families. The members of these families were consulted and involved in every part of the long-winded process. Pushpam was only informed that she would be getting married soon. Soon meant many months. Inquiries and arrangements were thorough. The Dutch pastor Baldeus, who had written the details of the culture of the north, said "An arranged marriage is laudable as it has the consent of the parents." "A single man is half a man," was an idiom in Tamil.

Though there was no prior love, romance or even acquaintance, the marriages lasted. The females regarded it as their duty to accept the chosen partners they got in life, and a wife apparently seemed to be the subordinate partner. I remembered an English proverb that said, "Hanging and wifing go by destiny." The Tamil version was, "The wife and teacher one gets are according to fate."

Divorce was unheard of. A traditional wedding usually did not fail as it was cocooned in a social, moral and religious hard shell. Dissension was not voiced, but swallowed with humility and, who knew, may have been with bitterness. An arranged marriage started essentially like a business proposition. Arranged marriages started with the marriage broker. Males were predominant in this profession, but in our neigbourhood the marriage broker was a woman. She was always referred to as Ponniah's wife. We never knew her first name. She was pleasant and garrulous. She had a pretty round face, and though buxom she rushed around with light steps. Her left nostril and the earlobes had diamond studs that shone brilliantly. Ponniah was hardly seen, and more hardly heard of. He was a shy retiring male who did a clerical job in the village council. She must have earned more than her husband, with cash gifted to her or with a percentage of the cash dowry given to the bride in every successful marriage brokered by her. In fact, when Ponniah fell ill and died shortly thereafter, his death was spoken of as Ponniah's wife's husband's demise. So much for her status in the village.

Ponniah's wife (the name stuck to her even after widowhood) was a constant visitor to our village and to the adjacent villages as well. Her conversation very subtly included the number of children in a family, their educational qualifications, jobs, status. Then she looked around the house, the compound and guessed the dowries it held for the daughters. News travelled fast. Ponniah's wife arrived promptly at my aunt's and offered her services for a nominal 'fee,' as she had brokered for so many members of our family. She asked detailed accounts of cash, land or house and the jewels that would be given to Pushpam. She then enumerated the suitable boys and their families.

The unspoken but first consideration was the correct caste of the male. He could be handsome, rich and famous, but the caste overrode all. Ponniah's wife had to be careful as a marriage proposal at the request of the girl's family and then refusal by the young man's family was not taken amiss. It was not the same if the male proposed was refused by the girl's family. It was considered an insult to the young man's family and to the strip of village he came from. The suitable bridegroom was found within our village itself. The final inquiry was very easy. The washerman, who lived in our compound, was an unfailing source of information. Suppiah washed the soiled clothes of many in our village but owed allegiance to us, the main householder. The washerman was also referred to as the *Kattadiyan* as he practiced the occult art too. He was the most frequent visitor to any home, giving washed clothes, sorting dirty ones, listing everything, spent much time bundling them, all of which were done on the back verandah. He carried them away after much gossip and drinking of tea. His mug was specially reserved for him, and kept apart for his use only. He met many members of each family he washed for. He would know their physical and other characteristics, whether there was any sickness or debility in the family. He would keep his ears open for any shortfalls, criminal or otherwise. If not the washerman, the barber, another member of the retainer caste, would also do the needful, but was not so thorough in his information. He knew less because cutting the hair and shaving the face was done under a tree. Each member of the household was attended to at different times and individually. The caste of the proposed groom was minutely dissected. Every family thought theirs was a separate higher caste. The inquiries of the groom's family pertained to looks, dowry and reputation of the bride to be. If the female was good at needlework and music they too were added to her other accomplishments and her worth in marriage! After caste consideration of the male, the education and employment were scrutinized, then his reputation and lastly his looks. If he had many unmarried sisters that was an encumbrance, as he and his wife would have to see to their marriages and their dowries.

Vijayan was found as a suitable boy. He was of a similar caste, educated, employed, had no illnesses mental or physical, and had no criminal record. Pushpam wasn't still enlightened about her marriage. She was told only after the horoscopes were matched. Ponniah's wife had done her duty and gave over the rest of the arrangements to both sets of parents. Vijayan's parents and an older female came on an 'unofficial' visit to Pushpam's home, saw her and approved of her appearance. Pushpam was tall, slim, pretty, with a dusky complexion.

After a few weeks an elderly relative, a middle-aged female, arrived with Vijayan's horoscope and exchanged it for Pushpam's. My aunt handed the horoscope to their family astrologer to do the most important part of the marriage – the comparison of the two horoscopes. Every child in our village had a horoscope; even we had them in our family though we were Christians. The time of birth of every child was meticulously recorded at birth in the village. Every mother hovered around the midwife and watched the clock till the birth occurred. The horoscopes with the nine planets predicted in the twelve houses of the chart were compared for agreement on physical fitness, temperament, sexual compatibility, longevity and children. The horoscopes should match at least up to sixty percent. If the horoscopes didn't match, it was an unwritten ethical code that they be returned to the respective family. It was never given to any other family.

Pushpam's and Vijayan's horoscopes matched in compatibility. Pushpam was then told of the partner she was to wed. She hadn't still seen him! To be doubly sure, an uncle of hers went to the Brahmin priest of the village temple with two packages – one enclosed a white and the other a red flower. After he performed the *pooja* he was asked to open one. It contained the white flower. The marriage would be successful! All types of mumbo jumbo was practiced because getting married was like a journey to an unknown destiny.

About ten days later four well-dressed strangers appeared at my uncle's house. They were expected. Sweetmeats and tea were ready. After some time Pushpam was brought in, dressed in a silk sari, flowers in her hair and she wore some of her jewels. She was looked over critically, approved, and the motive for their visit revealed. It was to discuss the dowry! They were offered the betel leaf and arecanut and they began the transactions. With the discussion of dowry, marriage became a business proposition. The transaction too ended with the offer of betel.

Pushpam was given the parental home. Under the *Thesavalamai*, the legal rules in the north, the house would be written only in her name. The house and jewels were a matriarchal inheritance. The husband would have no legal right to them. This was to safeguard the home for a girl in case the marriage failed. If it did, the husband then had to leave the house without complaint! Pushpam got the major share of the mother's jewels, which must have the equivalent of ten gold sovereigns. The jewels were hardly altered for a century or more. The dowry was settled amicably and the cash promised. Once dowried, Pushpam had no legal claim to the parents' wealth after their demise. Her male siblings would inherit it. Since Pushpam was pretty, her dark complexion didn't alter the amount of cash dowry. Usually more cash would have been demanded for a darker complexioned girl. Pushpam was then told the details of the proposed groom, but she still hadn't seen Vijayan! She was wondering whether she would see him only under the *Manavarai Panthal*, the throne of the wedding ceremony, but Ponniah's wife quickly told her that she could have a glimpse of him. This glimpsing was to be at the temple on School Lane on the following Friday. Ponniah's wife had also shrewdly informed Vijayan that he could have a glimpse of Pushpam at the same temple. So they both had a glimpse of each other and the glimpsing seemed compatible. Pushpam remarked that there had been no falling in love at first sight, but he was pleasant to look at! Since the dowry was settled, a date for the registration of the wedding was sought and it had to be an auspicious day. The *Panchankam*, the Hindu almanac, was looked into and a date was set. The event would be at home.

On the day of registration of marriage, Pushpam was dressed less glamorously than a bride and awaited the groom. I still remember the dark maroon and gold sari she wore. The *attiyal*, the pearl throat-set with a small pearl pendant and the longer pearl chain with a bigger *paddakam* that rested on her chest. She wore many pairs of gold bangles and long dangling earrings with pearl circlets at the ends. The other jewellery was in boxes and kept on a table together with the deed of the house in its scroll. If anything was promised it had to be displayed.

The groom arrived in a silk *verti*, shawl and unshod feet. The couple sat at a table and signed the legal registration forms in front of witnesses and a legal officer. Glimpses between Pushpam and Vijayan became glances, then conversation. Pushpam told me later that she was relieved that his voice was low and mellow. Only the closest relatives were invited to this event.

The registration of their marriage was really the beginning of their courtship. As Pushpam was legally married they were allowed to go out and meet the family casually, in lanes and doorways. Official visits were always done after the ceremonial marriage! The parents were not worried at their freer movements and any misdemeanour, as they were married! The preparation for marriage seemed endless, but the wedding was to be held soon. Usually the sons of a family saw to it that their sisters were married before they did. Pushpam's brother married later a cross cousin. It was a correct consanguineous marriage. He married his mother's brother's daughter, but it could have been his father's sister's daughter. They were considered *Machan* and *Machal*, that relationship denoted eligibility to marriage. This would have been in their parents' minds since their births. There was easy banter and camaraderie between them since childhood. Still orthodoxy reigned and they were not allowed to go out together till their marriage was registered! Ponniah's wife was disappointed with such marriages as there was no brokering to do. Horoscopes could be scrutinized or glossed over and dowry was taken for granted; it need not be much. Only the registration and marriage rituals were the same.

Woe to a girl or boy who wanted to marry a not-so-correct cousin, like his or her father's brother or mother's sister's child. There would be pandemonium in the village. The marriage, if it took place, would have to be out of the village and they would not be tolerated any more in their parental homes. Genetics was unknown but gut feeling told them that a mental or physical defect could be doubly possible and might mar the marriages in the village in the future. The correct cousin marriages were very common. In fact, it was the first choice of parents. An arranged marriage was considered if there was no eligible cousin.

Pushpam, whose marriage was legally registered three months ago, was to be married the following month in a Hindu ceremony, on an auspicious day. A wedding was the most joyful and looked forward to event within a closely knit household of a village. After the auspicious day was chosen and almost a month before the wedding, Pushpam's parents or a closely related couple visited the homes of their relatives and friends to extend a verbal invitation to the wedding. These visits took many days. Letters and cards were unheard of. The parents of the bride would never be forgiven if they forgot to invite a relative!

The first concern of the younger females was who was going to wear what, and what jewels would match the saris they wore. A shopping expedition to town was arranged by a group of females, accompanied by an older aunt. There was no end to the acquisition of saris. Nobody would dream of wearing a sari worn even for a not-so-recent wedding. Others would remember it!

The saris were of silk and colourful. No white, greys or light shades of coloured saris ever came into consideration. The saris must have some amount of gold work either on the border and headpiece or scattered with gold in embossed designs. Saris were strewn on the shop tables, thrown over shoulders, or held next to the face to see its suitability. A lighter skinned girl had a greater choice of colour than the duskier ones. Each one wanted a unique buy. Sari buying took almost a day. Once bought they were wrapped securely and covered within bags to prevent water splashing on them for the boat ride home. Each one had to budget within the money given to her by her father.

Buying jewellery was rarer. Only the younger ones of the family and of course the bride had new jewellery made. The favourite jewellery was of pearls on a gold chain. The closer the pearls, the richer the jewellery was. The pearl was a favourite jewel of the north. Pearls were plentiful and of good quality because of the pearl fishery. It was started by the Arabs and then taken over by the Portuguese in the north. Most jewellery was passed on from mother to daughter and the eldest female in the family got the best of them. Jewels were never altered, never redesigned - only given to be cleaned and polished.

A generation ago, the goldsmith had come to the house bringing his fine, delicate tools and a receptacle for red hot burning coals. The goldsmith was of the middle order caste. He was given a portion of the rear verandah where he sat and made the jewels. The heat of the coals was kept hotter by blowing through a long hollow iron tube. He melted the gold, beat it with an anvil to a sheet on a granite block, reheated it and made the outer gold design. A responsible female sat by him with the gold sovereigns and precious stones wrapped in a silk cloth, held securely by her. The stones for easy retrieval were sometimes inserted into a cut ripe pumpkin! The eyes of the female would dart to the hands of the goldsmith, then shifted and glued to the pumpkin when the stones, even the smallest diamonds, were removed by the goldsmith for insertion into the finely wrought gold base.

The *padakkam*, the pendant, was the most exquisite of the jewels to be hung on a pearl chain. The pendant in making had tiny spaces separated by delicate gold filigree. Into these went the rubies from Burma and the emeralds from India, both of which were expensive, and the pendant would give an indication of the owners wealth. If not by these stones the spaces would be filled by white stones like zircons. Invariably every pendant would end in a row of pearls hanging from delicate gold spikes. The pendants were either large semicircles, lotus shaped, conch or shell shaped. Smaller *padakkams* are won on an *atiyual*, a throatlet, which may be of a single strand of pearls or a gorgeous collar of pearls of three to four strands. The other pearl chain was longer so that the *paddakam* rested on the chest or even longer so that it lay on the bosom. The *padakkam* of the older generations were so rich with gems and so large and indicated that the owners may have had big bosoms! There was no family among us without pearl jewellery.

Pearls were easy to obtain when the pearl fishery flourished in the north, close to Mannar. The Arabs started the fishery from the seas of the Malabar Coast down to Kalpitiya. When the Portuguese arrived, Mannar became an important base with Mantota as the harbour. The pearl fisheries were money spinners and the

Portuguese exported them, exploited the industry and finally killed it, leaving hardly any of it to the Dutch who came after them. When the Portuguese started the fisheries they got down the Moor *Paravas*, a caste of fisherfolk of South India who learnt the trade from the Arabs. The *Paravas* came with a few Portuguese officials from Tuticorin in *thonis*, boats, and with the help of a few local fishermen of Mannar searched for a suitable and known 'bank.' Divers were sent down to bring up the oysters. If the pearls in them were good in number, quality and value, a buoy marked the site and a camp was set up on the adjacent land. Houses were set up for the *vedor*, the treasurer, officials and a church was built adjacent to these. The workers were in huts, separated by caste to avoid quarrels! Then notice was sent out to get more vessels and divers. Each master of a vessel had to be registered with the number of divers he had. The latter's names and religions were noted. A search was made of any unaccounted divers, in case he removed oysters surreptitiously.

Pearl fishing started in March and went on till the end of April. Many fisheries along this coast were started and closed at the prescribed time. Fishing was protected by soldiers of the Jaffna fort, and men at arms from Mantota. Oysters were opened after all the fisheries closed. The pearls were removed with great care. The Arab traders and the Chetties, the merchant caste of the north, were given chits entitling them to buy pearls and the sum to be paid too for them. Not only did they have to pay the purchase money, but also the levies on shops rented, goods sold and the right of winnowing the sand for dropped pearls! The Portuguese were hard task masters. Most of the money went to the treasury. A part went literally to 'shoeing' the Queen of Portugal. Some was used to educate the Roman Catholic children of the fisher caste.

Excessive taxes were the cause of the dwindling of the fisheries. Masters of ships and divers were made paupers as only one fishery per year was permitted. The Moors made more than the divers. The Arab traders took away their pearls. The Chetties graded the pearls according to lustre, perfection and size and sold them to the jewellers and private traders. There was a great choice of pearls in the north and pearls became popular, much admired and a readily available jewel. These natural pearls were highly prized and found a place in every piece of jewellery found in the north.

If a female wore a pearl chain and pendant she would have also acquired a long small pearl-studded cage-shaped dangler, *chimmiki*, for her ears. It was attached to a lustrous five or seven pearled earring. These too went from mother to daughter. Though gold was an investment in the north, chunky and heavy gold jewellery was not favoured. A gold chain would invariably be interspersed with gold beads, semi-precious stones or corals. Corals too were a great favourite of the females in the north. The only exception was the thick, heavy gold *thali kodi* worn by married women, which was an investment and income in widowhood.

The older I became, certain incidents and people of my early life became clearer. I remembered my brothers. The youngest was always with us. He was never inclined to study or go abroad but was my mother's pet and she spoilt him. He was quite happy to be a clerical servant after obtaining the minimum qualification in school. He was very keen to marry a cousin in Malaya, but even in that endeavour he didn't pursue it - agreeing to marry another cousin in Jaffna and having a large family. We, the four girls in our family, helped him along in kind and cash to make ends meet.

I was very fond of my second brother Seeva. He was born in Puttur hospital, a maternity hospital set up by the Methodist mission. The Methodist missionaries were allowed to come under the tolerant rule of the British, though the Anglican Church got more privileges from the British. The Methodist Mission, in addition to its churches and schools, set up a small hospital in Puttur, a few miles from Jaffna. My father too was teaching in Puttur. The hospital was primarily set up to prevent the increasing number of women who died at childbirth in the late nineteenth century. Puttur was famous for its deep bottomless well.

Seeva

My mother remembered the names of the English nursing sisters, Easter and Gertrude, who worked there. In fact the doctors and nurses came from Britain. Sister Easter delivered my brother and told my mother by intuition that he would be a great man some day! He did become a doctor, considered something great in those days. This brother Seeva studied at Jaffna Central College, a Methodist school, and then he went to Malaya, as my mother's five brothers had flown the nest to Malaya and Singapore. One of them offered to educate him there with monetary help.

One incident I remembered well was how concerned he was when I was bitten by a dog. He too was a young boy and still in school. I was much younger. He took me to the doctor a mile away by rickshaw, while he cycled beside me. I remembered it was quite early in the morning. He got my wound dressed, took me home and rushed off to school. He was always selfless. In fact, we depended so much on his help for every little problem that arose at home, as my eldest brother was already in Malaya. The uncle in Singapore, who was a teacher, remembered the help my mother gave him financially while he was at school and wanted to reciprocate. Seeva was clever and fortunate to enter the medical college in Singapore. He was fortunate that my older brother Nava was in Singapore too. His home became Seeva's home too during his holidays. From Singapore he had to go to London to complete his degree. Many students, one of them being my brother, were discontinued from the medical school in Singapore as they had supported a students' strike. My two older sisters financed him there with loans, which he repaid promptly when employed on his return. When he qualified, as a doctor, he came home. We wished that he could have stayed in Jaffna for a long period, but it was not to be. First, he was sent to rural hospitals and then district hospitals, from north to south and then east to west. My family was able to see many places in Ceylon as my brother worked in Mannar, Udugama, Batticaloa and then Weligama. He was sent in succession to Beruwela, Ampara, Tangalle and finally to Ratnapura, his last station, as Superintendent of the hospital.

My older brother Nava who was older than Seeva was also educated in Singapore. I hardly knew him as I was a year old when my grandmother took him with her to Malaya on one of her frequent trips and left him with one of her sons who educated him. I was seven when he came home. I looked at him without recognition. I remembered how he carried me, kissed me and assured me that he was my brother.

Nava was sent to study, which he hardly did, but became a wonderful and well-known cricketer in the local scene. In those days the British in Singapore had their own cricket team and matches against England were frequent. They were short of players and asked Nava too to join their team. He played so well hitting sixes and fours, and with this wonderful talent he was able to win many matches for them. When he was seventeen and studying rather reluctantly, he started looking for a job. He remembered an English cricketer in his local team who was the head of a government institution. Nava, very smartly and without hesitation, went to this official and asked for a job. However, Nava said he was eighteen when he was only seventeen, an age when he should be in school. The boss asked him to come to his office the very next day and appointed him as a clerk. Even in those days there were many job opportunities and employment as avenues opened for a sportsman who was not academically inclined. Nava was generous with his pay, sent money to mother and then to my sister who needed the money for her marriage preparations. To do this he didn't hesitate to borrow money from a *Chettiar*, a *Chetty* money lender and paid the huge interest the loan entailed to help someone of his family. His cricketing reputation grew greater. There was much anticipation and then rejoicing when he came home on holiday. Everyone in the village was eager to see him play cricket. He did so, and when he hit the ball it went missing as it had fallen into a neighbours well, a long way off. Everyone was delighted, but not the neighbour. My brother Nava was fond of partying and drinking and had a premonition that he would die young. Seeva, the younger brother, then a medical student, assured him that he would look after his family.

True to his fear, Nava's wife died at her last and eighth confinement. Shortly thereafter, he too died. His family was truly stricken with grief, especially my mother. The older two children of Nava decided to stay back in Malaya but the others, six boys and a girl, were brought to Ceylon and my brother Seeva looked after five of them. My eldest sister and I took the younger two. Seeva had the onus of looking after so many children including his own five. He didn't hesitate to send all seven of the boys to a private school. They all travelled third class, even though his children were entitled to first class berths.

The eldest girl of Nava, who was now married and lived in Singapore, wished to have her siblings back. One by one they went, except the one with my eldest sister who wouldn't part with him even though she had three children of her own. Seeva was sad and disappointed and saw the cleverest of them go back – a nephew who could not master Tamil, the compulsory second language. In Malaya he did very well academically.

We visited the south of Ceylon and its interior regions when we visited my brother Seeva and family when he was appointed to southern towns. That land was so green and luscious, compared to the brown earth interspersed with tall trees of the north. My younger brother would tell me that if one planted a walking stick in the south, it would grow.

It was a weekend spent in Karainagar. We were in Jaffna and trips to see grandfather were done during a weekend of a month. My father too was there on that weekend as he was on holiday from Malaya. It was rare to see father and grandfather seated at the old heavy table in the latter's house. Their relationship was strained. Grandfather did not approve of his son drinking so much alcohol. He had got used to drinking the refined stuff abroad and came back to enjoy the palmyrah toddy too. In fact the money sent to us was insufficient and we depended on mother's brothers to help us financially.

They were seated with sheets of paper and noting the extent of their lands and income from the paddy fields. Income tax to be paid was hotly debated.

Grandfather remarked that the British did not bleed them dry. His grandfather had narrated and grumbled about the horrible taxes that had been fleeced from the northerners by foreign rulers before the British. The king of Jaffna, before the Portuguese, levied taxes for the upkeep of the monarchy and to maintain defences. The all-powerful mudaliyars kept accounts of the king's revenue in cash and in kind. Taxed in kind was the *pingo* of goods, which was defined as two porters' loads hung on either end of a pole carried on the shoulder. The subjects of the king gave their share of taxes as such.

In the early sixteenth century the northern peninsula attracted little attention from the Portuguese, who were already in the southern kingdom, because Jaffna produced no commodities of interest to them. In 1560 de Bragnea, realizing the shipping lanes and the strategic importance of the north, conquered Mannar, which till then was subject to the king of Jaffna. The Portuguese exploited the pearl banks and the shipping of pearls between Tuticorin and Kalpitiya. They took the export of elephants from Urukuthurai, later Kayts, which in Portuguese meant 'elephant quay.' Though unconquered, the king paid tribute to the Portuguese in Mannar either in elephants or their value in cash. He still flaunted his independence. This was in 1582. After many attempts King Sangili was vanquished in 1619 and he was taken prisoner. The Catholic and non-Catholic mudaliyars tried to overthrow the Portuguese with the help of the Nayak of Tanjore. This they did a couple of times till de Oliviera, the commander of the Portuguese, defeated the local forces. Magapillai Aratchi, baptized and known earlier as Dom Luis, led another revolt. This time he got help from Tanjore and from King Senarat of Kandy, but to no avail. King Senarat was keen to break the ring of Portuguese rule in Jaffna, Trincomalee and Batticaloa, but failed in this too. The Portuguese, once established, asked the mudaliyars to give a statement of revenue and expenditure in the old kingdom. This was done in the highest value coin, the *pardaos* of the ruler. The document obviously proved that Jaffna was hardly feudalized. Money transactions replaced taxes of land and its produce. There were no feudal levies and even the king's soldiers were paid in cash.

The only tax in kind was a pingo, which was equivalent to one hundred *pardaos* - not even one percent of income. The other 'in kind' payment was elephants to the king. The Portuguese realized the former non-realistic nature of income not taxed and took advantage of it with the presence of the increasing circulation of money. From 1624 until the end of their rule, Jaffna was turned into a money-making machine for the Portuguese. Revenue was far ahead of expenditure, the excess was siphoned off to their territories outside Jaffna. De Camora was the author of the terrible register, the Tombo, improved by Raiz alias Rodriguez and then completed by Mascarenhas. In 1634 a detailed register of each plot of land, the name of the owner, his caste and its produce were listed. The plot could be of paddy, palm, vegetables or miscellaneous cereals. The northerner had small plots of land and the Portuguese didn't mind the tedious work of surveying each plot which was taxed! The revenue to be taxed doubled. In the south a village was considered one plot and its revenue was so much less. The mapping of each small plot, however, became helpful later to the local people in case of litigation. When the Tombo was completed by Mascarenhas it had about two thousand folios in about seven books.

Tombos were also prepared for Mannar, Mantota and Vanni. By now Mannar had lost its privileged position. It came under the Jaffna administration which in turn came under Colombo. Vanni was a separate entity. Inheritance laws of *Thesavalamai*, the local laws, were translated and incorporated in the Tombo. By these manipulations of land division the revenue to be taxed increased by forty percent!

The mudaliyars were not honest and were withholding taxable revenue. The mudaliyars and adigars were replaced by Portuguese collectors in 1626. Still not satisfied with this increase of revenue, the collector levied taxes on the palmyrah that grew wild! The rationale was that no one sweated over their cultivation. The shrewd northerner started cultivating it. The Portuguese were not far behind, taxing the cultivated variety after giving a few non-taxable trees to the owner.

De Oliviera, the commander, had sold lands to the locals at very low prices. Some of these reverted to the crown and were resold at much higher prices. This increased the revenue by five percent. Though he was the overall commander, De Oliviera was unhappy that he was not involved in the Tombo and thought this unnecessary. It was a pity, as he was sympathetic to the northerners, especially the poor, and did not agree with the regular increase of taxes. But de Cammora insisted that surplus could be used outside Jaffna and that the fort of Trincomalee could use this surplus. The taxes on elephants were increased and added to the revenue. The northerner was further burdened by the increase in arrack and tobacco taxes. These were introduced by the Portuguese themselves in 1636. The tobacco trade was very remunerative and became twenty percent of the revenue. When the Portuguese lost the cinnamon trade to the Dutch, it was a loss of 30,000 *zerafins* to Colombo. Jaffna had to compensate! The bishopric of Cochin was supported by Jaffna and Jaffna became so important that it had a separate *vedor*, treasurer, in 1648.

In spite of the small plots of land of the northerners, parcels of land were given to Portuguese settlers. They paid so much less to the crown. Land policy followed revenue policy and not much allotment of land was given to the Portuguese to settle on. It was not for the love of the Tamils but the revenue from lands held by Tamils was much greater. The Portuguese, however, got the most fertile land of Nallur and Valikamam.

The Tombo that was begun in 1623 had eight thousand eight hundred and ninety families in the register by 1645. Unlike in Kotte, the Tombo became onerous and tedious, not only as each land was described by boundaries, ownership and crops, but the rent was fixed and taxed on hypothetical income.

Non-rebellion by the northerners meant non-confiscation of land, but when the tax became unbearable many migrated to the Vanni to escape from the burden of this tax. The higher caste Vellalas became mapannars and vanniahs. The madapallies who were already there as the high caste Vellalas were asked to spy on the Vellala new comers. The spies were also from the *thavalams*, the caravan carters, who brought trade from the south to Jaffna. The only tax paid in the Vanni was in elephants. Two thirds of these elephants had to be males. Overall the Portuguese ignored the Vanni.

The Dutch arrived in the east in 1638. Trincomalee had a wonderful harbour. Ships of all types sailed into it from the Coromandel Coast and a large amount of arecanut and cloth were exported from there. Batticaloa did not have a good harbour, but the land was fertile and well populated. It grew much paddy and was rich in timber, wax, honey and elephants for export. The Dutch exchanged the east for the cinnamon land of King Rajasinghe in the south. The Dutch proceeded to the interior and then to Jaffna overland.

Like the Portuguese, they needed money and the most important persons in the council of administration were the revenue officers. They appointed muhandirums and mudaliyars from wealthy Christian families as collectors.

Jurisdiction was from Kalpitiya to the north, past Mannar, the great inlet, and then to Point Pedro. Many lands were flat and excessively fertile. Rice and cotton fields were plentiful and so were elephants, both wild and tame. People were passive and hardworking. Among them were weavers, dyers and handicraftsmen. The islands too engaged in handicrafts. The

Dutch added Vanni, Trincomalee, Mullaitivu and Batticaloa to the Jaffna administration.

Governance was entirely different and revenue recovered differently, and taxes were impossible to bear in the north. There was no information on lands from the Portuguese. Hundreds of folios and books of the Tombo had been destroyed in the war or wantonly destroyed. A few registers were found. The Dutch got ideas from them and improved on them at the expense of the ruled. They relied on native chiefs to endorse the tax system.

A cash system was made use of and land lease was taken by the Dutch. The Tombos were revived, and more details of the owner and his caste and demarcations of land were detailed. In taxing grain, lands were assessed for quality before the crop was harvested. Compulsory labour was extracted from the lower castes. If they were not given because of the hereditary rights of the Vellala caste, their non-rendered services were commuted as tax to be paid by the relevant householder.

A committee of five would inspect each plot of land in every village. The Dutch started their own Tombos. The plot owners name, caste, family details and families that it supported were entered. Paddy fields were entered separately with the quality of paddy noted. Every fruit-bearing tree noted in the garden was taxed including the Murunga and Glyceridia.

The register had the number of people of lower castes in a household. This made them liable to service. The nature of service and the number of days were stipulated as tax. By these wiles the number of people to be taxed increased by twelve thousand and the revenue increased by 75,000 guilders. The excuse was that 'these lower caste people were unlawfully used and had evaded their liability to serve the Lord of the Land.'

This overall increase in rent and tax on produce made Jaffna revolt. This was in 1676 when the Tombo was almost complete. The Dutch always thought that Jaffna was calm and quiet. This was a shock to them. Revolt was aimed at the new Tombo. People left their lands and went into the jungle or to the Vanni. The army was stationed from Jaffna to the Vanni to stop them. The Tamils had no idea of *uliyam* or compulsory service to the king and thought that service of the caste slaves should be theirs. The service of caste tenant to landlord, which was less exacting, was not realized by the Dutch. This revolt led to the Dutch being more exacting, more efficient and more violent.

Started in 1623 by the Portuguese, the Tombo was finally completed in 1699 by the Dutch. A new unit of land, the *lacham*, was introduced. It was one sixteenth of an acre and computed as four sowing measures instead of eight. Produce too went up with it and so too land tax. New lands were sold as *lachams* and at a higher price. A fresh tax was levied on the few arecanut trees too!

The Dutch now controlled the Vanni and its inhabitants. Palmyrah timber, the hardest of all timber, was taxed. The cultivation of female trees by the locals and the best in timber was drastically reduced in numbers to escape the tax. The tree was a great source of food and toddy in the north. The tax system of the Dutch broke the spirit of the Jaffna man. He missed the king during Portuguese and Dutch rule. In the past, of the ten thousand *pardaos* accounted to the king, half of it went to pay the soldiers, and a quarter went to pay the temples and the mudaliyars. Only a quarter was given as tribute to the king in kind, like the pingo loads and elephants or the equivalent in cash. The revenue then too came from lands and fields.

In the east, the tax was ruinous. The land was very fertile. It was the granary of the previous kingdom. It had a tenurial system. Peasants gave the sovereign a share of produce and worked in his fields for certain days. Each caste was dealt with separately. The caste chiefs had to pay the taxes even in kind, like bees honey, wood of plants, elephants and cloth. Paddy and other produce had to be delivered at fixed prices. There were no private traders, and they had to give it at much less a price, almost half to that of the western region. Only the surplus was bought by the Muslim and Chetty traders. What added to their woes was that fields were inspected even before the harvest to prevent the harvest being hidden. Sometimes no seed paddy was left and no allowance made for failure of the crop and no incentive for production of paddy. Through sheer anger, the paddy would be destroyed rather than sold for such a low price. The people went into the interior for their livelihood.

The Dutch realized rather too late the impact of their economy and the immense influence of the caste system and gave up all their attempts to go against caste and subcaste. It was too complicated to understand, nor did they make any effort to do so.

"Then the British came, and that is another story", so said my grandfather, still writing copious figures on the sheaf of papers.

My father and a brother of his were the first converts to Christianity in our large and extended family. The education in Jaffna College of the American Mission may have been a catalyst to their conversion. It was later that we became Methodists due to the Methodist missionaries' zeal and the Methodist school Vembadi, which we attended.

St. Thomas brought Christianity to the East. It was to South India that he travelled, preached in and was later martyred. Later in remorse an icon of St. Thomas was kept in a temple. Christianity was more than a thousand five hundred years old but reached us in the fourteenth century. Hinduism was the religion of the north and many parts of Ceylon. It prospered for thousands of years. Hindu temples extended from Keerimalai to Devinuwara. Buddhism later took root in the south. Islam was introduced by the Arab traders first to the Malabar Coast. The converts there brought Islam to the north of Ceylon and then to the south with the migration of the Muslim traders to the southern coastal towns. Buddhism was seen in patches in the northeast. Arahat Mahinda arrived at Senthankulam near Kankesanthurai. He preached and taught whilst travelling to the south, converting many to Buddhism. Manimehalai was an ardent Tamil Buddhist woman who was a great teacher and writer of Buddhist books. Black granite statues of the Buddha, typically Dravidian in style, were found in the north in addition to burial mounds.

I lived in the east after marriage. I remember Seruvila which was then called Allai, where small black granite Buddha statues were placed in niches under trees and worshipped. They were so much like the black granite Hindu icons that too were placed under trees and worshipped. However, when we went there again many years later the statues were missing. The icons had been installed in a museum and white-painted, tall Buddha statues scattered in the open spaces had replaced them.

Buddhism could not establish itself in South India or in the north of Ceylon as the Chola kings jealously guarded Hinduism and were averse to Buddhism. They promoted Hindu culture in the north as it was in their Pallava or Chola kingdom. Christianity as Roman Catholicism was first brought to the north by the Franciscan monks of the order of St. Francis of Assisi. The people of Mantota, the port of Mannar, the people of the coast and of Kayts, the elephant quay - the port of the Portuguese, were the first converts.

Then the Portuguese came to the north. The conqueror of Jaffna was de Oliviera, the most ardent Roman Catholic of the rulers. He devoted his energy to conversion. His subjects, realizing how the wind blew, became nominal Christians. Every applicant for office needed a certificate from the priest. The priest converted the higher social class including relations of the king, the mudilayars, vaniyars and even a few temple priests! The greatest boast of de Oliviera was that he destroyed five hundred Hindu temples replacing them with churches. He used the metal from the melted Hindu idols and made bells for those churches.

Parishes increased and a priest, called *kannadi*, the spectacled priest, was most fervent in converting the people. He even had the audacity to burn a mosque on the harbour quay and another on the street inhabited mainly by the Moors. De Oliviera was called "Philip Raja" by the Catholics, as he helped the locals a great deal during a hailstorm. He died the following year. He was buried in Jaffna in the churchyard of his favourite church, the Church of the Lady of Miracles, even though his wife wanted to take his remains to Portugal. The enduring memento of the Portuguese rule was Roman Catholicism. Their numbers were never overtaken by the Protestants.

Many embraced this religion more as a convenience than by conviction. Conversion ensured jobs and ownership of land. The Portuguese had a peculiar way of conversion. The village elders publicised a meeting by means of the low-caste drum beater who shouted out the imminent arrival of a Portuguese missionary. The village population would meet under a tree, a mango or tamarind. The priest, a Portuguese and the local officials arrived and stood in the shade of another tree. The priest then read out a transliterated Tamil pastoral speech and then commanded the crowd to receive baptism. This was called 'general baptism,' which entailed compulsory church attendance. Non-attendance meant a fine or corporal punishment. The number of conversions looked impressive. Actually these 'converts' were practicing Christianity externally but Hinduism within their homes. A large number of churches and monasteries were built and simultaneously a large number of Hindu kovils razed to the ground. The Portuguese had no desire to educate the people any further. The old schools were left intact and its vernacular education went on.

The Roman Catholic converts were also along the coast south of Mannar among the fisher folk. There was a concrete column in Arippu, a village near Mannar, which commemorated Dona Catherina's safe stay there. The Portuguese hid her there to escape the wrath of the royal family of the Kotte kingdom.

The Jesuits came later and started their mission schools. The Catholic Church had very little land in the north. The missionaries' and churches' upkeep was by extracting cash from their flocks, and the fisher folk gave their tithes in fish. This made the outwardly non-practicing Roman Catholics to be more vigorous Hindus. The absence of a Hindu king was a tragedy and a drawback to the local people. With conversions, names too changed in a peculiar way. The Tamil endings were kept in names like Pedropillai, Manuelpillai and Johnpillai. Jaffna never became solidly Catholic, but the Portuguese were wise to introduce Catholicism in a Hindu milieu and conducted annual festivals of the church like those of Hindu temples. They took the statues of Jesus, Mary and the Saints round the church and into the streets in a procession with load music similar to that of a festival of a Hindu temple.

At the end of their stay the Portuguese united Jaffna, Mannar, Mullaitivu and Vanni, and taxes were paid to Jaffna. *Uliyam* or free services extracted from Catholics and others were used to build forts in Jaffna and then Kayts. The nominal Catholics at the end of Portuguese rule had the capacity to say a few prayers and make the sign of the cross. The natives did not experience any of the blessings which the foreign religion was expected to bring.

The Dutch followed the Portuguese. The Reformation had taken place in Europe by now. Their Calvinist Christianity was more organized and systematic. They showed no mercy to the

Roman Catholics, expelling them from the main towns and closing their religious institutions. The Dutch gave more religious freedom to the others. The nominal Roman Catholics fled back to Hinduism. The Roman Catholic churches were converted to Dutch Reformed ones. The Baroque architecture and decorations of the churches were removed, and the churches became simple, airy, columned ones, with typical large Dutch doors and windows. They repaired only a few of the broken Hindu temples. Their type of Christianity looked cold and sterile with no rituals. The Roman Catholics grew in number even under the Dutch. The Dutch insisted that those employed under them attend Sunday service bringing their wives. Like in the temple, there was segregation of sexes. All sat on the floor of the church and its aisle separated the genders. When the wives refused to attend church, like my great great grandmother, her husband paid a few cents to another female of the household, probably of a lower caste, and sent her to church to represent his wife. Only the numbers of each sex had to tally! The Dutch were keener to change the names of places than to convert. The Tamil names of the islands were renamed by the Portuguese, and then renamed again by the Dutch. Only the name Delft remained. The religious minister was an ordained Dutchman from Holland. Educated natives were preachers and teachers for proselytization. The Dutch clergy took control of education, and a complete religious educational system was given by the Dutch Reformed Church. Catechism, prayers, reading and writing in the vernacular were taught. The school masters became responsible for the Tombo, the land register, the registration of marriages and deaths too.

The educational establishment of the Dutch held sway over all. The Dutch official visited the village once a year to see the baptized, and to baptize, marry and bury the dead if need be, but mainly to see the school register. The Dutch were in Jaffna for one hundred and thirty years. Conversions to the Calvinistic Protestant faith were more from the higher castes, but numbers were still much fewer than the Roman Catholics. All told, the 'pagans' were equal in number to the Christians! The Dutch brought more merchants than religious leaders.

The British arrived in 1795. They allowed the Dutch to continue education in the vernacular, but the British stopped them from serving the crown when they refused to pray for the king of England! The Dutch were allowed to visit the rich and pray over them. In 1805 the Protestant missionaries arrived. The British abolished direct proselytization or compulsory conversion. No religious beliefs were stipulated for officers and religious freedom was given to all. They repaired the Hindu temples but not to their pristine glory. The disabilities to the Roman Catholics were removed.

The Methodist missionaries started the schools in the north. By 1811 they had twenty-three schools. Most of them were set up in villages along the coast. Church and school began together, and education was in the vernacular. A few English schools were established in the main towns. The Anglican schools were fewer in number in the towns of the north and education was in English and Tamil.

The American Mission made the greatest impact in the west of the peninsula and islands. They set up ninety-five schools and three boarding schools all by mid-nineteenth century. Vernacular and English studies went hand in hand.

Vembadi, a Methodist school which I attended, was founded in 1839. It was preceded by the Methodist Central College, the oldest school for boys in Jaffna that started in 1816. My principal was Miss Lythe. I started education in a Tamil school till my English improved to be admitted to Vembadi. I loved school because I was good and earnest in my studies. We students would wear the stipulated uniform but other attire was permitted. The footwear was not uniform. Slippers and sandals were common but most feet were bare of anything.

Rev. Dr. Daniel Poor
The First Principal of
Jaffna College.

My grandfather told me that the Batticota Seminary and then Jaffna College churned out scholars. Mackenzie Canagaratnam, who founded the first Hindu English medium school in 1876, was a product of Batticota Seminary. With all these advances, in both construction of schools and education, the caste system could not be shaken. It was 1915 and when I went on holidays to Karainagar my uncles, who were staunch old boys of Jaffna College, related past and recent events in their old school.

Rev. John Bicknell came in 1911 as principal. He left an indelible stamp of his personality and beliefs on the school. It was still the era of bullock cart transport. There was no electricity and no instant communication facility. Rev. Bicknell wanted to change something he could. The caste barriers were still strong. No low-caste boy was admitted to the school hostel. Rev. Bicknell admitted the first boy from the lower caste to the hostel. There was pandemonium in the school and all the high-caste students stood in a line next to the school office and asked for their school leaving certificates! The certificates were promptly given and the schoolboys left school. The staff apprised Rev. Bicknell of the gravity of the situation. He was not moved. He said he would continue the school, stand by his conviction and teach that one boy. As days passed by, the high-caste students returned one by one. Education was of such great importance to them that it overran caste issues. The caste barrier in the school hostel truly broke down and the different caste students ate together and shared the rooms. The caste issue never raised its head again in the hostel. It did so in the school a few years later, when a low-caste boy was in the football team. A match was scheduled to be played against a Hindu college nearby. A telegram was received by the principal of Jaffna College – "If Abraham plays we don't play." The Jaffna College team met and sent back a telegram, "If Abraham doesn't play, we don't play." Rev. Bicknell was delighted that the students had started thinking differently. Of course, the elders of my family had thought differently. They thought the decision of the college was premature.

It was way back in 1820 that the first printing press was started in the north at Batticota and mostly used for printing the school texts, religious tracts and leaflets. In 1841 the island's second oldest paper, the first being the *Ceylon Observer*, was printed and called *The Morning Star*. The latter had an unbroken record of publication. As years went by the machines of printing were worked by members of many castes, as no caste was associated with the monopoly of any occupation associated with machines. The work of the machines temporarily broke caste barriers. The missionaries themselves became fluent in Tamil. Rev. Myron Winslow published the first comprehensive Tamil English Dictionary in 1862.

During this time, many converts by conviction or convenience reverted to Hinduism. Though Vairavanathan and Muthukumaru became Nevins and Mather, Carrol and Thamotherampillai reverted to Hinduism. Some of the Hindu scholars of Batticota Seminary founded Hindu schools, but much to the disappointment and sadness of the Christian missionaries, the Hindu schools admitted at first only the high-caste boys to them. One of the many converts who reverted back to Hinduism did so as he was thoroughly disappointed and upset at the treatment meted out to him by the missionaries. He was groomed to be the head of an American Mission school. He was baptized as Samuel Hutchins Taylor, named after one of the five missionaries who translated the Bible into Tamil. Taylor became a reputed scholar and was well known for his Tamil poetry and lyrics. He set the lyrics to violin music. He was also known for the Christmas carols he wrote in Tamil. He was appointed the editor of *The Morning Star*. Taylor was overlooked by the American Mission and had appointed a much younger foreign missionary to the post that Taylor was promised. He was determined to foster his own Hindu school. He changed his name to Taylor Thuraiappahpillai and started a school in his own home in Tellippalai. In his home he converted a room into a classroom with a blackboard and taught his daughter and a niece. He greatly desired to educate the females in his family. His wife was a nominal Christian, baptized either before marriage or even earlier at the American Mission's Girls' school at Uduppity where she studied, and her baptismal name was Rosabelle. She gladly reverted back to Hinduism when her husband did so and reverted to her former name, Thaiyalnayaki. Taylor then started his school on his own land and named it Taylor School, which he later named as Mahajana College. He was also appointed the editor of the newspaper *The Hindu Organ*. Years later his school grew in stature and great scholarship. All this history was spread by word of mouth by the older generation.

The arrival in Jaffna of the American missionaries with their liberal and wide education had unintended consequences. There was a concentration of efficient Protestant mission schools in Jaffna, which led to a revival among local Hindus led by Arumuga Navalar, and they built many Hindu schools within the peninsula. The local Roman Catholics too started more schools as a countermeasure. Later the state started its primary and secondary schools. Jaffna was saturated with educational opportunities and the majority of Tamils became literate. The British colonial government used this literacy to hire Tamils as government servants, not only in the south of Ceylon, but in Malaysia and Singapore. With employment the Tamils settled in the south and this influx of Tamils was used by politicians later to bandy the 'divide-and-rule policy' of the British. It was made the reason for standardization of marks according to community that came later and may have been the cause of riots and civil war.

In 1922 the centenary celebration of Jaffna College took place. The village was agog as most of the boys of the younger generation attended that school. The villagers decorated the school, its premises and even the public roads. The celebration was enhanced by the 10th anniversary of the opening of the library in 1910. It was opened during the stewardship of Rev. Brown. The school had an advantage, as the American Mission was rich, and it stocked the library with many books. Every worthwhile magazine produced anywhere in the world was available in the library. My daughter who was there many years later said that *Life* magazine and the *Illustrated Weekly* of India sat cheek by jowl on the same shelf. The students were even luckier as the years went by. The library was opened in the mornings for a few hours and then again in the evenings till ten o'clock with closure in between. This was to encourage the students to take part in sports. In the evenings, the male students were allowed to come in sarong or *verti* and shirt to the library. The westernized would even saunter in wearing a smart pair of pajamas and a matching coat! The females were expected to dress with decorum. The closing hours of the library was much appreciated by the local and foreign graduands and the people of the north. The undergraduate section prepared students for the degree of the University of London. It was the best school library for many years. It treasured books of the East and West, and the most treasured books were kept safe in glass cases. These were the English medical textbooks translated by Dr. Green and his students into Tamil in 1858.

The cockbird was a late riser in our village! The alarm was in the udder of the cow looked after by aunt Kamalam. At four thirty in the morning there would be a gentle moan from her cow that was affectionately named Ponni, though it was a white Sindh cow and not a golden one! If the moaning was ignored, louder and louder became the moans that followed. If still not heeded the cow bellowed, requesting immediate help to relieve the engorgement of milk in her udders. The calf, which was tied a little distance from his mother, clamoured to reach her. It had to wait its turn.

Kamalam jumped out of bed and wrapped a sari haphazardly over her long skirt and blouse. She as usual had slept in the latter garments. Nightdresses were unheard of. She tied her long black hair into a knot at her neck while she ran towards the cowshed. She hurriedly cleaned the already cleaned pails again, washed the udders and began her first chore of the morning. She deftly and quickly milked the udders of the cow alternately and very soon a pail or more was filled with milk. The calf, still young, nudged her shoulders while she milked, to get to its mother. The udders were never emptied as the calf had to be given its share of milk. With great joy the calf rushed to the mother after Kamalam had milked the mother. Every young and willing female of that large household were at the same task in the large cowshed with four or five cows in it. Each cow would be tenderly spoken to by its name. The calves were kept until they were weaned and then sold or kept if the mother was getting old. Kamalam took the pails brimming and frothing with milk to the rear verandah of grandfather's house.

Then she began her next chore. Kamalam sold the excess milk to villagers who had no cows. The villagers had brought clean utensils and bottles and had left them on the *thinnai*, the front porch, the previous evening. Kamalam cleaned them again and left them on the back verandah. She was so particular to clean the villagers' utensils as any souring of the milk would be promptly blamed on the drawn milk. After she took sufficient milk for the use of her household and ours, she poured the milk into a brass vessel with a beaked spout and filled the bottle up to a pint or more as requested. The purchasers ambled in and took their share of milk. Cash was paid promptly at the end of each month. She collected about ten rupees, a large sum it was at that time. Prompt payment was the rule as the northerners realized and appreciated the hard work that went into the production of grains, greens or milk.

My mother was given her share of milk and she boiled part of it in a large saucepan. While it was boiling she added the ground coffee and the brown sugar. Water was unheard of in the making of coffee. The milk was stirred and the thick cream that came to the surface was also stirred into the coffee. Each of us was given an enamel cup of steaming coffee. We enjoyed every sip. What a glorious taste it had - I can still taste it! Kamalam did the same and my grandfather relished his coffee. It tasted different from ours! Coffee seeds had been ground with coriander seeds and then brewed. We did not care for that taste at all.

It was five in the morning and still dark. Soon the night was nudged away by the sun. I never saw a colour tinged dawn. The sun rose suddenly, fast and hot. I saw the sun creep over the live fence. It sat awhile on the margosa trees at the edge of the *valavu*. Then it stealthily but quickly made bright the mango tree. The almost black palmyrah of the dusk became brown, tall and distinct at the further end of the garden. In the blink of an eye the whole garden was bright and hot. The sunlight poured into every space and very soon the heat rose from the ground.

The men who walked the 'well sweep' descended from its height. They had been walking the well sweep since four in the morning to escape the hot, steamy sweaty mornings.

Kunchu, the old female domestic help, came with her *ekel* broom to sweep the ground before the heat made her physical work uncomfortable. She swept the garden, bent over the broom as it had no long handle. *Ekel* brooms with long handles took time to arrive at our village. Kunchu swept the ground spotlessly clean, bereft of every dry leaf. She made piles of the dried leaves and refuse, gathered them painstakingly and deposited them into the nearest compost pit. Deep pits were dug in many parts of the garden. She collected the dung too from the cowshed and put it in these pits, and covered them with a layer of soil that was kept on the side of the pit when it was dug. Her daily work saw the pits filling with compost. Vegetation was so precious, even the dead ones. When swept, the compound was so white, clean and sandy that we sat on it.

Kamalam was still busy. She took a part of the milk to make buttermilk for a midday drink for grandfather and I went there on time for it too! To make the buttermilk she poured some milk into a deep container. Into it she immersed a wooden churning rod which had a serrated oblong base. She held the rod between her two palms and rolled it to and fro, with speed and agility, churned the milk. I watched mesmerized and with admiration when she made the buttermilk. The cream rose to the top. She scooped out this yellowish tinged cream, which was left aside for days to become *Ghee* – clarified butter. This was a great favourite in which vegetables were fried and lentils tempered. Ghee was also be poured onto cooked lentils before eating. The lighter skimmed portion *moor* or buttermilk was poured into a brass container, and when sliced onions, cut green chillies and salt were added to, it became a savoury tasty drink. Any visitor who came by was given this drink. Grandfather would drink a tumbler full of the drink with his lunch as well.

A little curd, saved from the previous day, was added to some of the milk kept aside. This milk became curd overnight and was eaten the next day. Curd was eaten by us with rice, and as dessert with sugar or jaggery. Most northerners, being wholly vegetarian or vegetarian many days of the week, depended on curd, buttermilk and milk for a complete and nutritious meal. The cow was treated with much respect and affection. They were celebrated and made much of on the day after the *Pongal*. Many a time I saw aunt Kamalam's cow led away from the stall by an unfamiliar young man. I was told that the cow was taken to be sired by a stud bull of repute that was in an adjacent village. New blood was always sought for to improve the cattle stock. The owner of the bull was paid handsomely. My other aunt Nirmalam reared goats and their kids. Goats milk was much in demand by the villagers who had allergic problems especially asthma, which my grandmother had too. Drinking goat's milk reduced greatly the recurrence of these allergies. So Aunt Nirmalam had good sales for the goats' milk.

Most of the outdoor work had stopped by ten in the morning. The washerman living at the end of the compound would have washed our clothes and hung them on clothes lines. The women had gone to their smoky kitchens to cook the lunch and everything seemed quiet except the cawing of the ubiquitous crows and the barking of the mongrel dogs, the pets of the household. They barked for no apparent reason.

The churning for buttermilk and ghee in Jaffna

Ceylon history was hardly taught by the British missionaries of my school. We were taught that in the prehistoric period Ceylon was part of India. We paid little attention when our teacher droned on about the Paleolithic period of ten thousand years ago and the Stone Age in which the stone tools used were the clumsy heavy axes. These evolved into small lighter ones and later in that period to more elegant cutting tools. The inhabitants' occupations were hunting and cultivation. The Mesolithic period with more Stone Age industry followed. It indicated settled communities that lived with hunters and fishers. This age was followed by the Iron Age which was about one thousand B.C.

Agriculture and domestic animals were prevalent in this society and during this period, ethnic types appeared. This was due to the migration of dark-skinned Australoid and Negroid types. The latter is still seen in the Andaman Islands where little mixing of people took place. Migration of physically similar people to Ceylon took place as land was continuous from South India. Even after separation, migration took place by the land bridges in the sea. These mixtures of people were the ancestors of modern day South India and Ceylon. Human traffic went to the islands off Ceylon, which were also stepping stones between India and Ceylon. Dark complexions made them Dravidian ethnic types. It was common folklore that when a visitor saw Ceylon he had gasped at the beauty of it and exclaimed *Ilankai*, which means beautiful in Tamil. Tamil was a dominant language among other languages in that protohistoric people of South India and north Ceylon. Tool technology was similar in both South India and Ceylon. They were made of quartz and had similar shapes. They were similar in southeast India and northwest Ceylon.

Mesolithic people migrated further to the south of Ceylon rather than staying in the north, because of a lack of water, and then migrated from the south to every part of Ceylon. Common physical features were seen in both populations. The Veddah seemed to be the last of these Mesolithic people. Their pubertal rites are similar to those of the people of the north of Ceylon. This

Mesolithic period might have existed for twenty-five thousand years before the Iron Age.

I read more than I was taught of that Mesolithic age. In the north the Mesolithic people settled in Tambapanni. They grew into many tribes and spoke many dialects. Tambapanni with Mantota, the earliest port, had a direct route by sea to the port of Matirai in South India, which brought a constant flow of traders. A tribe in Tambapanni was the Nagars, who regarded the cobra as sacred. It was the dominant tribe. The land was then called Nagadipa. Legends and history became intertwined. Kuveni was the queen of this tribe in Tambapanni. The ruins of her kingdom were still seen between the Gulf of Mannar and Wilpattu sanctuary. In recounting history there was the story of Prince Vijaya of India who came and married Kuveni, and had children by her. Prince Vijaya then deserted her, went south and established a kingdom there.

More important to the tribe was the harnessing of water, as Naga civilization was agrarian. One of the better known landmarks of this Naga civilization was the reservoir, the Nagarkulam. It was created southeast of Mannar. No chronicles mentioned it. It was as isolated as the north of the country. Extensive ruins near it pointed to a large settlement near Nagarkulam. Names like Nagativu and Sivanagarkulam were prominent as names of villages. Nagarkulam was a reservoir with a channel system. It had two parallel embankments toward the sea and a curved bund that joined them. The tank was enclosed on three sides. Irrigation of lands was from the front and flanks. Earlier the tank was named Akatimuraippu. The Arippu Aru's branches flowed to the left and right of it. The origin of these branches was the Malwatu Oya. The tank was surrounded by barren land when first discovered by the Dutch. They were amazed at its size and promptly renamed it as the Giant's Tank. They discovered that it fed one hundred and twenty two smaller tanks by channels, which in turn watered the numerous paddy fields. Detailed examination of the ancient engineer's skill found that the centre of the tank was shallow and unfinished, which may have been the cause of it drying up ever so quickly in the very hot weather of that region.

With the rise of the Pandyan kingdom more of the Tamil drama and literature came to the north with the demise of the other dialects. The Pakrit language brought in by Jainism and Buddhism did not take a permanent place in the north. Trading with the west at Mantota flourished. The single and most sought after article was the valuable pearl from the Gulf of Mannar near Karkai and Pookulam, where pearl fisheries flourished. The other articles sought for were the chanks, the conch shells. They were used as ceremonial trumpets, libation vessels, symbols of good omen and charms against evil.

Legend said that King Solomon's ships sailed by the Phoenicians took ivory, gold, hyacinth (the blue sapphire), apes and peacocks from Mantota. The Hebrew names of some of the above were from syllables from Tamil and Sanskrit. The Phoenicians were great traders. The written symbols of the Tamils were Brahmi, but that may have been influenced by the Phoenician alphabet introduced earlier by traders, maybe in one thousand B.C. The ships were not able to sail to the southern ports of Ceylon as huge rocks in the sea, blocked the ships' passage.

Overlooking the Bay of Mannar was a hillock, the Kuthiramalai, the horse hill. This may have been the pasture land of the horses that were to be shipped abroad and other breeds of horses that were brought in. This horse trade flourished during Portuguese and Dutch rule. Horses were bred in Delft. The name Tambapanni was derived from the lovely copper coloured sand that covered that region and Kuthiramalai too. There was also a long tomb and a little temple in the vicinity of Kuthiramalai.

The other prehistoric legend mixed with history is that of Ravanan. Legend blending with history or vice versa was anybody's guess. Ravanan, considered a dark skinned Dravidian, must have been of the Yaksha tribe and ruled Ceylon from the verdant parks and gardens of the south. He was considered at first a good king. He was pious, a devotee of Shiva who gave him superhuman powers. He was cultured, a music lover and a maestro on the *veena*. Excess love of power made him feel like God.

He was so famous for his fighting prowess that any icon of his showed ten heads on one body which meant that he was able to see every foe in every direction. Every face had a bristling moustache, a typical Dravidian feature, unlike the Hindu Aryan icons. He was supposed to have had a wonderful kingdom, family and many siblings. He was not only a warrior but a good and clever physician and a musician.

With his extraordinary powers he thought he was equal to God. He went to the foot of the Himalayas, stood there and challenged God. God Siva, seated on the pinnacle of the Himalayas, put out his foot and placed his big toe on Ravanan and crushed him. Overcome with remorse and still prostrate, Ravanan fashioned a *veena* out of his back bone and one of his heads. He played the instrument so beautifully that God relented, lifted his foot and let him go back to his kingdom. Much later in his life he made the fatal mistake of abducting Sita, the wife of Rama, an Aryan prince and brought her to Lanka in his legendary aerial chariot. While bringing her to his kingdom he had hidden her many times in many places. One of these was in a deep cleft in Swami Rock in Trincomalee, called Ravanan's cut. While there, he heard of his mother's death and was sad that he could not get back to do the last rites. Vishnu in the form of a hermit approached him and offered to perform the last rites at Kanniya, a village six miles from Trincomalee. Needing water for the rituals, the hermit pierced the ground at Kanniya and the hot springs leapt out. The hot springs had water which ranged from mildly hot to boiling hot. A small Sivan shrine was built and many went there to perform the last rites for their dead.

Ravanan then took Sita to the south and kept her hidden in a beautiful garden in the interior of his kingdom. A battle raged between Ravanan and Rama, and finally Ravanan was killed. The outcome may have been different if his brother Kumbakarnan didn't lapse into sleep intermittently and his younger brother Vibeeshanan did not betray him by joining Rama. Vibeeshanan was later crowned king of Lanka. Ravanan's wife wept over him and sang a dirge, still remembered, praising his exploits and what a wonderful king of Lanka he was.

Years later, my doctor brother would tell me that Kumbarkarnan suffered from narcolepsy and could not help falling asleep intermittently. These tales were more interesting than history itself. Dates of historical events were difficult to remember, but not the legends, true or false, that were associated with history.

We moved to Jaffna. We were to occupy the Dutch house on the Second Cross Street, right in the heart of the town. I was thrilled in anticipation of Jaffna, and attending an English missionary school, Vembadi. The only thought that clouded this enthusiasm was that I was leaving my grandparents and a whole host of uncles, aunts and cousins who lived in that large compound that was our *valavu* in Karainagar. I felt sadder to leave my grandfather whom I tailed wherever and whenever he roamed in his garden.

We went a few months before the school commenced its new academic year, which was January. We had to take only our clothes to the new house as the three uncles, who jointly bought the house, not only generously gave it rent free but had furnished it with the essentials. That was good enough for us. Our village home was also furnished simply like most homes in the north.

I remembered the house as we had seen it before, but, again, its large size, its thick walls, enormous doors and windows, typically Dutch, were simply staggering to my young eyes. As we entered through a long and broad verandah there was the combined sitting and dining rooms. A large room and two smaller ones opened into it. There was a large hall-like room which was to be the girls' bedroom with its simple beds and a cupboard. The roof was so high that I craned my neck as far back as possible, and even with that effort I only got a glimpse of the roof. Dutch houses had no ceilings. The beams that supported the roof were broad and strong, probably of teak. The large windows faced each other so that the breeze swept in and swirled about in the room and made it cooler. The Portuguese houses had been small, two storeyed, with a central courtyard and the rooms opening from it were also small, as were their windows and doors. The Dutch made everything big, which made the house and the rooms cool by the breeze coming through such large windows. Ventilation was the ultimate for comfortable living. The colonnaded courtyard was behind the main house. The kitchen lay beyond it, reached by a verandah. The verandah had smaller rooms opening into it, probably store rooms and servants rooms. There was a combined toilet and bathroom. One of its two doors led into the bedroom and the other opened onto the back verandah. The Dutch had still not introduced the water closet. The night soil was removed by the scheduled caste, coolie, who trundled his noisy cart stopping at every house.

They entered the premises by a side door, removed the night soil liberally covered with sawdust, and emptied and cleaned the enamel buckets into a larger pail in the cart. They unobtrusively left the premises.

The front of our home also had a colonnaded verandah. The house sat right in the middle of the compound. Garden space was a few feet round the house. The space between house and road was even smaller.

Old Dutch Houses in Jaffna

Our neighbours' houses were close to us and in some streets where the land was more expensive the walls of the houses abutted each other. Each house was literally a step from the road. The gables of the Portuguese houses were not seen in these houses. They were considered dangerous during the monsoon storms. Instead, fan lights had been installed.

My younger sister and I were not admitted to Vembadi immediately, as our village school hadn't made us proficient in English. We were sent to the primary school attached to the

Anglican Christ Church for two years and when we were considered proficient in English we were admitted to Vembadi Methodist School. I was so proud on the day of enrolment at school. Right throughout my schooling I had six friends and we went from one class to a higher one, together. Three of them from orthodox Hindu homes left school after the Junior Cambridge exam which was equivalent to the eighth standard and were groomed for marriage, but the rest of us went on to sit the Senior Cambridge examination. Our uniforms were simple. In fact, the missionaries introduced the white, calf-length uniforms but we wore no shoes!

Among the communities who lived in Jaffna there were hardly any Sinhalese families, but there were plenty of Dutch Burgher families. The British took over Ceylon from the Dutch by treaty and not by war, as it had been between the Dutch and the Portuguese. The Dutch preferred this treaty rather than a three-pronged war with the French and the British. Before the arrival of the Dutch, the British and French were more antagonistic to each other trying to capture the harbour in Trincomalee, a stepping stone to the forts in the coastal region. With the conquest of Jaffna by the Dutch there were many Dutch families in Jaffna. The British, now the rulers, did not allow the Dutch to sell their possessions and move south, so the Dutch preferred to stay in Jaffna for several generations rather than lose their homes. The longest lived family was the Koch family who were there for three generations. There were also the Jansens, the Van Sandens, Speldewindes and quite a few more but now forgotten names. We met them mostly in church as most of the girls went to the convent and the sons were sent to St. Patrick's College. The parents knew their sons would be disciplined by that great disciplinarian, Father Long at St. Patrick's. My husband too studied there and would relate how his brothers and he travelled by bullock cart from Trincomalee to Anuradhapura for three days and nights. They got down frequently, pushed the cart that held their iron trunks over hillocks which were rudely called by them 'buttock breakers'! Hurricane lanterns and fires were lit, from night to morning, which kept them safe from animals while they slept.

At Anuradhapura they would take the train to Jaffna. This railway was started only in the last years of the nineteenth century. Unlike in our society there was no caste system among the Burghers but the northerners did not fail to repeat that the 'good Burghers' came from Jaffna!

The Methodist Church in Ceylon, the oldest in Southeast Asia, was founded in 1814. The boys' school in Jaffna, Central College, was founded by it in 1816 and it took twenty-three more years to found the girls' school in 1839. This reflected the prominence given to male education.

Miss Tweedy was the first principal at Vembadi. I looked up to Miss Lythe, my principal, for her sense of fair play, justice and humour. I was a keen student, good in my work too, and that made my school days at Vembadi very happy. I managed to be among the top five of the class.

During my early school days at Vembadi, my oldest sister Harriet Chellamah left school after the Junior Cambridge Exam. Most of her schooling had been at the American Mission School in Karainagar. My grandmother took her to Malaya on one of her frequent visits. They returned when my youngest uncle was to be married to his cousin in Ceylon. My sister was about eighteen years old and she was pretty. She brought with her a considerable wardrobe of pretty frocks and saris. She was even prettier when she wore these frocks. She could speak English a little better than us and was haughty. My younger sister and I fumed with anger when she insisted on walking almost a hundred yards ahead of us as she considered us village girls, inferior to her. It was such a joy when we mastered English and left her far behind in it, though we never grew up to be pretty like her.

I was one of the first girls in our family to sit the Senior Cambridge examination. The Junior Cambridge examination was what most school girls sat for and then left school to be groomed for marriage. A few of us sat the Senior Cambridge exam and I did very well, getting better results than Pakiam, who was considered cleverer than I. In addition to the main subjects, English dictation and spelling were included in the English language examination paper.

The principal called me and gave me the wonderful news of me being selected for the matriculation and then First in Arts examination. I was truly over the moon at this news.

I felt I was flying home, rather than walking, to tell my mother this wonderful news. She looked at me with great pain in her eyes and told me that she could not educate me further as education meant money. She didn't have the money nor could she ask her brothers who had already educated two of my older brothers. I was stunned and shocked but felt a great empathy for her as she did so much for us over the years.

My heart and mind were in a whirl but the following day I went to the principal and with sadness told her that I was unable to enrol for the matriculation examination. She was sympathetic but could not help me as scholarships were so rare. She offered me a teaching post in the primary section. My friend Pakiam was lucky to go on with her studies and become a medical doctor. My friend Faith took a teaching post in another school. My teaching years were my happiest as I had a great gift of teaching children. This inability to go for higher studies may be the reason for my

Fellow Teachers

ambition to see my daughters go on to get their professional degrees.

Later on in life, I would gladly volunteer to teach my neighbours' and friends' children. Many nephews too came for the extra tuition during their school holidays, and told me years later how they appreciated the time I spent with them.

The British arrived in Ceylon. The Dutch had become militarily weaker by now, but Jaffna to them was a profitable commandment as communication with South India was so easy. The British East India Company had eyed Ceylon, ages before they came, for its cinnamon. The Portuguese, however, were well entrenched. So were the Dutch. They had guarded this source of wealth. Dutch power declined due to their wars against France. Both France and Britain eyed the eastern harbour to berth and repair their ships. King Keerthi Sri Rajasinghe wanted the Dutch out and to give the Trinco harbour to the British. France captured Trinco harbour but gave it back to the Dutch! The Dutch didn't want a three-pronged attack with Britain and France. Holland was at war, which spread as far as Batavia. The Dutch made a peace treaty with Britain and gave them Trincomalee with the cooperation of the king. The first aim of the British was to repair all the forts that the Portuguese had built in the maritime provinces. They made Trinco their headquarters.

The Dutch changed their minds and kept vacillating about their colonies. The British decided to conquer the island. Stuart attacked Trinco and breached Fort Ostenberg. Batticaloa was easier to capture. The garrison there, in fact, ran away into the countryside even before the British arrived. The British captured Jaffna in October 1795. A British regiment was sent from Nagapattanam to Point Pedro, and Jaffna was conquered on October 16.

The British were dead broke after the wars. Whether they were Portuguese, Dutch or British, the conquerors sat down to tax the conquered even before the bugle sound of victory ended.

Frederick North was made the first governor of Ceylon in 1798. He made many changes. He introduced the rix dollar notes in 1801, a substitute for copper money. The rix dollar was equal to one shilling and six pence of English money.

The Dutch left Ceylon in a pecuniary state. The British had given the Dutch government promissory notes at the final peace treaty. No silver was available. Silver was the currency in trade. There was hardly any trade and consequently no silver. Governor

North thought he could bring back the silver, anticipating the pearl fishery. He may have been a good man, but not a practical one. He thought that the famed pearl fisheries would be a source of revenue. In fact, he built a two-storeyed house out of a portion of the old Dutch fort in coastal Arippu, near Mannar. It was strongly built of coral stone and concrete. I used to imagine him seated on the balcony of the fort, eagerly awaiting the boats returning brimful with pearl oysters.

The Portuguese exploited the pearl fishery. The Dutch scraped the bottom of it and the oysters may have fled by the time the British arrived. That fort used by Governor North at Arippu stood long after the British came and went, and even now the ruins, still strong, gives an idea of what it had been. Success in the pearl fishery would have meant a flow of silver into Jaffna. Taxing the local population's revenue was the answer.

Robert Andrews was sent to Jaffna for the collection of revenue, assisted by Jarvis. In addition to Andrews' salary, he was paid one percent of the revenue collected, as commission. Governor North introduced the revenue system of Madras, and he brought the revenue officers from Madras as the local mudaliyar was not familiar with it. Revenue collection was from Mannar, Jaffna and their dependencies. The revenue officers had judicial powers in punishing crimes related to revenue dues. The mudaliyars too helped in the collection of revenue.

In 1799 the Dutch criminal procedure was replaced by the Supreme Court for criminal jurisdiction. Following that, the civil, town and district courts were established.

The maniagars in Jaffna and the vanniyars in Vanni were subordinate to the mudaliyar. They had the duty of collecting coolies and cattle for public service. They arbitrated in petty disputes of the inhabitants. They took a two percent commission for themselves on the cost of all articles imported to Jaffna. In addition, their lands were cultivated free and they obtained fish free too for their needs.

Though the Dutch were past masters at collecting revenue, they refused to do so under the British.

Bureaucracy, departments and centralization of administration was the hallmark of the British. The surveyor's department was the first to be established in 1800, and then the land registry to replace the Tombo. Though the Dutch had some sort of postal arrangement, it was greatly improved and post offices were set up in the north and east by 1804. Daily post began. Dispatch was by single runner during the day and by a couple of them by night carrying lights and firelocks to keep the animals at bay. Postal services brought no revenue because letters were official. "The natives have no correspondence, and the Dutch little", so said the British. The British, however allowed the locals to keep their titles which they had retained even during the Portuguese and Dutch eras. The titles were mudaliyars, muhandirams, maniyagars, aratchies, kanganies and kanakupillais.

The Dutch had bred ponies in the island of Delft. The horses were sold in Jaffna at attractive prices. The British within a few years of their rule abolished the breeding and sale of the Delft ponies. The British followed the Dutch practice of taxation. One of the heavily taxed products was tobacco and closely behind it was cotton. Cotton was introduced by the Portuguese. It grew very well in the north. The renter, the one who bought the cotton, had

Wild Horse Trade in Jaffna

to pay a heavy tax. Most of the cotton went to India via Point Pedro, which in its Tamil name meant the cotton harbour. There was a weaver caste in Jaffna who made use of the cotton to weave cloth for local consumption. Indigo and other dyes grew in plenty in the northern islands. Dyeing of cloth was done on a moderate scale in Jaffna. When the Dutch took over the administration, they were keen on more taxes. The taxes were unbelievably high for the locals, especially for cotton. The Dutch sent the cotton to Indonesia and the woven material was sent back to Jaffna for dyeing. The Dutch were suspicious that the indigo dye was surreptitiously used by the local weavers, and they forbade red material to be worn by the Tamils, a colour very popularly worn at celebratory occasions.

The British came along and reduced the tax on cotton by five percent to compete with Indian cotton. They found that the Dutch laws of marriage and legitimacy ensured an adequate labour force, so they retained them.

Governor North did not have an easy relationship with the Kandyan kingdom. It was in a perpetual state of rebellion. When North arrived, the king was Rajadhi Rajasinghe, of the Malabar dynasty. He died childless, even after having five wives. The Maha Adigar Pilimatalawa was wily and ambitious and installed a supposedly illegitimate son of Rajadhi, naming him Sri Vikrema Rajasinghe. A revolt began against the Malabars. A brother-in-law of the king, Muthusami, who supported the rebels, was sent to Jaffna. Muthusami held court in Jaffna, and was paid a handsome salary by the crown. Pilimatalawa claimed the coast from Trincomalee to Tampalakamam that supposedly the Dutch had promised to him, but it was of no avail. Pilimatalawa was suspected of treachery by North. Then followed a treaty with the Kandyan kingdom. The king was irked by the British keeping Muthusami, a rival to the throne in Kandy. When the rebellion started again, Muthusami was given up and was executed in Kandy. A number of Kandyans invaded the northern territory. Pandara Vanniyar of the Vanni, a British subject, also rose in revolt as did Viravahu from Mannar. Madugalle made him a puppet king in Mannar. The ten Bhikkus who were involved in stealing the tooth relic were

Jaffna Hospital – 1800

confined to Jaffna. Finally, with counter invasions, the victorious British ruled Ceylon.

Smallpox raged in Ceylon and Jaffna didn't escape it. Vaccination was introduced in 1802. A charitable institution served as a hospital in 1800, maintained informally by the churches. The fines imposed as punishment by the British, for any wrong doings of the natives, was also given to maintain the hospital.

Like the Dutch, North thought of the caste system as slavery but enforced it for his own purposes. He, however, imported the Kaffirs who became slaves to the British and the remaining Dutch. He appointed Barbut as collector of revenue in 1798 in Jaffna.

In Jaffna lands were free holdings. North agreed to tithe the revenue at ten percent, one tenth of revenue from paddy sown on the land, together with house and trees. Barbut who replaced Jarvis as collector of revenue was wily. He separated the grain tax from the house and tree taxes because the separation brought greater revenue. The mudaliyars' powers were also cut.

The British, unlike the Dutch, who practiced a subtle form of proselytization by giving education in an ecclesiastical form, did not compulsorily convert nor stipulate a particular religious belief for official appointments. In fact, they kept the official appointments themselves and it was much later that it was extended to the local educated elite.

The British removed the disabilities of the Roman Catholics imposed by the Dutch. The Roman Catholics were much more in number than the Protestants. Jaffna had the most number of them and Galle came next. Governor North wanted the Dutch clergy to stay back and teach but the majority of them were reluctant to do so. When Governor North arrived there was only one local priest and two catechists in the north. North then sent one educated Tamil every year to study for priesthood in England.

The first missionary society was that of the Baptists in 1792 followed by the Anglican London Missionary Society in 1794. The latter only wanted to preach not teach and be under the government. They founded no schools. The Church Missionary Society was established in 1799 followed by the Methodists in 1810 and this was followed by the American Board for Foreign Missions bringing their education to Jaffna in 1816. The London Missionary Society left in 1795 rather like abandoning their calling. The Roman Catholic missionaries held sway with its churches scattered all over Ceylon. The Dutch Reformed Church confined their churches to the maritime provinces.

The Dutch mission left, as state support for it was stopped. They made it out as if they left as an obligation to discourage other religions. They were more against Roman Catholicism than the Buddhist and Hindu religions. The Dutch gave the impression that half the population of the maritime regions were Protestants and North too believed it.

In the first three decades of British rule, the missions brought the first changes in education. Their school system was used for evangelization. The Dutch had elementary parish schools, where reading, writing and Christianity were taught in the vernacular. North became even more fervent for vernacular education. He repaired the churches and schools of the Dutch and converted them to Anglican ones.

He set up special schools for the Muslims. However, in Jaffna he refused the establishment of Hindu schools, as the Dutch had given the impression that the majority in Jaffna were Christians. He created many departments for economic growth. Each department had an inspector. He made a superintendent of pearl banks, another for cotton plantations in Jaffna, one to oversee the breeding of horses in the island of Delft, and another for the salterns.

North, like the Dutch, made school masters the registrars of births, deaths and baptisms. They distributed stamps too. He restored *uliyam*, the compulsory service of the locals that had been stopped by the Dutch.

Governor North's administration was successful and substantial but not practical. He left Ceylon in 1805 though he intended many times to leave earlier.

Governor Maitland succeeded Governor North in 1807. He was more ambitious than North. He found Jaffna economically viable with trade in tobacco, cloth and indigo dye. He promptly increased the tax collected and appointed a comptroller in overall charge of Customs. In Jaffna he appointed a comptroller over the muhandiram who had collected taxes. There was rampant corruption in Jaffna as the collector was a victim of native insubordination over which he had no control. Governor Maitland overturned the revenue boards and revenue came under his personal supervision. He gave the collector power to examine and punish criminals.

Maitland insisted that the British collector had to supervise the revenue returns personally and not to rely on local subordinates. Collection was done every three months in Jaffna. The collector was to see the exact population, their occupations and revenue to be exacted. The Land Registry of the British was abandoned as Maitland thought it was like transporting the English legal and economic ideas to an unknown land. He revived the Dutch Tombo, and took over military as well as civil powers. He thought the military had greater power under North and that it had precipitated a lot of problems in the Kandyan wars.

Maitland had a completely different view about caste. He thought that the high caste had a right of servitude and restored caste obligations of the lower castes, some of whom had been the property of the Vellala caste. Their relationship was considered symbiotic and he maintained that no service meant no protection of the lower castes. He confirmed the social set-up as before. He was very particular and somewhat difficult.

He was the first to insist that all private lands should be enclosed and street spaces kept clean. Prices of bakery goods were fixed. He subtly practiced a divide-and-rule policy between the Buddhist temples of the south, and between the Hindu temples of the north. He made the Protestant churches as a whole to be under the Bishop of Calcutta. He created police divisions with *Vidanes* over them and he further diminished the power of the mudaliyars.

Where the Kandyan kingdom was concerned, he requested the king to release the British prisoners especially Davie and worked towards forming a treaty. A seaport was the bargaining card of the Kandyans and this was refused. He preferred to keep the status quo as war would be expensive.

Education continued in the vernacular and schools were improved. The Christian missionaries started learning Tamil to teach and preach. He found that recruiting young civil servants from abroad was expensive as they retired young and received a pension. Twelve years' service was sufficient for a pension. He appointed military officers as civil servants and appointed Major McNab as collector of Batticaloa. This was promptly stopped by the Crown as there was no gradation of services.

He was keen to connect the religious with the political establishments, but when the London Missionary Society sent a Dutchman, de Vos, as pastor, he suspected schism. He tried to revive the pearl fishery in 1808, but it was not a success.

Governor Maitland stopped public servants from trading and wanted the whole of Ceylon to be under the British. This was not accomplished during his tenure. He was ambitious and successful but he bit off more than he could chew and could not complete his programmes.

Strangely, he restored caste obligations with servitude of the low caste and confirmed the *Thesavalamai* in the peninsula. Before he left, he made a register of caste slaves that included the Kaffir slaves of the Dutch Burghers. The Burghers promised the gradual abolition of slavery and finally this was achieved in 1816.

Maitland left Ceylon due to ill health in 1812.

My uncle Chelva was coming home! His mother had arranged a marriage to her brother's daughter, a cousin marriage, the first choice of the parents of the old north. My grandmother was very lucky indeed to have had five sons. They had their secondary education up to the First in Arts level at the oldest and premier Methodist mission school, Central College. They left for Malaya one by one as one brother encouraged the other to migrate. Grandmother Augusta Jane was a constant traveller to Malaya to see her sons. She would say that the journey was quite tiresome as the boats were cargo cum passenger and the deck was converted to sleeping quarters. Whenever she came back, she would bring the latest in ceramic ware which replaced the brass and aluminium utensils and a few pounds of white sugar. She would dole it out on our outstretched hands and also on the palms of the other children in our compound. We would look at the glistening and beautiful tiny crystals on our palms licked the sugar long and greedily to lengthen its taste and enjoy the novelty of it.

Uncle Chelva accepted the wedding arranged for him and of his mother's choice. Of course, in a marriage like this there was no *suliodi*, the broker's fee, nor the dowry discussed. Any dowry given was accepted. There was no hassle of glimpsing and meeting as the relationship made everything easier. Uncle Chelva arrived to take a wife back!

Grandmother was with us in Karainagar. This was in 1910. Uncle Chelva came to Jaffna and he, with the money earned abroad, bought a vintage motorcycle. He had ridden it and brought it by boat to Karainagar. That day, like most days, was hot, dull and quiet. Suddenly there was an unearthly noise as Uncle Chelva roared into our lane and then into our compound on his gleaming machine. This was the first motorcycle that the village had seen and the first time the village had seen Uncle Chelva. He was handsome, dashing and the best looking of his five brothers. I looked around and found many people of the village had crowded into our compound and were staring at the machine and its rider. The noise that we were used to was the slow creaking noise of the fulcrum of the well sweep or the squeaky noise of the threshing wheel. The first noisy but elegant machine had come to the village, but, of course, there was no helmet on the rider. The younger ones looked at it first from far, then drew closer, and finally they touched the motorcycle and declared it warm and smoking. After spending some memorable time with it and with their curiosity satisfied, the villagers trekked back to their homes.

When Uncle Chelva was assured that his motorcycle was parked close to our house and in the shade, he walked into our home and without much ado invited us to his wedding. As usual in our village, a visitor must have a meal and rest before he gets back. After the meal he again swung over onto his motorcycle, pleased with the admiration and curiosity it produced, and roared back through the lane and to the boat.

Of course, as soon as he left there was much discussion about the wedding, the bride whom we had seen and what we were to wear. The day before the wedding, we packed our luggage with care and travelled by boat, then by buggy cart to the large Dutch house in Jaffna town.

The engagement of the couple had been a private event, but the wedding was a splash of colour and celebration. A family's status was measured by the ability to have horse-drawn carriages for a wedding. There were the carriages drawn by brown horses for us too, the guests. The carriage drawn by two white horses was for the groom and best man to travel in. They travelled a distance, about eleven miles, to the old church at Tellippalai. As we took our pews, a hymn was sung and the bride in a white silk and silver-bordered sari walked down the aisle with her retinue. Everyone was in coloured attire except the bride. She was in white, a colour introduced by the missionaries. I had the impression that the missionaries always wore dull colours, and colourful clothes to them were heathen. Uncle Chelva looked so handsome, but comparatively the bride wasn't. It was a great disappointment to us but he didn't think it was so, as Uncle Chelva could have had a choice but did not take it.

In the midst of the hymns and the homily, a very Hindu tradition the Christians clung to, took place. It was the tying of the marriage necklace, the *thalikodi*. It had a thick stiff gold chain, the *kodi*, and a pendant, the *thali*. It was made of an odd number of gold sovereigns, the pendant of one sovereign and the chain on average of ten sovereigns. It was given as a financial asset. It was never removed till widowhood and then it was the first asset that could be sold if a financial crisis loomed for the widow. This made her a little independent of her relatives. If she was rich, she kept it and reused the gold. The *thali*, the equivalent to a pendant, worn on the chain had Christian symbols. The commonest symbols on it were either a cross, a Bible, an anchor or a combination of these. It had Hindu symbols before the Christian converts changed them.

This was the first wedding I attended and I was agog with excitement. We sat in the front pews. I remembered uncle Chelva lifting the face veil of the bride to tie the *thali*. Suddenly there was much amusement and twitter in the congregation as uncle Chelva had instead of waiting, demurely at the back, assisting his married cousin to fix the clasp of the chain, had gone in front to have a better look at the bride. The Christian service was solemn compared to the noise of music, colour and rituals of the Hindu weddings in the village. However, the Christians didn't let go of Hindu practices – a *pottu* was on the forehead, flowers were in her hair, the throatlet of pearls, a chain and a *paddakam* and the diamond earrings with pearl danglers were all worn.

The service began and ended with hymns mostly in Tamil and a homily in between. The registration of the marriage was done by the pastor who was appointed an official registrar by the government. This was in the vestry of the church, in the presence of close family and witnesses. The face veil, another piece of western attire, was removed and she walked with the groom down the aisle to the entrance of the church where the thunderous noise of fire crackers was heard. Everything so far had been introduced with missionary zeal. The carriages for the family took all of us to the bride's place, which was not too far from the church. At the doorstep the groom's page boy poured water from a brass vessel close to the groom's feet and collected a gold ring due to him. The Hindu custom was that the water should be poured on the groom's bare feet but the Christian groom wore shoes! The bride and groom were garlanded as in Hindu weddings, by couples who were married and were close relatives. The couple was garlanded both at the church and at the doorway of the bride's home from where the newly married couple was led to the settee which was covered with a rich colourful sari on which they sat. When everybody was seated, whether on a chair or a mat, the cake was served, another western custom at the wedding, introduced by the missionaries. This was much enjoyed by us instead of the usual local sweetmeats.

The richly covered settee on which the couple sat was a poor substitute for the flower covered throne, the *manavarai* of a Hindu bride and groom, but the ceremonies reverted back to Hindu culture. The sari given by the groom was maroon in colour. This colour was considered by the Hindus as one of the 'sun colours.' The sari and a garland of jasmine for her hair were placed on a tray and taken by the groom's sister and her husband among the guests to be blessed. Those guests who were married and had children blessed it by placing their hands on it. The groom then draped it around the bride's shoulders. She retired to change into this sari from the colourless sari she had been wearing. When she appeared again the couple was garlanded by another married couple. Vegetarian sweetmeats and fish pastries were served.

It was dusk and time to return. The bride went to the husband's home that first night unlike the Hindu practice. Honeymoons were unheard of. The main meal was at my uncle's home in Jaffna town and we travelled back the eleven miles to it by carriage again. Dinner was served in a typical northern style. Folded mats were laid on the ground along the walls of the drawing and dining room. The guests sat on them while square-cut plantain leaves were laid in front of them and a vegetarian meal was served on them from brass vessels, with the additional dishes of curd, ghee and *rasam* – a pepper water. There was a protocol for dinner. The most important male guest was invited first to wash his fingers with the water poured out, from a brass vessel, held by the father of the bride. I cannot remember us children washing our fingers to sit for the sumptuous meal! Dinner was followed by plantains and sweetmeats. Unlike in Hindu weddings, the couple didn't go back to her home but stayed at the groom's home.

Two or three rich, silk, bright 'sun coloured' saris were given by the groom to the bride, to be worn on successive days to meet relatives and receive gifts. Uncle Chelva was leaving for Malaya, so he preferred staying at his place to receive the visitors. Weddings were such wonderful but tedious affairs.

Following uncle Chelva's departure, his mother stayed with us in her sons' house and recalled incidents of her son's life. He loved to dress in saris and went to the neighbours' or aunts' homes, and frequently fooled them with his disguise. He told his friends that moustaches, much favoured by the northerner, were out of fashion. He offered to shave them and then only shaved off half of it. He went missing for an hour, and then came back amidst much consternation, and shaved off the other half!

Grandfather and his immediate family members lived a stone's throw from each other within that large *valavu*. The compound was very green with plants and trees that grew in it nurtured by man. Nothing sprouted on its own from seed dropped by bird or man! There weren't many palmyrah palms. Clusters of them were found at the very rear of the compound.

Except for our home which was non-vegetarian, a characteristic of conversion to Christianity, most relatives were vegetarian totally, or on certain days of the week. They kept to the orthodox Hindu practices and were dependant on their home gardens with their fruit trees and the extra vegetables that were cultivated on the paddy fields after the harvesting of paddy. The paddy field was at the rear end of that large acreage of land and was separated by a well-built bund. The siblings of my father shared the labour entailed in both the paddy field and the home garden. The members of the lower castes who lived in the compound, together with the *Koviyars* became the labourers when needed. A few coconut palms stood in a corner. The trees that provided shade were the mango trees of which there were four varieties, the two kolumbans, kili and ambalavis. The largest trees, the tamarind and banyan, were not grown in the garden, as they took up space and nothing grew underneath them. The tamarind tree was considered unlucky to be grown in the garden. These trees were plentiful in the lands surrounding the village. The mango trees were cherished. They were pruned after every harvest of fruit. This ensured a better harvest to follow.

The ever-present tree in a Jaffna garden was the margosa. These were at the borders of the garden within the fence. They were elegant, shapely and their pretty leaves which made a soft sibilant sound in the slightest breeze. They were planted in the belief that they medicated the air. The fronds of margosa leaves were brushed against the skin to repel insects. The twigs were broken in the late evening and burnt on coconut shell charcoal in long-handled brass incense burners. This kept away the insects, especially mosquitoes. These burners were, like in a ceremony, taken around the house, and then slipped under the beds. Margosa oil was always at hand in any home, extracted from the small, pretty, yellow oval berries. The timber was too soft and only planks could be made from the tree trunk. They were used as cross bars fitted into the notches across the ends of beds. The bed heads were of satinwood or teak. The margosa oil extracted from the berries was sufficient for all of us. I would watch the berries being dried for a few days in the ever-present hot sun. Then they were sent to the *chekku*, a crudely made contraption, to extract oil. I would accompany my older male cousin to a small community of the *Chandor* caste, the oil pressers. Only a few villages had these *chekkus* and Karainagar was one of them. The closest town to us, Vaddukodai, had one too. Crushing of the seeds was done on a casual basis, a few times or several times per month, depending on the harvest of berries. A separate *chekku* was used for the extraction of gingelly oil.

I watched and heard the *chekku* machine working, with my fingers thrust into my ears. There were such harsh and high-pitched creaking noises. The *chekku* was a large granite stone or a

The Chekku

trunk of a large tamarind tree hollowed out like a mortar. It had a pestle made of strong satinwood or teak. The pestle, deep and firm, was worked round in the mortar by a pair of bullocks yoked to a transverse beam attached to the pestle. The pestle withstood the pressure of the movement and crushed the seeds. This contraption was rough, crude and basic. The crude oil was scooped out, a bottle or two of it given and money paid. The older generation daubed this oil mixed with saffron as a remedy for all skin rashes. It was also used for arthritic pains or simply applied with the belief that it prevented everything! The smell was unpleasant, and we would get away from whoever had applied it on his or her body.

I seem to have digressed. The paddy field occupied one third of the land. While walking towards it with my grandfather, I saw small houses, huts and children. Their mothers were busy with household chores. "Were they our relatives?" Grandfather said "No," but explained the feudal caste system within a family household. There was no feudal system in Jaffna, he said, except within a large compound of a landowner. Most landowners were Vellalas who were in the majority in Jaffna and every Vellala had paddy land and therefore the means to maintain such a system of caste. Grandfather had this great love of going back to the past, its history, literature and, of course, the caste system. He applied a utilitarian point of view to caste! He told me that "affection between castes was severely restricted, so too courtesy." Only alcohol seemed to break it down temporarily. *Kulam* was a nicer word to use than caste. "Now caste is no guide to work. It was so a long time ago" he continued. "Palanquin bearers and hand weavers are no more." They were considered as separate castes in the past. There was an aversion of one caste to do the work of another, unless the whole process of work was mechanized. The lower-caste males filled the vacancies left by carpenters and blacksmiths who were considered of higher caste, but who had moved out of the village. In the printing press of Jaffna College all castes worked as a team during working hours. The Vellalas were called *Nainars* or feudal lords who had vassals, the Koviyars of the *Adimai* caste. They were the personal servants of the house holder. They rendered their social and ritual duties at the behest of a particular Vellala master. They were not exchanged or sold to other householders. The Koviyars lived in huts or small houses at the rear end of the garden of the householder.

The Koviyars had a peculiar relationship with the Vellalas. In fact, Koviyars may have been the southern Govias captured in one of the many internal wars. Living as household servants to Vellalas, marriages were taboo between the Koviyars and the Vellalas. The Koviyars received land to build their houses and received subsistence too. The land given to them was termed *manian*.

The Vellalas ate the food that Koviyars cooked. They were always hired to cook for weddings. Vellalas would have mistresses or concubines from the Koviyars of the same household. *Sinna veedu*, small house, meant a mistress's domain in that garden. The children born of this union were accepted as Vellalas but they had no hereditary rights. Koviyars were allowed to touch the bier of a deceased Vellala, while other low castes could not. The Koviyars carried the bier to the cremation ground. Vellalas would be guests at Koviyar weddings, but never at of the lower castes. Koviyars were socially inferior but ritually equal. Grandfather said with a chuckle that his mother was annoyed but hid her anger, if anyone remarked that the child from the back garden looked like her husband!

The *Kudimai* castes, the retainers, were the *Pallars* - the agrarian casual labourers, and *Nalavars* - the toddy tappers. They too were given land near the palmyrah patch at the bottom of the garden. Nominal rent for land was obtained. If they were hired, cash was paid for work done for the householder. They, however, looked for work outside to enhance the little money coming from the land. They worked for other Vellala households of the village. The other strata of castes had within them the artisans, goldsmiths, masons, musicians and so many of other subcastes. When the Portuguese conquered Jaffna, the Mudaliyar Vellalas held considerable power and wealth under their former rulers. Though the Portuguese feared that the Vellalas would incite a revolt amongst the population, they found that the locals were passive people, with no military training, and were only cultivators. The Vellalas were sixty percent of the population.

The Vellalas loved to trace their genealogy. They climbed the family tree and discovered their ancestors for about four, five or even six generations above them. Above that the blank space was invariably filled with dots and dashes up to king Sangili. The king had so many claimants he must surely have had hundreds of Vellala concubines.

My sister, the one just older than I, was groomed and ready for marriage. The house we lived in, which was my eldest sister's, was spring cleaned and colour washed for the forthcoming marriage. In the garden of that house and compound there were two structures that had travelled from village to town. One was the not so deep or broad well of our village. The well was only a short distance from the back verandah, secluded by shrubs especially the hibiscus and crotons. They thrived there and formed almost a continuous green fence and made a wall of privacy. The well, like in the village, was the site of communal or individual bathing. Washing of clothes and kitchen ware was all done at the well. Running water from water tanks and pipes had not yet arrived.

Marriage proposals went to and from eligible families and ours. With little or no scope of higher education for females, her age determined the eligibility for marriage. In our village seventeen years of age was right to start the proceedings of a marriage. The girl may be immature for a wedded life, but she came last in the consideration for consent, as parents took the initiative in marriages of their children.

However, with education and moving into a broader-minded society the age of marriage was in the twenties. My sister Nesam was never ready for marriage. She was pretty, had such culinary gifts and also a flare for housekeeping. She harked back to the fact that she was not educated enough. The Senior Cambridge was not good enough for her, though I did better in that exam. I accepted the fact that higher education meant money and my parents didn't have it, but she did not. She would hark back to my father's reprimands and the corporal punishment she got for running a race with a boy. She declared vociferously and very strangely, so many years later, that it was an unfair and terrible incident. Her nature was such that she would have found fault with every marriage proposal brought to our family.

My mother was truly relieved when a proposal was sent from Malaya. It was a proposal of intermarriage. The marriages would be for my brother Nava, who was already in Malaya, and Nesam, to a sister and brother of a suitable family equal in status and education. In this type of marriage there was no discussion of dowry and no long drawn-out search for pedigree. Everything had been seen to.

My sister as expected opposed it. She declared that the photograph of the young man sent from Malaya was just not enough. She wished to meet the proposed groom before marriage and to get to know him well. This was not possible even with a local proposal of our times. Coercion and persuasion by the older members of the family, together with the letters from Malaya that gave glowing accounts of the groom and family, made her a reluctant party to the marriage. My sister, a gregarious and outgoing person, may have looked upon this marriage as an adventure to a foreign country.

She was not given much time to vacillate in her decision. With acceptance she packed her clothes and everything else she fancied in her wardrobe in a suitcase. My mother with many instructions of safety gave her share of the jewellery which was taken by my sister in her handbag. In between her packing and leaving, she cried out the unfairness of it all and threatened to come back. She went sadly and reluctantly on the next available boat to Malaya. We missed her sorely for her chatter and quick repartees in her speech.

Mother was truly anxious and, knowing Nesam's impetuousness, thought that she would turn back. She stood at the gate with trepidation and awaited her for a couple of day. Days became a week and mother was relieved. There were many relatives in Malaya, by now, who attended Nesam's wedding. Her letters arrived without recriminations and very soon a letter with news of starting a family. Mother was at peace. She would not be coming back. Nesam added to her family regularly and finally had a brood of eleven children. We were amazed that she had finally become truly domiciled and domesticated.

However her attitudes and boldness had not changed. She always wanted to be different and the next thing we heard about her was her fondness for smoking cigarettes. We were truly shocked and kept the news within the family. Women smoking cigarettes was unheard of in Jaffna but females smoking cigars in the village were not so rare.

When she came, which she now did once every couple of years, my mother would request that she smoke on the back verandah and not in front of friends, or worse, relatives. She obliged her but the nicotine stains on her nails were not hidden for long. She had not lost her manner nor the gift of the gab

She had a house of her own in Jaffna and brought her younger children and spent a few months in it. The next thing we heard was that she had taken a fancy to the Jaffna cigar and liked it too in spite of that horrible smell! That seemed to be the last straw of decadence to us. It was incongruous to see the black fat cigar sticking out of a still attractive, light-skinned face. There was the tell-tale pigmentation that appeared on her lips too.

She was still a good conversationalist. She was still garrulous, and became a great favourite of her nieces and nephews, who young and modern enough, overlooked her habits and appreciated her bantering speech. She sewed dresses for the nieces and cooked meals for them; age had not diminished her culinary talent.

She came to Ceylon many times until her age made these journeys physically tiring, though her spirit was ever willing. She stopped coming after a few more years. My younger sister too married a cousin of ours, who was domiciled in Malaya. She readily agreed to the marriage as she knew her cousin well, an eligible *machan*. She was the absolute opposite of my sister Nesam in every way, timid and soft spoken in her speech and demeanour.

My mother though now in her eighties was still trim in her figure and she walked to visit her old friends and relatives, at whatever distance they lived in Jaffna. She broke her leg on one of these jaunts. The doctors told her that she would be confined to bed, if not she would be on crutches. Six months went by when she left her bed behind her, threw her crutches away and went walking again and visited her acquaintances. She had long flowing white hair but suddenly appeared in a short hair style and would be referred to by friends and relatives as the modern grandmother. Mentally alert, she would insist on leading long prayers before dinner. The grandchildren fidgeted, ate dinner in between prayers and interrupted the prayers with many Amens too. The scene would be reminiscent for me of prayers with my grandmother so long ago.

There would be many messages sent to her children of her imminent death following recurrent illnesses. I would rush to Jaffna by train. My niece met me at the station as she always did. I can still visualize her standing on the station platform, with an umbrella for all seasons. She took me to my sister's home, which had become hers. Like my mother's recurrent illnesses my trips to Jaffna were also frequent and I did not mind them at all.

When my mother died, it was still the age of horse and carriage to take her remains to the cemetery.

The years had gone by after my schooling and teaching in the primary section of Vembadi. I was told that a marriage proposal had come. Compared to my eldest sister's marriage, the ages at which my younger sister and I were married were considered old. I was in my mid-twenties. The better educated girls delayed marriage compared to the poor and uneducated, who had nothing to look forward to than a happy marriage and children. My parents arranged an intermarriage for me. This meant a double wedding for a brother and sister to marry a sister and brother of, usually, an unrelated family. My family was large with four girls and three boys. The brothers were preferentially treated in education. My brothers Seeva and Nava were considered very eligible. They were also eligible for the simple fact that Nava was in Malaya and the other was a medical doctor. My brother Seeva and I married Kanmani and Kanags, a lawyer, of a similar large family. The families were socially equal. This was a convenient form of marriage in the north for both families. The usual subject and wrangling over dowries never occurred. However, the males sacrificed a large dowry, an asset when starting life, to see the sisters married. I was only given cash and jewellery.

The wedding itself was not wanting – a simple church wedding and a simpler reception. My father-in-law, a mudaliyar, however, gave my husband a few acres of land, away from Trincomalee town. He felt that his daughter married a salaried professional, and a young lawyer's life was difficult. The land was scrub land and left untouched for decades.

Moving to Trinco after marriage, we lived in rented houses. The first was a spacious Dutch house and what was wonderful to me was that it was right opposite the town library and the sea beach. The latter was wonderful in the late evenings, but the constant breeze brought the dust too into that house. I did endless trips to that library to satisfy the appetite of the bookworm. I was religious and Kanags was gregarious and fun loving. Our four children kept us together.

Having come from Jaffna, my great ambition in life was to have my own home, as most girls did in the north. Though I pestered my husband to buy a piece of land in town, the price was beyond us. We decided to build our home in the large tract of land given to us in a village. It meant travelling a distance of three miles to and fro by the jeep we owned. The jeep was handy as the roads were bad. These were the years of the Second World War. Soldiers of every colour walked by our house. The tall turbanned and bearded Sikhs looked formidable, and the younger children rushed back to the house on seeing them. Still other soldiers shouted their 'hellos' and handed bars of chocolate, brought from the 'navvy' shop of the navy, to the children they met on the roads. There was such pandemonium on the streets when the Japanese bombed a ship in the harbour. It seemed that all the people of Trinco had rushed to the railway station to catch the first train out. The army assured us that it was futile to rush away as the daily trains could not possibly hold all the people. So we stayed on and saw the people return home in a few days. The sirens blasted and blackouts occurred daily, the rooms were made darker by the dark blinds which had to be put over windows. The children rushed under beds, with cotton wool in their ears and a piece of wood held between their teeth. The younger ones were terrified of this repetitive exercise that they were made to do at every blast of the siren.

My husband was a volunteer officer in the army and kept busy going to the army camp whenever he had to. The batman when needed came to spruce his shoes and medals. When I look back, it is ironic that our first Sinhalese friends were from the army: Sepala and the Sams. Many were our trips to the army base camp at Monkey Bridge, a few miles from the town and many were the times these friends came home for a home-cooked meal.

My ulterior motive in building a large house in the village was to finally sell it and buy another in town, but when the house was built it looked so solid and striking in that large garden and we lived there for decades. The building commenced after the Urban Council gave its permission. I remember getting up in the mornings, anticipating the supervision of the building. It was a family joke that I counted every brick that went into it.

It was 1945, the war almost over. The British who had a large naval base sold its stores of materials and household effects. I actually bought a stove to fit into a future house! A contractor estimated the prices and bought cement blocks from carters who made a penny as middlemen for the navy. Rangoon teak was sold in very long and broad pieces. Doors and windows were easily shaped out of them with enough left over for the beams. Indian carpenters hired by the British were looking for work and that suited us very well. We were truly lucky to get the materials so cheap. Initially I thought of building three small houses for the daughters, but my husband wanted one large house. He was six feet tall. He needed large cars too, and he was proud of his American Packard and changed to another American make whenever he needed to replace the older car.

I started building the house but my husband finished it. I was glad of it as getting money from him became an ordeal. Like an officer he took control of it and finished the roof and ceiling. His army friends dropped in frequently to see the progress of construction. On its completion, Sepala wanted it named 'Kanags Lodge' and so it was.

The garden was very large. Mango, jak and margosa trees were the trees of choice planted and they interspersed with coconut and palmyrah palms. There were still spaces for vegetable plots. We were so close to the sea but fresh water bubbled out from the numerous wells that were dug there. Most of the villagers had small houses or huts, roofed with tin or asbestos and many of them were casual labourers. They built a shack near their dwellings and made them into little 'boutiques' in which they sold sugar, flour and other essential food items! Their children made our acquaintance very readily. I remember the three younger boys of a family of seven who came and slept the nights under our large dining table, as their house was so small. They would clamour to pour a few pails of water to the growing plants in return for breakfast of bread and jam. They were always at hand and ran errands with the hope of getting something to eat as their reward.

The house was of solid concrete and stood up to the cyclone of December 1964. It was a terrible morning. The youngest daughter had the house spring cleaned and its red floors polished to a shine for Christmas. She was so particular that she made her father walk on newspapers spread on the floor of the dining room. I saw the snakegourd with its creeper plant fall to the ground. I wondered why and was amused by it. Suddenly the wind howled, and the rain pelted the earth and both battered the house. Then I saw the huge tamarind tree fall with ease, cruelly crushing a man who took shelter under it. The garden became strewn with coconut and palmyrah palms uprooted and thrown away. Three of us rushed round, closed the doors and windows which were incessantly banged. We could not control the water pouring in from the ceiling, now exposed, as the tiles had sailed away to quite a distance with the wind.

There was knocking and banging on the back door. Our neighbours and their families stood there with their bag and baggage and anything that could be retrieved, seeking shelter. Their homes had been blown away, the roofs literally taken away to distances unbelievable. Suddenly our home was filled with people who occupied every available space and we were left with two chairs between the three of us. The beautifully polished floor had disappeared under a layer of mud. David Paynter's paintings, much cherished by us, were splattered with mud. There was nobody who was not praying aloud. Jesus was called on, so too Mary, Siva, Vishnu, Krishna – in fact, every God known to our neighbours. We shared the little food we had. My heart was filled with anxiety not knowing where my nephew was. He had been sent to fetch the Christmas cake from the baker. We prepared it but everyone trusted the local baker to bake it to a nice brown.

The storm went on for about twelve hours until midnight and suddenly there was a palpable stillness, followed by the sound of stampeding feet. The neighbours rushed back, picked up theirs and others' bits of roofing and clothes they came across. They rushed to salvage and rebuild their homes. The compound, that was spotless the day before, was a sight with wet clothes on the ground amidst fallen trees and tins. The fallen tin sheets and kitchen utensils had run merrily across the garden.

My nephew returned with the cake. Family members were expected. Those who came by train walked the three miles lugging the suitcases, not recognizing any known landmarks, till they came home. Those who came by car drove over rail tracks and any available piece of road that led home. Everyone was safe.

Help poured in from the generous south with provisions of food, cadjan, bamboo and cooking vessels. Strangely, very few deaths occurred, but not a single house was a complete one, or more often with no roof at all. I had bought some mutton requested by a friend which now came in useful for our X'mas lunch. We did have a blessed X'mas in spite of the cyclone. The neighbours' children were there as usual at Christmas for gifts and cake.

I remember that most of the villagers' social life took place on the *thinnai* – the front verandahs of their homes, a short distance from the gate. So it was in my grandfather's home. It seemed to me that the whole world came to his home, met him, sat for a few or many minutes, and left, especially if another visitor arrived.

There was a predetermined protocol of seating arrangements. A person of lower caste stood outside the verandah, removed the towel or shawl from his shoulder, and spoke to grandfather with courtesy constantly changing the posture of his legs. My grandfather too spoke with courtesy but the endings like 'him' and 'you' were different to that of his equals.

Though most of the lentils and leafy vegetables were grown in the garden, the most constant visitor was Meena, the woman who sold vegetables. Over the years she seemed always tall, slim, dressed in colourful saris and blouses that did not match in colour. The sari was more bundled in front than neatly pleated. The blouse was very short and exposed a large bare midriff. If she came later in the morning her face and neck would glisten with sweat, more visible on her dark brown skin. When she walked to face the world, her back was arched with a concavity at the rear, which made her straight as a palmyrah tree. The head held erect carried a large, hollow, palmyrah-leaf-woven basket filled with vegetables. The drumsticks seemed to stick out and seemed to me for yards. The basket never shifted on her head even when she manoeuvred the gate, coming in or going out.

The verandah was a rectangular, long, smoothly cemented platform, a foot and a half above the sandy soil. It was not enclosed. A few chairs were on it and grandfather's chair was the most constantly used one. The vegetable seller knew her position there. She would leave the basket on the ground and demurely sit on the verandah with her feet on the ground next to her basket. Her manner of selling was not humble though. She was equal to the bargaining and banter of my grandfather. I was sure that she got the price she had decided on and left with the money tied within a knot made at the free end of her sari. She got up, smiled and said the usual "I'll go and come," and sailed away through the gate.

Fish was never brought to the door as a respect to the vegetarians in the household. They were unhappy even with the smell of the fish that might pervade the compound. Grandfather loved to market and offered to trudge, with me in tow, to the centre of the village. There were no permanent structures, and the market was women and men with baskets and boxes sitting under spreading trees. There were innumerable women selling vegetables, each seated on their prescribed patch of earth which was sacrosanct to them. These women were cheeky, loud and would rudely tell off the customers who found fault with their vegetables! They even insulted their customers at their taste for cheap vegetables that they would not dream of selling. My eyes sought out the wooden boxes filled with coloured plastic wares and the glass bangles sold by the younger men. The bangles were not only colourful, but would be either embossed or wrapped with gold or silver beads. I would pester my grandfather to buy me at least a pair of them. Every household article was sold here. The brass ones which were more popular were the most expensive.

The fish and seafood stalls were further away and their smells would guide the customers there. The sea around us was rich in fish and not less in other seafood. Fish was sought most and crabs least except when there was a visitor from the mainland who craved them. The mullet fish was the tastiest of the fish, the seer less so. Beef was sold away from the market in some particular area. Pork was unheard of. Even the Christian converts like us never ate beef.

Though mutton was sold in the market, the villagers had a peculiar way of getting it. Families got together and shared a portion of a goat killed for its meat. The family that took the best cut paid more. This method assured us of good and cheaper meat. Mutton was the favourite meat on Sundays. The males imbibed the toddy and applied gingelly oil generously from their heads to their toes. Their *vertis* were tucked in like loincloths so that as much body as possible was exposed for the oiling. Their bodies glistened as they stood in the sun, lounged around or got about their work. They kept the gingelly oil on their bodies for three to four hours and did a quick bath at the well anticipating a lunch of rice, a curry like murunga and their favourite curry, the mutton spiced, oozing with oil and thick coconut milk, literally called *piratel*, milk fried mutton. Every curry tasted delicious in the north, probably the brackish water added to the taste and flavour.

Sometimes going home from the market or from school, I saw a few strangers seated on a cemented portion of land a few feet from our gate. On a raised portion of this was a large clay pot of water and a beaked tumbler. My grandfather and those who could afford to be generous with their money built these simple structures so that wayfarers who came from the interior of the village to Jaffna could rest, drink the water and even cook on it. Well water would be drawn for them and left in a large aluminium pail. Sometimes at the break of day, chatter was heard outside the fence, but we, the curious children, were never allowed to meet them, as we were told that nobody knew where they came from and their antecedents!

On the front verandah of grandfather's house, visitors sat on mats spread or on chairs according to their social status. Status may go up with education, but caste did not and such visitors sat on a bench which was directly opposite to grandfather's chair. Chairs and even furniture were minimum. If more were needed, someone went up a few steps at the rear of the verandah and then through a heavy door to fetch some chairs from within. Coffee, if served, was in beaked tumblers so that it could be held aloft and coffee poured into the mouth.

My grandfather would occasionally be summoned by an urgent ringing of the bell of a cycle. The Hindu priest had arrived. He had put one of his legs down but had not got off his cycle. He, as usual, was in his white *verti* with the shawl thrown over his bare chest. A cotton thread traversed his chest from the left shoulder, a symbol of the priestly caste. His forehead and upper arms had traces of holy ash and sandalwood. By caste he was probably next to God! This was one of the very few instances when grandfather would get up promptly from his chair and walk to the gate to meet the priest. The Brahmin hardly came in or sat down and never took any refreshment.

The visit was to discuss matters that pertained to the village temple as grandfather was one of the patrons of it. The exchange of words between them was always courteous. The laity managed the temple and the priest looked after all the religious ceremonies. The relationship was beneficial to both. There were a few small temples in the village. The Kannagi or Pattini temple, one of six in the north, was in our village.

The most prestigious temple was the Sivan temple, further towards the coast. It was also known as Rudra temple, but what made it more beautiful were the surroundings. There was the Casuarina Beach on one side, scrub land on the other. In between there were large green trees, vegetable plots, palmyrahs and a solitary coconut tree, all surrounding this temple. The temple was embellished with two *gopurams*, the intricately carved tall towers, at the entrance. Siva was depicted as a *Lingam*, the phallus installed within the inner sanctum. Festival time was in December coinciding with the festival of the South Indian Chidambaram temple festival. In fact, it was called the Southern Chidambaram. The whole scenery then was a mass of people.

The temple, built in the sixteenth century, was razed to the ground by the Dutch in 1648 when they sailed the coast to capture Fort Cays of the Portuguese. It was rebuilt in 1848. To me it was a great adventure to accompany grandfather to the evening *pooja* on Friday. When conversion to Christianity took place in our family, I was given strict instructions to stay outside the temple, and not eat any food offered at the *pooja*. I would obey the first rule and stand at the entrance and stare at the ceremonies. Before entering the temple Grandfather broke a coconut at the entrance of it. He said that it was a symbolic gesture of breaking one's body and spirit which meant in fact one's ego, before God. To me it seemed that the ceremonies and rituals with many libations took hours. The second rule was harder to keep and I did not refuse to eat the hot gram lentils, the sweet milk rice nor the banana while we walked back home. It was tastier because it was forbidden and was eaten away from the temple.

Friday service was long as the *pooja* was special. Ceremonies started with the blowing of conch shells and the beating of drums. It was explained that a lot of the ceremony involved the rituals offered to a king and God was a king. The icon was bathed ceremoniously with milk, curd, sandalwood, coconut water and then water. Holy ash was then poured over it and it was wrapped in colourful cloth, gold being the prominent colour. The icon was garlanded, and incense in a brass censor was held aloft and circumbulated. The flag, the sceptre, the fanning whisks and various other ceremonial items were held or waved before the icon. A lamp which looked like an upright exquisite gold chandelier with a myriad lighted wicks was held. The lighted wick lamps of various shapes and sizes were circumbulated and the wrist of the priest gave the circumbulation various patterns and directions. Movement was always clockwise. Finally the priest held and circumbulated a single lamp lighted with camphor. The devotees would shout their salutation, "*Arohara*," and that would be the end of the *pooja*.

Grandfather would receive the holy ash, milk and food prepared by the priests. I would be impatient by now, as the most wonderful part of the trip was to rush down to the Casuarina Beach which had groves of casuarinas trees. Probably the seedlings came up by chance or they may have been planted to break the harsh howling wind and water of the monsoon. The casuarinas trees made a wonderful green backdrop and relieved the harsh brown ground but they were not comfortable to brush against.

The beach was broad and beautiful. By evening the seawater was cold. We as children stood or waded into the sea and got our legs and invariably our clothes wet. Sea bathing was rare, except by the fisher folk who waded in and out of the boats; swimming was a rarity in these islands. Dusk fell quickly. Sunset over the islands and lagoons in Jaffna was something one could hardly erase from one's memory. The sun went down as a big ball of fire. The descent was rapid and it was chased by the disappearing colours of the rainbow which went down much more slowly. The colour indigo was the last to go. It was something different when the sunsets were close to the beginning of the rainy weather. The beauty of the setting sun vied with silver streaks and splashes of the colours of a prism. The silver streaks lingered long after the sun had set and suddenly disappeared with the fast falling dusk. The moon would come up over the sea. An upward glance at the northern sky would show it filled with more than its share of stars. The twilight and dusk would make pretty silhouettes of the tall palmyrah trees. The moonlight would make them look like tall black giants but the coconut tree's shadow was so sharp and beautiful as if an artist had sat under it and painted, with a sharp stylus dipped in Indian ink, the palm and its leaves on the ground.

The stars seemed to be in millions. As a young girl I would hope that one would get pushed out to the ground by sheer overcrowding of the stars. The sky with its stars was a constant feature in the north till clouds covered it during the monsoon. Twilight and dusk gave a beauty to the usually bleak open coastal places of the north.

Grandfather would occasionally take a few of us to the temple in neighbouring Vaddukodai. The anticipation of arrival a little further away even made the trip by boat more pleasant. We were hurried along the way so as to be on time for the last *pooja* of the day. The walk back to the sea and the boat was the most pleasant walk in the north. The road was dead straight, bordered on both sides by lush green waving paddy interrupted by a few Tulip and Flamboyant trees. The late evening breeze was gentle and came at you, it seemed, from all sides. The sun was sinking. The walk was enervating with plenty of time to gaze at the empty spaces. Flocks of swallows went overhead and parakeets screeched as they found some ripening paddy.

Dusk would seem to fall suddenly in that open space. The sound of a high-pitched, frequently tolled bell of the village temple would travel across the paddy fields and across the road to the farther paddy fields and homesteads. The temple bell was a contrast to the familiar church bell to us. The latter was low pitched, sombre and tolled slowly. The temple bell had an urgency, calling its people to worship at the end of that Friday. The walk became lovelier with the stars above and, if we were lucky, the moon above too. We reached the boat and were taken safely by the boatman with his oars and lanterns across the inlet. We stepped onto that sandy shore with much banter, chatter and fatigue.

It was October. The northeast monsoon was anticipated and that meant many days of drenching and skin-hurting showers. Bucketsful of rain poured from the skies and gave us thirty to forty inches of rain in one season.

The majority of the people in the north were agrarian, lived in rural areas and grew rice mostly as a source of income. Grandfather's family cultivated the field and the rice from it was enough for his own and his extended family's consumption. The acreage of the land was not large at all, just a few acres at the back of the compound. The Jaffna farmer was never called a peasant; he was a model farmer with regard to working his fields, with crop rotation and his readiness to try new ideas.

October meant, to us children, quite a few days leave from school. We kept away a week and the older ones for a few more days. No one gave written or verbal excuses as the missionaries at school knew that sowing the fields was anticipated. We were

Vellalas of Jaffna

simply excited bystanders and watched others and older cousins work. I had mastered the Tamil alphabet, a few numbers and progressed from writing on sand to the slate and pencil and wrote words in print. English was confined to a few spoken words.

After the last harvest, gingelly, lentils and kurakkan had been grown in the field as rotation crops as their roots were rich in minerals and fertilized the paddy that followed these crops. These crops needed little watering from the well. After the harvest of these crops the field was ploughed by the sturdy bulls tethered to the plough but mostly by the long-handled hoes. Then the fields were left forlorn and fallow till the deluge of October.

A few weeks of rain and grandfather was busy cutting branches of the local Tulip and Glyceridia plants into thin pieces and spreading them on the field. This was the green manure, a peculiarity of the north.

Even before the rains came the herdsmen of the village were summoned and hired to send their cattle to graze on our fields during the day and to be kept overnight. The cattle became the manure manufacturers. Grandfather would pay a few cents per head of cattle. If a pregnant cow calved during her stay on the field, he would have to pay for the calf too. This process of cattle grazing and manuring the field once every few weeks went on for a couple of months.

With the first rains, the handy source of manure was the contents of those large pits in the garden. The garden refuse and the cow dung, put into the pits mostly by Kunchi, had become rich slushy compost. The dung was precious manure. It was never used as fuel in the north.

The Thirukkural says, "In rice plants distance is required. In kindred closeness." The males of the extended family and the males of all the castes living on the land would work together fertilizing, sowing and then harvesting the fields. Uncle Ratnam who lived close by would send his labourers and he himself would come over. This labour would be reciprocated by grandfather's labourers when they were needed by Uncle Ratnam. Relationships and work were symbiotic.

Grandfather had long cadjan-roofed carts, twice the length of the normal bullock cart. Yoked to it were his two huge white sindh bulls. To us, the horns of the bulls, long and curved, with bells tinkling on them, would be a terrifying picture. The cart was in constant use in the garden. The compost would be hauled out from the pits by long spades and hoes, the cart filled and taken to the field. There the manure was spread generously on it. Kunchi was most enthusiastic about manure. She balanced a palmyrah leaf-woven basket on her head and walked along the lanes and by ways where stray cattle grazed. Her eyes roamed around looking for the dung. When she did see it she picked up the dried dung and tossed it into the basket. She did it so dexterously that neither she nor her basket lost balance. She would spread it over the field with great satisfaction and get a few cents for her trouble. There was always excess and unused manure. This was hauled back into those sturdy bullock carts that trundled away. The manure was sold profitably to those farmers who had insufficient compost or cattle.

When the soil was wet, sturdy, broad but not elegant ridges were built by the workers. These bunds were boundaries and paths between squared spaces and retained within them, the maximum water. The grey clay below the loam of the soil retained the water better than the rich red soil of the fields in Inuvil, which percolated the water rapidly. The family lavished a lot of loving care and labour in the fields. We too would be rushing around dragging small cut branches over the fields to be a part of the work of cultivation. The pelting rain had a great attraction for us. We rushed in and out of the rain till we got soaked and reprimanded. The latter didn't stop us standing under gutters for more rain baths! The sharp and cold rain on our bodies was the most perfect and pleasant sensation after the sizzling heat.

Although grandfather's family lavished a lot of loving care on that paddy field, the return was disappointing. Religious rites were always done before sowing, but that didn't seem to increase the yield! Coconuts were broken, lamps lit and the rites of sowing were done to get even that normal yield!

Sowing was done with great joy, with the females and older children joining in. The seed paddy had been preserved with great care from the last harvest. One corner of the field was sown thickly, and when these seeds sprouted and grew to a few inches they were transplanted to fill the spaces where the seeds had not taken root. Weeding was hardly done. Even the weeds may have needed a better soil! The sky opened and gave those fifty inches of rain till January. The paddy grew, and the climate grew colder as the dew of the misty months of November and December came down. It was the only time that people even spoke of the cold and the miserable weather. Dew fell fast and made everything hazy in the mornings. For a few weeks the early risers and there were many of them, wrapped warm woollen scarves over their heads, and round their necks to keep warm and the dew out. This season meant that my maternal grandmother was planning the next trip to Malaya to ease her asthmatic attacks.

The paddy grew and when it was a few inches high the normally arid brown northern ground was transformed into a beautiful green, moss like carpet, contrasting with the still brown ridges. The green paddy extended to the horizon or to any intervening village. The clumsily made scarecrows, with stick hands jutting out and old clay pots for heads on which turbans sat, appeared among the paddy.

The ripening of the paddy was heralded by the screeching of parakeets. They were greener than the paddy and had rose ringed necks. Their screeching meant the harvest was near. They swooped on the paddy, pulled up a whole plant, found a perch and ate it grain by grain.

Our harvest time was March. The harvesting too was a cooperative effort. On an auspicious day, the lamp was lit again, the coconut broken and other rituals done. Paddy was cut by sickles and laid in neat rows on specific large palmyrah mats, kept for this purpose. In a couple of days the women would take handfuls of the paddy and shake or beat the paddy on the dry ground. Over eighty percent of the grain fell. The stalks were gathered and stacked for a couple of weeks to be threshed. There was no specifically built threshing floor. The paddy field had dried hard enough to be a threshing floor. The threshing wheels yoked to the bulls were driven round the threshing floors many times.

The grain gathered was about forty bushels, so my grandfather told me. The stubble fields would then be gleaned by the poor neighbours. They would dig out paddy from holes made by rats too. The women and children were great at this foraging. No paddy was sold.

Paddy was stored in a corner of a room, reserved for grain and garden produce, in large palmyrah-woven baskets and covered securely with palmyrah leaves. Country rice, the brown rice was preferred by all. When it was needed, the paddy was taken from those baskets to be pound in the largest mortar and pestle that we had. It was a backyard job, with women of the dependant castes doing the chores. The pounding of paddy was a back-breaking job as the husk of the paddy sat securely round the grain. I still remember the pair of tall slim women dressed in bright saris and unmatched blouses who brought the pestles down into the mortar with the paddy in it. They brought the pestles down alternately, bending and stretching their bodies forward and backward with a regular rhythm which became soporific if looked at too long. Some of the grain was boiled, dried and then pound. A good number of measures of rice were kept with great care for the next Pongal festival.

On returning to my village many years later, it was sad to see the field gone. The fragmentation of land meant each member of the next generation had only a piece of it. Small houses had replaced grandfather's big house. Many had left for Malaya, having sold their shares to relatives who preferred to stay behind. There was no sign of the live fence. Palmyrah was the only tree that seemed to have survived.

Holidays away from home and seeing new places were pretty much rare in our younger days. If we went anywhere it was to visit the coastal belt of Jaffna. If a sojourn at a place visited was for more than a day, we would invariably stay with some relatives or friends close to our destination.

There were no guest houses and hotels were unheard of. The Hindu relatives who came along with us would combine a visit and worship at a temple on the route and even they would be happier if a *pooja* coincided with their arrival at the temple. They would adhere to a strict vegetarian diet long before the journey from Jaffna. Buses, bulky, ugly-coloured ones, infrequently made their appearance on the route. Buses arrived in Jaffna long before the arrival of the motor car; the latter did so only in 1902. Tarred roads and buses came to the north long after they made their appearance in the south. Lorries for transport of goods however came long before the passenger buses.

We waited patiently for the bus, and on arrival, we got in with great anticipation. The bus was restarted with its crank with a loud spluttering noise and very reluctantly too. Black ugly smoke trailed behind its uglier back and every acceleration of the bus added to the thick smoke already blown out of the exhaust pipe.

The journey was on a straight, hot road. Thankfully the breeze from the ocean percolated through the always open windows of the bus. Visiting temples on the way became only a dream for my cousins, as the whole process of disembarking and embarking would have been exhausting and time consuming. Our first destination was Keerimalai, the spa hamlet of the northern coast. It nestled among the rugged and rocky shores that hugged the blue serene sea of the northernmost coast. It provided an ideal retreat for pilgrims and travellers alike. The people there were simple, religious, friendly and were like the people of an unspoilt village. They regarded us as people coming from the outside world. Keerimalai became famous for its mineral springs, which gurgled out of the depths of yet unfathomed coral beds. These springs, well known for their healing power of body and mind, attracted many devotees. We dug pits on the shore of Keerimalai and were amazed to find fresh water at the bottom of some of them.

When the tide came in at dusk, the seawater rushed in and diluted the fresh water. The early morning pilgrims queried loudly whether the water was fresh or salty. If salty they waited, for the tide to return and the water to turn to fresh mineral water. It was unbelievable that a spring of such fresh water could be so close to the sea. The waters of Keerimalai were contained within a walled tank, and steps led from a side into the water. As is usual in a conservative society, the males and females bathed themselves in two separate, divided portions of the tank.

Legend spoke of a rishi called Nagulamani who had a face like a mongoose, bathed in these sacred waters and was cured. For this reason it was called Keerimalai, meaning mongoose rock.

The temple here, named Naguleswaran, was one of the five Eeswarans or abodes of the God Siva. Koneswaran, on the east, was the one I was familiar with.

Maviddapuram, which meant 'where the equine face left' and the temple here with the tallest *gopuram* was built by a Chola princess, Maruthapuraveegavalli, who was cured of her equine face by bathing at Keerimalai.

This temple was across the land from Keerimalai. Hindus considered it a great privilege to have the ashes of their dead family members immersed in the sea next to the Keerimalai temple.

The temple like all Sivan temples had rows of large granite pillars, which were a thousand when it was built. The icon, the lingam, had circlets of smaller copper lingams and was referred to as Tampaleeswaran.

The Portuguese arrived and like the fate of many temples this temple too was destroyed by them in 1621. After four hundred years, the Hindus under the guidance of the Hindu

Gopuram

reformer Arumuga Navalar built it again. It was destroyed again by fire and rebuilt yet again. It was occupied by the army in 1983, and the worshippers needed permission to visit it. To those who were not concerned with the spiritual values of Keerimalai, it was still a wonderful haven of peace and quiet, and a place for picnics.

Relaxation for the males came when they sipped the refreshing sap of the palmyrah blooms, served in the palmyrah palm frond cups, while watching the swarthy climbers in their protective climbing kits. Thankfully, we avoided the festival time of July and August, as then we would be jostled by the unprecedented crowds who would gather to have a dip in the sacred waters, in the firm belief of having their souls cleansed and their sins forgiven.

It was more picnic than a pilgrimage when our next break in the journey was Point Pedro. Pedro was the name given by the Portuguese. It was literally the highest rocky point on the north coast named after St. Peter. In Tamil, it was Parithithurai, the cotton port. This had been as busy as Mantota when the Portuguese introduced the cultivation of cotton to the north, which grew and flourished in the Jaffna soil. Cotton was sent to Indonesia and India to be made into cloth. Some of it was brought back to Jaffna to be dyed, as indigo and other plants used in dyeing grew verdantly in the north. The dyed cloth was then sent back again to Indonesia. The cloth for the local population was brought from India! The cotton of Jaffna was a great source of income to both the Portuguese and the Dutch.

Point Pedro boasted of a lovely beach but Thondamanaru, close to it, had a wider and lovelier beach. The lighthouse was even taller on closer inspection. It must have beckoned all the trade ships ashore, and when commerce died down in the north, it revealed and guided the many fishing boats that went out at dusk and returned at dawn, bringing their shoals of fish. The harvest of fish made the fisher folk rich in the northern coast. The market was filled with shouts of sales talk, mainly of the fishmonger who shouted the prices of the fish. In the market square stood a concrete stone, which was inscribed with the information that the spot on which it stood was where Baldeus preached his first sermon, standing under a tamarind tree, which gave the only shade for him and his listeners.

We were now impatient to traverse the desert of the north, Manalkadu, which literally meant 'the sand forest'. We left the straight main road and enthusiastically walked briskly on a side road to Manalkadu. We were filled with energy and enthusiasm of the young. However going further in we became nervous to find ourselves in more sand and among numerous sand dunes with another stretch of sand further out. It seemed foolish to have ventured into this desert. We looked around and there was a bullock cart, nonchalantly ploughing its way through the sand on tracks familiar to the carter. We hailed the carter and did not wait for his permission but jumped onto the rear of the cart, our backs to the carter and with our legs swinging over the end of the cart. We recalled the story of Laila and Majnu and wondered whether we would have met the same fate if we had not met the carter. To our young eyes the desert seemed endless while we were trundled and rocked along the path. We saw a bluish grey haze in the distance and then a lighter blue, and there was the north coast sea again.

Baldeus preaching under a tamarind tree at Parithithurai (Point Pedro)

Thanking the carter and jumping off the cart at the same time, we rushed across the remaining sizzling desert sand to the seashore. Weren't we thankful when we saw St. Anthony's Church looming on the seashore. We rushed towards it, away from the blazing sun and our feet touched the cool, cemented floor of the church. Having exhausted the water we had brought with us, we rushed towards the niches in the walls of the church which had cemented receptacles holding holy water. We dipped our fingers in it and poured that cool water on our heads and tongues. It refreshed and revived us. We were told that the distance from the north coast road to the church was only a couple of miles but to us it seemed like a mini Sahara.

The whole trip was an adventure to us, but was so prosaic when recalled. We returned along the same wide open spaces of the coastal road. Dusk fell quickly and the tall palmyrahs seemed to be etched on the sky, which still held some light of the sunset.

The trip back home was full of chatter about the forthcoming wedding of Pushpam. The wedding was to be in September, a convenient month with innumerable auspicious days. The Hindu almanac had been perused diligently to find the date and time of the tying of the *thalikodi*.

The two events that were celebrated most in an agrarian and extended family were Pongal and a wedding.

We not only had a daily dose of Christianity in school with prayers and scripture lessons, but it was continued in Sunday school as well. In addition, we had a fortnightly prayer meeting and Bible study at home conducted by the Christian missionary Miss Helen Elizabeth, who looked after the spiritual welfare of quite a few families. Preceding the visit our sitting room would be cleaned, the chairs rearranged, and the small table would be covered with a beautifully embroidered table cloth, that was sewn by my eldest and accomplished sister. The simplest fare of sandwiches and tea would be made, to be laid on the table after the meeting. Christian friends in the vicinity of our home joined us. The missionary arrived wearing a dull coloured dress. It was of a cotton material printed with small dull flowers. It had a collar and a low waist band. The dress covered the knees and trailed to her calves. She wore very practical shoes. It seemed a uniform, of the missionaries as every one of them dressed inconspicuously like this. She had freckled skin. We had never seen freckles before. Later I saw these freckles on a very light skinned Tamil friend denoting probably some European lineage. The meeting started with the singing of a hymn and a passage read from the King James' version of the Bible. If the missionary felt confident of her knowledge of Tamil, she then read from the Tamil Bible.

We used the Fabricius translation of the Tamil Bible, of 1791. However, the first translation had been done in 1723 by Ziegelbalz and Schultze. The American missionaries had a great desire to translate the English Bible to Tamil using simple language. A committee of six members was headed by Peter Percival, the principal of Central School, Jaffna. Percival had a tremendous fund of scholarship like that of the other western missionaries, and spoke Tamil like a Jaffna man.

The other missionaries were Spaulding, Horshington, Samuel Hutchins, a great scholar of Tamil, Rev. Poor and Winslow - all of the Batticota seminary. All of them knew Greek and Hebrew too. In addition to their translation, they sought Tamil pundits to rewrite their translation into good and simple Tamil. Arumuga

Navalar was one of them. However, his version of the translation was rejected as he had introduced many Sanskrit words which were strange to the Jaffna Christians. A new translation modelled on the Tamil translation of Fabricius was and is still used in Jaffna.

The Bible study itself was short and interesting but the prayers that followed it were too long and reminded us of the prayers of my grandmother's, back in time, in our home. As teenagers, we found the long prayers hard on our bended knees and concentration. We were eager to say Amen many times before the prayers ended. The dreaded part of the prayer was when the missionary requested an individual prayer from each one of us. My usually garrulous sister, now out of her mind with nervousness, suggested that we pray in silence for a few minutes! She was glared at by mother while the rest of us giggled quietly. That stare from mother made her mumble a few words and a quick, loud Amen. Unlike us the missionaries had so much zeal for these meetings and shepherded their new flocks with the same zeal.

The missionary knew that the eldest of our family was being groomed for marriage and suggested a suitable Christian boy from a family she knew but failed in her endeavour as most of the time they were unaware of or knew little of the stratifications of caste. The eldest girl Chellam and Nesam the younger, very close to her in age, were groomed for marriage. They were taught the basics of good housekeeping, which included sewing and cooking. It was difficult to say who the better cook was, and we diplomatically praised every dish whether meat or vegetable that was set before us.

Both would wear the sari elegantly with perfect matching of the sari and blouse. The eldest, however, wore softer colours. Nesam would look glamorous in the darker-coloured saris with matched and stylishly made blouses. Her skin colour was a shade darker than her sister's and the bright colours blended with her skin colour and made her more glamorous. She would not wear a sari until a perfectly matching blouse was made for it. It might take months to get the combination right. Mother would grumble at her fastidiousness, but was grateful that she was a good seamstress. My eldest sister became, with age, more particular in her attire. I would watch her getting dressed to attend church. She draped a pretty blue flower printed Robia voile sari with meticulous elegance. She wore her hair in a coiffure. She changed her ordinary gold ear-studs to brilliant diamond ones and changed her gold chain to a heavier one. She then dabbed pink face powder to bring out her light complexion. Her feet slipped into an elegant pair of slippers. She left for church invariably with a not so elegant umbrella.

We were living in my uncle's home when earnest endeavours were made to find a suitable boy for my eldest sister. If she had lived twenty years into the future, she would have attracted a male with just her good looks. Love marriages were unheard of at that time. The groom had to be sought for, though not in our village as it had only a few Christians. He came from Araly where there was a moderately large Christian community. Being a Christian was not enough. He firstly had to be of the same caste. The young man, Thurai, considered the proposal and came to visit my sister. This of course followed an agreement on the cash and jewellery to be given as dowry. The jewellery of twelve sovereigns of gold instead of the usual ten and a piece of land in Jaffna was stipulated. Thurai and a couple of his close relatives had formal talks with my parents, after which savouries and sweets were served as refreshment. In contrast to my petite and pretty sister, he was stockily built, tanned, had thick eyebrows that met in the centre of his forehead, and an even thicker handlebar moustache. We, the younger three sisters, were quite disappointed at his appearance but knew that sister would agree to the proposal.

The eldest girl in a family had little choice in it, as she must marry to make way for the younger female siblings. The extended family was surprised that my parents considered a groom who was not a government servant with a foreseeable pension! This pension was so important in the north as the salary was the backbone of the family's economy. There were no plantations or large acreages of paddy fields that brought an additional income. He was a clerical hand in a British establishment in Colombo. This was a shock to us as it meant she was going very far from us and Jaffna. This was the first time a member of our family was to set up home in Colombo. Colombo meant, to us, a place of great distance. The northerner hardly looked to the south for jobs, before the British arrived. The British found the English-educated northerner and sent him to the now centralized public service posts and to the private establishments both in the east and south of Ceylon. The British also made Colombo the pinnacle and last station of the public service, both of which meant that the Tamils worked and retired in Colombo. Most of them stayed on while others came back to their homes and *valavus* in Jaffna.

Thurai was not aware of the number of sisters-in-law he would acquire. We and the children of the neighbourhood were running wildly in the garden when he was visiting us, and he wasn't told who was who! A brother-in-law was responsible not only for his wife's welfare but also for his sisters-in-law. When his visit ended, there was much discussion among the adults and they assented that a pensionless groom was a great drawback. An old couple or a young widow could only be sustained on a pension once the gold asset of the *thalikodi,* the nuptial chain and pendant was sold for immediate financial needs. My aunt told us of a funeral she attended of her still young cousin's husband. There had been great sympathy and regret. The visitors at her wedding had remarked, very tartly, that she was marrying a pensionless groom.

My parents and sister accepted the proposal without demur. A suitable young Christian man was hard to find. We had endless chatter about his looks and job. My mother insisted that he was reputed to have a good character and a generous heart but we retorted that they were not apparent! Horoscopes had not been compared as Christians were not expected to do so. However, a Hindu relative found a good date in a good month, to be on the safe side, for the marriage. The time of the wedding could not be looked into as church services for weddings were fixed at particular times to suit the clergy.

During those halcyon days before my sister's wedding and departure, we would trek to all the familiar and beautiful places in Jaffna. We never got tired of visiting the old Dutch fort. The original remains of the fort were what the Portuguese built. Though the fort at Kayts was the first, Oliviera opted for Jaffna town as the site for a fort, as the kingdom could be defended by land and sea. It was begun in 1625 using *uliyam*, the free services of the locals. The added tax to the already taxed individual crop contributed greatly to the building of it. It was on the edge of the Jaffna lagoon, on the south of Jaffna. The Portuguese never finished it and it lacked a part of a wall and a bastion.

Painting of the Courtyard of the Jaffna Fort

The Dutch conquered Jaffna after incarcerating the soldiers and civilians inside the fort and starving them out. In 1658 the Dutch demolished the not so fully up-to-date square-shaped fort of the Portuguese and built it afresh to its pristine glory. The inner pentagon was built first, and later on the outer circuit. Everything was done in the latest design. Stone and lime were used in plenty. The best of military architecture was seen. It became the strongest fort in the East and a perfect defence against shell and artillery fire. It was the only fort that qualified with a designation of Citadel, which meant it was a large independent, garrisoned, administrative and military centre without civil inhabitants. This fort protected the town, and the town was in awe of it.

The approach path was 'S' shaped and we walked this path that would have had the drawbridge. Trees shaded it beautifully. The gate had the date 1792, the date of its completion. The inner circuit was through another gate which had the date 1680 on it, denoting the commencement of building. There were the ramparts, ramps and bastions. The thick entrance door had pointed iron spikes to prevent elephants breaking the gate with their heads. The walls were almost six feet thick with lettered panels, which probably marked the tombs within it.

The most attractive building within the fort was a solid Dutch house of one storey with a typical long verandah. It had security as it was used by the highest government officials, who came on official duties from all over the island. It was called the 'King's

Dutch Fort and Lagoon

Entrance to the Dutch Fort

King's House in the Fort

Dutch Church within the Fort

House.' It had old antique furniture in the drawing room and bedrooms. There were portions of tree-lined roads, which today gave a glimpse of the beautiful courtyard of the distant past. There on the ground was the remnant of a once beautiful sun dial. Walking further, there were the remains of a drawbridge and a bell tower. The bell had tolled the hour, tolled at the time of church services and was kept safely in the vestry.

Inside the Church within the Fort

The Dutch worshipped in their church within the fort. The church was in the form of a 'crab' cross. This meant that the nave and sides were of equal length. Plaques denoting tombs were part of the large floor. This Reformed church was a major and stable element for the Dutch, who ruled Ceylon, and this church was a fine memorial to that. Within the church were impressive bits of furniture, such as the four stalls and a roofed pew for the highest in the land. The metalled communion rail was added by the British.

We tried to see the gallows last, as its presence frightened us still. It was close to the church. We rushed past it to retrace our steps to the gate. Ghosts were expected to be seen at dusk. When walking back home, we saw two small underground buildings within it but were frightened to go there. These were for the Dutch prisoners. We admired the moat and drawbridge and noticed the guardroom at the gate, originally built by the Dutch. The garrison later became a prison.

This beautiful and inspiring fort lasted for so long, but finally crumbled to artillery and canon fired between the rebels and soldiers.

The Jaffna Lagoon at sunset

Thankfully I never saw the ruins after 1984, as I had stopped going to Jaffna. The fort was close to the Jaffna lagoon and our repeated visits to the fort and Jaffna lagoon never became common place. We strolled to see the ultimate in extraordinary beauty - the sunset over the Jaffna lagoon. The waters would become still and dark. The fishermen on their fishing stilts and in their fishing boats would become silhouettes. Our eyes would literally turn to heaven to see the colours of the sunset. It seemed that each colour, from indigo to green, stood by itself on the stage of the sky, flashed its colour, took a bow and then disappeared rather reluctantly. Every colour took its turn mixed with the silver of the clouds. The sun set as a huge red ball that competed with the other colours. We waited patiently and quietly as our usual chatter diminished to respect the sanctity of the scene. We waited till dusk came on and the twilight filled the space between us and the sky. Only then we turned back home. We saw the crowds that were near the lagoon, appreciating that sunset. A scattering of missionaries and other foreigners with their cameras were often seen at the edge of the lagoon. The waters of the lagoon became black and unreal.

The Rest House - Jaffna

On our return we passed the church where we worshipped. A service took place many times during the day. A large number of slippers of every shape and hue were scattered outside the door. This was a habit left over from our Hindu forefathers, who went with unshod feet into their temples as the ground within it was considered holy. Many women covered their heads too. The large church looked even larger in the twilight. We then passed the clock tower on the opposite side of the road. It commemorated the visit to Ceylon of the Prince of Wales in 1875 and was a gift from Sir James Longdon, who became the governor of Ceylon. The architect of the tower was Smither.

We passed the rest house, a typical Dutch house with wide verandahs which ran round the main building. The main street had a mixture of old Dutch and new British buildings, especially the schools. At least three of them were on the main street. The bakery was closed. We truly enjoyed the bread and pastries made by Wijedasa who to us was the best baker in Jaffna. He came from Matara in the deep south, and lived with his compatriots in Jaffna. Their families did not reside in Jaffna but the bakers travelled regularly to their villages. With slower feet we turned towards home and discussed the next outing. Mother brought us back to mundane things and reality, when she queried if we had done our homework and spoke of the coming marriage of my sister. All her words were contained in one long sentence.

It was a thud to earth from sunset to homework. In bed, I recollected that sunset and admitted to myself that in its beauty, it beat the sunset at Casuarina beach.

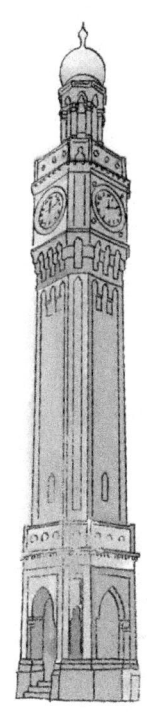

Clock Tower

On looking back, school days always seemed to be wonderful. Disappointments were easily forgotten and examinations a thing of the past. There was no such thing as extra tuition for lessons learnt. Homework was done with the help of my mother in the primary grades of school. She had studied till the Junior Cambridge examination and had been a teacher herself. She would sit with us every evening and supervise our homework, just as I would emulate her many years later with my own children. The missionaries, who were so keen to give a basic education in English, would insist that every student should be erudite in Tamil language and literature. We would memorize chunks of the poems and sayings of Thiruvalluvar and Avaiyar and struggle through the poetic interpretation of Kamban of the Indian epic *Mahabaratha*. The language of that poetry seemed to be above and beyond us as we struggled to understand the classical Tamil of the poems. There were a thousand proverbs to memorize, as the Tamil language was full of them. There was no letting up on this, even up to the Senior Cambridge. Then there was then a leap to England's Shakespeare and Jane Austen, great favourites of the missionaries, which later became ours too.

I remembered not only the school, but the church that we attended regularly. It was the Methodist church close to home and school. It was the former Calvinist or Dutch church that the Methodist missionaries made their own – St. Peter's. The church seemed so huge and airy, made more so by the high roof. Windows were large and unbarred. The aisles were long and broad. As children we sat on pews which were also long and rather broad. This made us push right back to sit and lean on the cane rattaned backs of the seats. Our legs and feet dangled over the edge of the seat. Cement, wood and coral stone had been equally mixed and used in the church's structure. A flight of long steps led into the church from its gate that abutted the road. I would compare the church with the temple of the village worshipped in by grandfather. It was of granite with one large heavy door at its entrance. The floor was cemented and cool to the touch. There were no side doors or windows. The roof was tiled, resting on palmyrah reepers. It had always been filled with the haze of smoke, the fragrant smell of incense and camphor. The temple was still cool within the thick granite walls and pillars, the granite stones made it so.

With us in church was a fair sprinkling of the Dutch Burghers who made Jaffna their home. They came in their 'Sunday Best' as we too did. They wore high-waisted flouncing skirts, gossamer blouses and beneath them were seen petticoats with pretty lace shoulder straps. We seemed so inelegant in frocks which we wore when young. Elegance came only when we wore saris to church in our late teenage years. However, every new frock sewn for us was first worn to church.

When quite young, we went to Sunday school. We spent an hour singing hymns and listened to Bible stories. Sometimes we had to draw incidents and figures from the Bible. My artistic talent was so poor that my figures had no resemblance to anything human. However, Sunday school was fun and at the end of the year we had a great Christmas party.

The church was a meeting place for the young. Friendships and sometimes romances began in the church, some ending in matrimony but mostly not. The church was equidistant from Vembadi and the Boys' Central College, and the Christian boys from the latter would be the first young non-related males we met. A church similar to the one in Jaffna but smaller was the Calvinistic church in Trinco that became the Methodist church. The congregation there was a mixture of the local Protestants and the British naval establishment. The pastors came from England, and like the American missionaries of old, were so keen to master Tamil to preach in that language and be part of the Tamil congregation. They were persistent in their study, and we were amazed at their proficiency attained in such a short time; their accents though made us smile very often. The British worshipped in that church till independence was granted to Ceylon.

The liberal education and a Christian environment made us accept every one of every caste as equal and we did so in our classroom and in extracurricular activities. However, the caste radar in-built within us detected the caste from their conversation, and the places they came from. Names did not specify caste.

Yoga was very proud of her clan that lived in the locality of Velvettithurai, a village on the north coast. Her caste, she told us, was Thimilar, also referred to as Thevar, a caste separate from Karaiyar, the fisher folk. Both were in the middle class order of the hierarchy of the caste system. *Thimil* in Tamil meant boat. They were seafarers in the boats they built. They built the *kattumaran*, anglicized as catamaran. This literally meant a tree, probably of satin wood, which was hollowed out into a boat, and another tree made into an outrigger and tied to the boat. They built barges, lighters and frigates, which resembled the British ones they had seen. They brought trade from Tuticorin to Jaffna and from Cochin to Kayts. Since Chola times, the *Thimilars* sailed the seas eastwards. *Chettiers* from South India bought their boats and made the *Thimilars* their employees. Thimilars were also well-known pirates of old, who raided the ships that travelled from the southern coast of India to any port in Jaffna. If a vessel sank anywhere along this sea route, they would claim the contents, even if the boat sailed and sank between Kayts and their village. The Portuguese met their match in these boatmen, and it took years for them to take control of the sea routes and claim all sunken ships. The Thimilars were very prosperous. Their wealth was seen in the red roofs of their houses, whose walls were of cement, unlike the mud walls of the fisher folk. They never married into the fisher caste. They registered their marriages, like the upper castes did, and their womenfolk did not work after marriage.

The boats that the Thimilars built were painted in bright colours, and flags fluttered on their masts. They were brought out in large numbers during the last day of the festival of their own Amman, Siva's consort's temple. This was the day of the *Theertham*, the ceremony of immersion of the iconic idols of bronze with gold plating that were colourfully dressed. The immersion denoted the end of the temple festival, which lasted a few weeks. On each day a particular ceremony of the temple took place. The immersion ceremony was in the sea, as the temple stood on the seashore. The inland temples, in contrast, had in their vicinity large dug-out tanks, with steps on all sides leading down into it, filled with water for the immersion ceremony.

The boats surrounded the area of the immersion. There were shouts of worship and joy when the idols were brought down the temple steps and then placed in a boat. It moved a few hundred yards into the sea, the priest and his helpers holding onto the precious icon. The priest chanted the prayers, the 'gods' were immersed and taken out. Then with shouts of exuberance, the boatmen and the onlookers jumped into the sea as they believed the waters to be blessed by the immersion.

All this was brought to mind when Faith, my friend of fifty years, wrote me. Faith was one of the seven close friends who continued our friendship, it seemed, forever afterwards. She was the only one who stayed back in Jaffna after marriage with her family. We had a correspondence of well over forty years, the letters took two to three days to reach me and each came every two or three months. They were thick with news of Jaffna. There were tidbits of news of Vembadi, our school, the church, common friends and who married whom. There was news of new Methodist missionaries and whether they had mastered Tamil to preach. Photographs were rarely included in those letters.

In the late nineteen thirties she wrote of seeing a news item in the Tamil newspaper giving an account of a ship built by the Thimilars for a Chettiar, a money lender. It was built like a British frigate, which the builders had seen after the British colonizers came to Ceylon. This boat was about one hundred feet in length like a schooner but probably in appearance looked like a frigate. It was used as a cargo ship that plied between the northern shores and the east towards Burma and Indonesia that carried spices, palmyrah products, tobacco, cotton and brought back teak and sugar. This boat stood tall and majestic among the smaller fishing craft and numerous other festive cargo boats that had assembled for the *Theertham*, of the Amman temple. The boat was named *Annapoorani*, in honour of Siva's consort, the goddess, the provider of food. An American, William Robinson, saw it on his travels to Jaffna, desired it, and bought it from the Chetty owner for a handsome price. He rechristened it *Florence Robinson* in honour of his girlfriend. He took the ship's crew of five Hindus, the chief of whom was Thambipillai. They set sail to a port near Boston on the other side of the world. Probably the crew had never before steered any sailing ship towards the West. Robinson first sailed to Gibraltar. An American, Dostoer by name, joined the crew in Gibraltar. They then sailed via Bermuda to America, but the journey was not easy. Before Bermuda was reached, water and food had to be rationed. The Hindus had to forego the washing of the head and body with fresh water before their religious rituals for a safe journey. Finally rice was rationed, which was their staple food for all three meals.

Food and water was replenished at Bermuda and they set sail for Gloucester in America. Their journey had taken six weeks. The Hindus had never seen fog or dark skies and must have prayed fervently when crossing the Atlantic. The ship and its crew must have been a sight to the Americans at Gloucester – the crew dark skinned, bare bodied, daubed with holy ash, sandal wood and with red round *pottu* marks on their foreheads. Their *vertis*, which were tucked up, gave them the appearance of wearing skirts. Crowds gathered to see the ship and its crew. Since they were British subjects they did not need visas to stay on American soil. They did so for almost six weeks. They returned richer and famous, but gladly went back to boat building and sailing them to the East.

These boat builders and seafarers of Velvettithurai and Point Pedro were also warlike and fearless, and had been welcomed even during the Chola rule of the Pallava kingdom. The Thimilar's prosperity waned after Colombo became a port too.

For almost forty years I had a correspondence with Faith. Finally I met Faith on a trip to Jaffna. We stood on her doorstep and queried the identity of each other! We had not recognized each other. Our writing would not have changed, but physically we had changed beyond recognition. The families would recall this episode with much fun, laughter, unbelief and wonder.

We hardly met each other after that. I was in my early nineties when Faith's daughter sent me an unblemished sepia print of a photograph in which the seven of us, just out of school and in saris, posed next to a school building. So many memories of school flooded my consciousness, especially memories of Faith who passed beyond. Images of her as a slim, tall, smiling young woman would be before my eyes ever so often.

As much as we enjoyed seeing places in the north and revised our history, the same occurred when we lived on the east coast. Friends visiting us were taken to Sigiriya and Dambulla, as Trinco was close to them. Sigiriya meant, first, the visit to the frescoes, colourful and lovely to look at, the artist unknown. The younger ones ran ahead with agility and ease and reached the very top of the rock with ruined structures on it, probably of a palace. Just as quickly as they went up, they hastily descended the same rough stones, with the help of a long iron rod that stretched along the steps.

The wind on top of the rock was too strong even for the sturdy young ones. From the Lion's Paw we crept up quietly in great fear and respect for the hornets whose nests seemed like small boulders on a larger rock face. The older ones would reach the Lion's Paw, rest, and admire the view, the trees and what remained of the gardens and glades of ancient times.

Dambulla meant climbing that beautiful large sloping grey rock at leisure but the ascent was hot on the feet and head. The rock led by an arch and a long path to the temples in caves. How refreshing it was to step from the hot granite to the coolness of the caves. We admired the statues of the Buddha in various seated, meditative, sleeping, and standing poses and we saw the reverence of the many Buddhists who came to worship them. Our trip cum picnic took us through a whole day and we returned tired and ready for bed.

However, what we enjoyed most on a Sunday or many a school holiday was the trip to Kantalai. This would mean driving alternately through thick jungle roads and then, in contrast, we were surrounded by luscious green paddy fields of Tampalakamam. The latter was famous for its Sivan temple. When the Portuguese in 1624 destroyed the Koneeswaran temple at Swami Rock, the Brahmin priests took some of the loveliest processional bronze icons of Siva and Parvati to the Kalanimalai hills, twelve miles away, where a temple built by the Cholas remained untouched. The main icon, a lingam, a Thambaleeswaran, was placed in the inner sanctum of this temple.

History recalled that Rajasinghe II, who hated the Portuguese, helped with his donation to build this temple. These icons had more gold in them than other bronzes, which reflected the Chola influence in making them. Devotees of this shrine built a village round the temple, which became a symbol of the destroyed Koneswaran temple, and the village was named Thampalakamam. The British renamed it Tambligam. A small Pattini shrine too was in that village. Thampalakamam was a rich fertile place made so by the waters brought by many channels of the Kantalai tank. Overlooking the Kantalai tank was a beautiful old rest house, a great favourite for picnics and relaxation for the day, especially for the nieces and nephews who spent their holidays with us. Food was not taken, as the amiable rest house keeper provided cooked meals.

Architecturally, like in most state rest houses, there was a broad and long verandah with old-fashioned chairs and loungers. It was always cool, with those large shady ficus trees at the edge of the tank. When the younger males got bored they threw empty corked bottles into the tank and shot the bobbing bottles with a borrowed rifle and this kept them entertained.

Kanthalai Rest House

The legend of the Kantalai tank would be repeated and it always enthralled us. It was the Dutch who came upon this tank and its legend. The Dutch were meticulous in their search for tanks, the existence of which they were sure of in an agrarian society. They rebuilt the roads which were in great disrepair. The Portuguese had sold land for revenue and parts of the roads were included in these lands. The Dutch took back these lands that were previous roads and meticulously rebuilt them. They brought to Ceylon the great republican ideas of administration and rule. Every road and tank was considered to be public property. They brought Malay soldiers and policemen to help rule the native people. Whenever a tank was discovered, or a road made, detailed deeds and maps were drawn and kept for posterity. They discovered the Giant's Tank, the former Nagarkulam, but found it uneconomical to repair it.

During their search for tanks they stumbled upon a large lake full of light and life. There were trees standing in the water and their glory was truly seen in the hot months. When the northeast monsoon arrived the trees got submerged. The Dutch discovered not only the lake but the legend that gave its name to the tank. The legend was that in prehistoric times, a prince who ruled that area and his wife came upon this vast collection of water. They realized that if they built the periphery, it would hold nature's bounty of water that could water the fields near and far. A gigantic granite boulder embankment was made, each individual boulder fitted perfectly into its adjacent boulder, with no adhesive used. Boulders were put on piles of earth. The overseer while building it found a constant breach at one section of the bund where the force of water against it was great. The water for the tank came from the Elahera canal from the mountain region, whose ridges were visible from the tank. Soothsayers were consulted, who suggested propitiating a demon responsible for this. A human sacrifice, a virgin's life, was needed. The overseer had no children. One day at dusk, when the sky was at its most beautiful he enticed his niece to stand in the breach. He quickly got his workmen to throw earth on her. She had desperately put her hands to her face and cried out, "Amman kan", "maternal uncle, my eyes". Then she cried out,

"Amman thalai", my uncle, my head. The uncle resolutely urged his workmen to cover her quickly and she was buried alive. That part of the bund was called the 'woman's bund.' When people walked by it, they heard in the lap of the water a mournful plea of "Kan" and then "Thalai." The tank got its name Kantalai from this legend. A Sivan shrine was built near the breach as atonement for the young girl's life. The kings and princes who ruled these territories used the water of this tank for cultivation. The bund of the tank was repaired when needed but the embankment never needed repair. The Dutch mapped it in 1760, and it was the earliest document of the irrigation projects. They discovered a strong construction of conduits under the granite boulders. The extensive area of the lake reflected the vast area it irrigated. It filled with the monsoon rains and the water overflowed the bund and fell into another hollow tank in the northeast of the main tank. This storage tank was named Vendevasa Kulam, named after the white and pink lotus blossoms that covered its surface during its season of flowering.

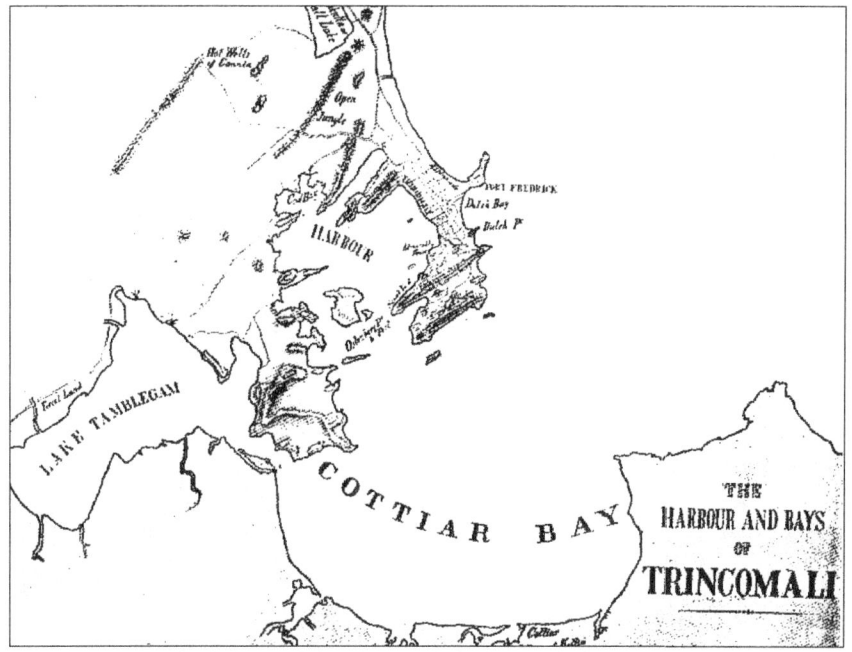

Lake Thampalakamam and the bays of Trincomalee

The Dutch engineers found evidence that water from several catchment areas augmented the water from the Elahera canal. The waters of the Kantalai tank and the *Vendavasa Kulam* drained into the *Peri Aru*, the big river. The *Peri Aru* flowed into a valley, the Thampalakamam Lake, before it flowed into the sea. The land between Kantalai and Thampalakamam was ever so green and fertile with this water.

The tank when viewed from the rest house appeared unbroken. The expanse of water seemed to rise to the range of low hills far away. Legend too recalled that the area between the tank and the rest house was haunted by a ghostly blur in the late evening of Tuesdays. We did not see it to prove this, as we rarely stayed late. We truly enjoyed every view, the breeze, and the whole atmosphere of the tank.

Many years later, President Premadasa wanted to commence a water scheme by tapping the waters of the Kantalai tank. He was advised against it by the engineers, as the insertion of a large pipe through the embankment would breach the tightly fitted granite boulders of it. He knew best and a large pipe was pushed through the wall of the bund. The boulders fell apart, and the water surged out of the tank and submerged the fields and villages of Kantalai. It was repaired, but with much difficulty.

When it was time to get back in the evening we saw the familiar flocks of teal and cormorants skimming the surface of the tank. Dusk would come on suddenly. There would be excitement and anticipation of seeing elephants, which we invariably did on our journey home. They would be there, right in the middle of the road and on its sides. We waited patiently with the windows of the cars closed and silent till the elephants decided to amble off into the jungle at their own pace. If there were large herds with young ones, it took more time for them to leave the road. We were truly lucky to see a leopard. The Eastern Province had long stretches of jungle and leopards were not rare. Chena cultivation and colonization saw an end to their habitat.

On our way back, the village of Kanniya was a small detour from the main road and had a Kannagi shrine. Kannagi was Pattini's former name. Kanniya was much visited, not only for the shrine, but also for the seven hot wells in it precincts. Legend said that Vishnu came as a sage and brought forth these springs up by piercing the earth seven times so that Ravanan could perform the funeral rites of his mother, but science pointed to volcanic activity below the wells. Each well was probably of a single spring as its water had a different temperature to the others. Whatever the reason, a visit to the wells was always looked forward to by the older generation, who thought that the hotter the water, the better it was for their arthritic pains.

Kanniya was a sylvan and quiet place. There were no dwellings nearby. Shops and vendors were few and far from the wells. The wells of these springs were below ground level, and the ground on which we stood to draw water from these wells was sandy and covered with small and large smooth pebbles. They were bounded by a short square wall of concrete. Steps led up from them to ground level. The bather bent over the well, dropped a small bucket with a rope attached to it and drew water out. There was no modern convenience for a change of clothes. A sari stretched out was a curtain behind which the females tied their bathing cloths. Swim wear was taboo. The older ones got down gingerly and relished the water from each well, while the youngsters dashed around, with shouts of glee and bathed from the less hot to the

Kanniya Hot Wells

almost boiling hot water of a well. No soap was allowed at the wells and nobody bothered about it, not wanting to nullify the effects of the hot water. The fastidious ones went to a nearby well, soaped themselves, washed and got back to the hot wells.

We tried to be the first to arrive there at dawn, as the springs had bubbled up and the wells were full. Later in the day the level of water went down and then came up again in the evening. The Hindus went to the small temples of Siva, Parvathi and Ganesh after a bath, which were situated adjacent to the wells. The men said their prayers and performed rituals in their wet clothes.

The Ravanan legend said that many Hindus, after performing the last rites for the dead, went to Kanniya for more rituals. It had a great attraction for all the locals and visitors. It was overgrown by the jungle during the conflict and an unfortunate accident occurred when a land mine injured a few people while they were performing funeral rites for their dead.

A Tamil proverb often quoted was: "By the time a man is forty, he is his own doctor or a fool." The northerner thinks he knows his ailments, and the medicine for them too. Having failed with his 'home medicine,' he went first to the native doctor, the *pariyari*, but decided for himself how long he would take his medicine, and how much of it. If he did not recover, he went to the doctor of western medicine and in this too he decided how much and for how long he would try the medicine. If not healed, he went back to the native doctor who was also referred to as a *Siddha*. Alternate treatment from the two types of medical men was commonly tried in the north.

The Siddha system of medicine in the north had its roots in the ancient Dravidian culture and belonged to the Saiva tradition. Tradition said that it was given by Lord Siva via his wife to the Siddhas. Siddha medicine was a combination of medicine and yoga. Then it got complicated with incantation, penance, meditation and elixirs. Siddha Medicine was practiced in Jaffna and even further south. Unani Medicine was the choice of the Ceylon Moors in Jaffna.

The best known of the first eighteen Siddhas was Agasthiyar who practiced medicine with extraordinary powers. He was also thought to be the founder of the Tamil language.

The Siddha medicine made use of metals, minerals, chemicals and herbs. The alchemy practiced had many references to the Chinese system. Siddha was similar to Ayurveda, but still different in that the physiological humour of air was a predominant factor in childhood, fire in the adult, earth and water in old age.

The old Siddha in our village was our friend and physician and would tell us, as part of his discussion that began before treatment, that the body had seven elements of blood, bone, muscle, nerves, and so on. Disease, he said, occurred when the ratio of the humours was disturbed by diet, stress and lifestyle. He touched the skin of the patient, looked at the tongue, eyes and their colour. He was keen for the patient to talk, for voice change may be a clue to illness if a blocked nose was excluded. He did all this to Mahen, a young cousin who was ill with a stomach pain.

The Siddha was keen for Mahen to pass urine on a piece of cloth. He was looking for the straw colour which meant indigestion, rose hued in blood pressure, saffron in jaundice, reddish yellow in a heart ailment and 'meat washed water' colour in kidney disease. However, he spent most of the time in feeling the pulse. This was of fundamental importance. He waxed eloquent about it and became almost poetic, and said that it did not leap like a frog or dance like a peacock, or step like a fowl, the latter denoting a sluggish system.

When it came to medicines, Mahen got pills and powders to swallow. The most important metal used was mercury and its salts; if not, chemical sulphur was tried and next herbs. The pill given was red or black in colour or was made into disgusting in taste, black, slimy balls or syrup. The syrup he got was probably powdered herbs in an aromatic liquid sweetened with honey or sugar. If not honey, then ghee was used. Nobody left without a *Thailam* - medicated oil. It had gingelly seed oil, coconut or castor oil. The medicines seemed impressive in their numbers.

Mahen took the medicine but his stomach pain became worse, so he was taken to the doctor trained in western medicine. The easiest place to meet him was at the local hospital, the Green Memorial Hospital built in our village in 1897 by a former student of Dr. Green. The hospital was built with the money sent by Dr. Green's brother and money donated by the past students of Dr. Green. The doctor examined him in the same manner as the Siddha, but the physical examination was more intense and the doctor thought that Mahen should go to the Green Memorial Hospital in Manipay, probably for surgery.

My grand uncle Ratnam offered to take Mahen and me in tow on that long journey by buggy cart, a more elegant and fashionable alternative to the bullock cart – only the bulls were common to both. The boat ride followed by a cart ride took us to Manipay.

Grand uncle Ratnam not only knew the history of his school founded by the American missionaries, but also the history of their medical mission. He started his monologue as we travelled.

Various groups of American missionaries and medical missionaries came to Jaffna from 1816 and the last one left in 1923. Most of them came to teach, preach and found schools. Invariably each group had a missionary trained in medicine, who looked after the health of their colleagues. The local people became aware of their presence and requested to be treated by their western medicines, which was never used or seen in Jaffna or in Ceylon before. They were only used to the Siddha medicines.

The first medical missionaries, Drs. Warren and Richards, had a basic knowledge of medicine, having had a two-year course in medicine instead of the regular three in the United States. Governor Brownrigg had welcomed the American Missionaries and allowed them to establish their mission. They went north to Vaddukodai and Tellippalai. Their travel to the north from America had been tedious. Their boat trip took almost four months via the Cape of Good Hope, where they had established a mission station. On their arrival in Colombo they were taken by palanquin to Kalpitiya and then by boat to Mannar and then by another palanquin ride to Jaffna. Their goods, books and medicines followed them in bullock carts. By treaty restrictions, the governor could not give those lands and buildings, as they were reserved for the Protestant missionaries. However, he gave them the three-hundred-year-old, but now ruined, Portuguese buildings in Tellippalai and Vaddukodai. The ruined buildings seemed large but only the coral stone pillars and floors remained. The missionaries, with painstaking zeal, built their missions, the money coming by subscriptions and donations from America.

When the locals in larger numbers requested treatment, the missionaries saw that not only were they ill, but malnourished as well, and they needed longer treatment. Small hospitals were built with public funds. Each station had a missionary to assist either Dr. Richards or Dr. Warren. Cholera and small pox were rife in Jaffna, with many epidemics. Children were more stricken by cholera. In the north the Hindus associated cholera with an offence against a goddess and the patient was whisked off to goddess Parvati's temple and made to prostrate him or herself at the temple door, while chanting went on to appease the goddess.

Cholera was also thought to be contagious and everyone was afraid to go near the patient. It was considered fatal. The medical missionaries gained the confidence of the local people and cured many of them. They used mercury salts and opium. Mercury was the cornerstone of Siddha medicine but strangely had not been tried in cholera.

With confidence gained, surgery was practiced, probably under opium sedation. The commonest surgery was setting bones after falls from tall palmyrah trees.

Both doctors fell ill with tuberculosis. Dr. Richards died and was buried in Tellippalai, aged thirty-eight. Dr. Warren died in the Cape Town mission. These missionaries started their life with the American Board for Foreign Missions in their twenties. They gave of themselves and the few short years of their lives, to Jaffna.

The first fully qualified doctor was Dr. John Scudder. He had the regular three years of training in the States. His father, a lawyer, opposed his entry to medical, pastoral mission work. The son persisted and set sail and arrived in Trincomalee via Calcutta in 1819. The northeast monsoon was raging and sailing on to Jaffna was impossible. He went to Jaffna by palanquin. His wife and the rest of his group went overland to Colombo and then by boat along the Dutch canal to Puttalam. From there they went by boat to Jaffna. Dr. Scudder, like his predecessors, took with him a large amount of medicines and more surgical instruments that included those for cataract removal.

Dr. Scudder, like all missionaries who came before and after him, wanted the preaching of the gospels to be a more important aspect of their mission of healing. Medical practice would begin by the doctor who told a prayer, preached the gospel or else had a conversation of salvation with the patients. Each patient needed a ticket to see the doctor. Medicine, at the start, was free, but later the mission could not afford it and charged a little. Each ticket would have a biblical verse printed on it. Scripture tracts were given to the patients. Those written on palmyrah leaves were given too. They were easier to be read by the patients and these were cheaper too. Dr. Scudder was ordained in 1821 and preached as a regular pastor.

These missionaries managed with the little Tamil they knew, but found no time to train locals as assistants. Dr. Scudder made his name in his surgical skill, removing tumours on one day and cataracts on the other. He, however, trained George Koch, of Dutch descent, and Whelpley, a baptized local. Unfortunately Koch left after his training and Whelpley died young after ten years of training under Dr. Scudder. These assistants were graduates of the Batticota Seminary where they gained knowledge of English and science.

Dr. Scudder opened mission stations at Pandaterrupu and Chavacachcheri villages. A printing press was much needed by the missionaries, mainly to print Christian tracts, a newspaper and other literature. It was ordered in 1816, but the printer missionary John Garret came in 1820. He did not stay long as Governor Barnes refused to give him residency status. He refused to allow any more American missionaries to come to Jaffna. His reply to the letter from the American Mission was that his government and the Anglican clergy were able to convert the heathen population. When the American missionaries came there were only five Methodist and one Baptist missionary and no Anglican clergy. John Garret left to continue his mission work in India.

Dr. Scudder had a large family of ten children, all born in Jaffna. Then another fully qualified doctor, Dr. Ward, arrived. In 1835 Rev. Poor, the head of the Batticota Seminary, was keen to start a medical school and hospital near the seminary, to train catechists and Christians as assistants. This was not to be and Dr. Ward was the sole medical missionary. Dr. Scudder was sent to India, as the British now allowed non-British doctors to work there. He and generations of his family worked in India, the most famous being Dr. Ida Scudder, the founder of the Vellore Medical College.

Dr. Ward began training the graduates of the seminary in medicine. He trained a dozen of them, of whom Gould and Evarts were well known. There was another severe epidemic of cholera and a greater recovery in those who took the treatment from Dr. Ward. He left Jaffna in 1846 due to ill health. He was keen to return after recovery. He was ordained as a priest but sadly died at

Dr. Scudder's Dispensary

sea returning to Jaffna. Before he died Dr. Ward had left Evarts to carry on teaching.

All the missionaries had to sign a contract for life with the mission. They went home on leave on rare occasions, and only due to ill health, which often prevented their return. Governor Barnes had refused permission for any more American missionaries to come from 1820 for eleven years.

After that there was an influx of missionaries. The most loved and most successful of the medical missionaries was Dr. Fisk Green. He graduated from a medical school in New York which was the precursor of Columbia University. He was very religious by nature and keen on mission work. He met the missionaries Dr. Scudder and Rev. Spaulding in the United States to learn more about the mission in Jaffna and the Batticota Seminary. He was appointed as a medical missionary by the American Mission Board. He was twenty-five years of age and had great progressive ideas. He lost no time in going to New Jersey and met Rev. Samuel Hutchins to learn Tamil. Rev. Hutchins had been in Jaffna for ten years and was associated with the translation of the Bible into Tamil. Dr. Green was a linguist too, and found no difficulty in adding Tamil to his knowledge of Latin, Greek, French and German. Rev. Spaulding encouraged him to take a sturdy and elegant carriage as it would make travel easier than in a buggy cart. Horses were plenty in Jaffna, as the Portuguese and Dutch had bred them commercially in the island of Delft. Rev. Spaulding had been the first to take an American horse carriage to Jaffna in 1828. Dr. Green took with him a large amount of medicine, medical books, an anodyne vapour machine (anodyne would have been the anaesthetic), a primitive photographic apparatus and even dental instruments. He travelled by ship to Madras, overland by horseback to the coast, then by *thoni*, a boat, to Velvettiturai. He arrived in Jaffna in 1847, a journey of four months. Dr. Green had stopped at all the American Mission stations on the way.

Rev.Dr. Samaual Fisk Green, MD
(1847 - 1884)

On arrival he started his Tamil studies in earnest. His ambition was to teach, preach and write in Tamil. He made a name overnight with his surgical skills, more so as the Siddha physicians did not practice it. He moved to Manipay, the centre for all the other stations, set up a dispensary and a small hospital there. Dr. Ward's students, then doctors, manned the other stations. Dr. Green gave them the title 'Doctor.' There was no governmental regulation to follow. Dr. Green's vision was immense. He wanted to train the locals in the practice of western medicine, teach medicine in Tamil and have a doctor for every ten thousand locals. He had the best tutors in Tamil, Mr. Nevins and a Tamil pundit, Mr. Muthuthamby.

Percival Dyke

He lost no time in starting the medical school. Selection of students was advertised in *The Morning Star*, the oldest paper in Jaffna, first appearing in 1820. Three students were selected. They were ex-Batticota Seminary students to be trained for the regular three-year course. The medical school was the first western medical school in Jaffna and in Ceylon, and it started in 1848. It was the first time in Ceylon that a human body was dissected to teach anatomy. The students were paid a stipend. The students themselves tutored the teacher in Tamil. The names of the students were their baptismal names, carried from school to medical school and thereafter. A new batch of students was selected every other year, and the British government gave a yearly grant to the medical school. Dr. Green was now proficient in Tamil. He made translations of the medical books needed for the first two years, and later went on to translate the books of the final years. He was determined to start teaching in Tamil.

At this time, Percival Dyke was the much loved government agent of Jaffna, which he served for thirty-four years. He died in Jaffna. He did so much for Jaffna that he was considered a rajah. He travelled to work on an elephant, and this added to his stature. He was a friend of Dr. Green and wanted to start a hospital in Jaffna itself, so that many would not have to trek from far to obtain western medicine at Manipay. Mr. Dyke founded the Friend-in-Need Society of Jaffna. Donations were called for and the new Jaffna hospital started in 1850. The treatment was free and that made a drop in the number of patients at Manipay.

Dr. Green's motive to teach medical science in Tamil was to keep the doctors within the peninsula and he hoped that cures and conversion to Christianity would go hand in hand. In fact he encouraged his students to come in their national attire to the medical school. The medical students came in their *vertis*, a shawl over their shirts or even over their bare bodies. Many wore turbans and some had their long hair tied in a knot, either behind or on top of their heads. Educated and dressed like this, Dr. Green was sure that they would not be attracted to go south to better their prospects.

Dr. Green's Medical Students
L to R: S. Miller (Velupillai), C. Mead (Kanapathi), N. Parker (Arunasalam), J. Danforth (Periyathamby), J.H. Town (Poobalasingham) and A.C. Hall (Kumaru)

Dr. Green was also keen to have joint discussions and clinical work with the Siddhas so as to learn from each other. He hoped to have a few of them on the permanent staff.

The first batch graduated and with the intake of the second, Dr. Green earnestly started to prepare a Tamil Medical Glossary, naming the parts of the body in a simple manner denoting appearance, shape and function. In addition to this, other medical books were translated and illustrated with the help of notes sent by the authors themselves. In total, eleven batches were taken in, each batch had from three to eleven students. The graduates who passed out helped with the translations of the medical books. The fourth batch started by taking down notes in Tamil, but was taught in English. The sixth batch was taught entirely in Tamil, and so were all the other students that followed this batch till the eleventh batch which was taken in 1879. Dr. Green for some time, and many of his graduates, worked in the Jaffna hospital. His ambition to keep the doctors within the peninsula was thwarted when the British government took them to work in the hospitals in the south, as doctors to the Planter's Association and insurance companies. Many of the graduates became teachers of their medical schools too. This included Mills, McIntyre and Adams. They became the teachers of the last batches and acted for Dr. Green, who was on leave at that time. Dr. Ewarts was sent to work in the Colombo hospital which was founded many years later. These doctors with baptismal English names would have been on the registers as British doctors and not doctors from the American Mission Medical School.

Dr. Green finally left due to ill health. The government started reducing the grant and finally stopped it. The grant looked after salaries of those working for the college. The college could not function without these funds and it was closed.

With the closure of the medical college there was an appeal to start the medical school at Vaddukodai within the seminary, but the missionaries were not keen on it. Manipay hospital was still popular and carried on with missionary doctors sent from America. The first female medical missionary was Mary Irwin. She was actually Mary Ratnam, as she had married Mr. Ratnam, a Tamil, in New York. She had been sent by the American Mission to Mr. Ratnam to be taught Tamil. She was discontinued abruptly as it was considered scandalous and dishonest of her for not informing the mission of her marriage. She went to Colombo and became a well-known doctor and social worker.

Dr. Curr came to Jaffna to take Mary Ratnam's place and worked in Manipay for many years. The hospital was renamed the Green Memorial Hospital in 1897 in honour of its founder.

When Mahen went to that hospital there was a doctor, a graduate of the Medical College of Ceylon. He examined him and ruled out surgery for Mahen. They returned with another handful of pills and liquid medicine paid for. Grand uncle thought he should see the Siddha *pariyari* again. Mahen informed us, in a loud voice, that he was going to see the 'wind, fire and earth' man and did go as it was the done thing.

Thankfully Mahen was not old with body and joint pains. If so the Siddha would have sent such a patient to be checked at a better established and equipped Siddha hospital. Thereafter, if treatment with herbs and decoctions failed, the Siddha would resort to more sophisticated therapy. There were the steam and oileation therapy where the patient was immersed in a hot bath. The bath would be of granite, probably brought from Mammalapuram in South India, the centre of granite workmanship. The water in the bath would be enhanced with herbs or hot oils. A fragrant or pungent steam rose from the hot bath to make the patient feel better if not good. If that too failed, bloodletting was tried before yoga therapy was resorted to.

Lakshmi, Pushpam's cousin was not able to attend Pushpam's wedding. She had given birth to a lovely baby boy a week before the event. In the north, births, deaths and any significant event in an individual's or more so in a female's life had its own rituals, customs and taboos. The whole household in which the birth of the child occurred was relegated to that of an untouchable caste. They were not visited, neither did they visit or come within the threshold of another household. Visiting was taboo and remained so for forty days. This was followed by the purification ceremony of the mother, entailing religious rituals in her home performed by a Brahmin priest. The following day she would attend the local temple with the child or, more so, they would go by boat to Nainativu to Nagapooshani temple, named after the consort of Shiva who is depicted there as an icon protected by the five-hooded cobra. The island was believed to have been inhabited by the Naga race, and one form of their worship was the veneration of the cobra.

It started as a small shrine, built by two traders who saw a cobra visiting that site daily with a flower in its mouth. It was observed to have swum across the waters to arrive at this place, which then became a shrine. Nainativu, also called Nagadipa, had a small Buddhist *vihara* in honour of the legendary visit of the Lord Buddha. Lakshmi and family took the baby to the Nagapooshani temple and placed him on the floor before the inner sanctuary where a special *pooja* was conducted to bless him.

A week after his birth we saw people bringing herbs and barks to Lakshmi's doorstep. These were used for the hot baths Lakshmi would have after the delivery. The herbs and barks were boiled in a cauldron at the back of the house. The hot herbs and barks were then picked up, placed on soft square pieces of cloth, and made into small bundles. In a secluded part of the house, the mother would then have these packs pressed onto various parts of the body, especially her abdomen. It took about half an hour to do this. She was then bathed with the remaining hot water in the cauldron. The belief was that this almost sauna-like treatment was good, not only for her skin and muscles, but helped the womb to regress and to go back to its former size. Her body was dried vigorously and then she was enveloped in a cloud of incense smoke. A tot of brandy or even toddy given and it was followed by the midday meal. This procedure was repeated daily for about five days. Her food was made rich with eggs fried in gingelly oil to increase lactation. Murunga, jak and fish of the 'milk shark' variety was given in plenty for the same reason. She was pampered as a girl after puberty. For the forty days of seclusion, she was not allowed any work, especially to carry water. The belief was that the soft post pregnant womb would be dragged down by strenuous physical work. Later, when I was familiar with the Old Testament of the Bible, I read of the strictures, the stringent isolation and the purification of the Jewish mother after the arrival of the new born. I was surprised it was so similar to our taboos.

I remember the time when we, a few teenagers, accompanied some older females who came to Jaffna to visit Lakshmi. She had had the baby, not at home, but at the private McLeod Hospital at Inuvil, well known for its maternity care. Lakshmi moved to Chundikuli, a half mile distance from our home, to be with her in-laws. This made it easier for her to attend that hospital for her antenatal visits.

Chundikuli was a fashionable part of town with very elegant Dutch and more modern houses enclosed within flower gardens and shaded by spreading tall trees. Many of the Christian families belonged to the Anglican Church and they had, within walking distance of their homes, the school and the church. Chundikuli, the girls' school, was always in competition with Vembadi in both studies and sports. Chundikuli was made even lovelier by the park dotted with very old spreading trees. In the midst of it was the old official government agent's home and office.

The northerners were fortunate in having two private hospitals, the first one in the early nineteenth century. Inuvil hospital was founded in 1898 after a gap of fifty years from the opening of Dr. Green's Manipay dispensary in 1848. The hospital came long after the founding of Uduvil and Udipiddy boarding schools in 1823. The hospital was started with the enthusiasm and tirelessness of

Government Agent's Residence in Old Park, Chundukuli

two sisters, Mary and Margaret Leitch. They were attached to the American Mission and worked for seven years from 1880. They started a fund-raising campaign in Scotland, England and America for expansion of the existing Manipay hospital, but mostly to build a hospital for women and children. In fact it was their women's medical mission. Their target was to raise thirty thousand pounds, but they were so successful that they raised triple that amount. They added to the fund from their own wealth, as they were rich. They helped all the projects of the Jaffna mission, but missed the opportunity of setting up a private medical college attached to Jaffna College.

Shortly thereafter the sisters left the American Mission and went abroad. They came back to Jaffna as workers of the Zenana Mission of the Church of Scotland. Zenana missions worked on behalf of Christian missions for the welfare of women; *zenana* meant female in Arabic. They purchased a few acres of land in Inuvil, close to the mission school in Uduvil. The hospital buildings were very large in comparison to the other American Mission buildings. It had lying-in wards, children's ward, surgical wards and private rooms. They had enough money to pay missionary doctors from abroad. They started a school for training nurses and a home for female doctors.

The first patients were admitted in 1888 under the care of Dr. Curr, a graduate of Scotland selected by Misses Leitch. The Inuvil hospital was renamed McLeod Hospital in honour of the biggest financial donor, Reverend and Mrs. McLeod, to the fund of the Leitch sisters. The hospital was then gifted to the American Mission, the Zenana Mission taking no interest in it thereafter. Nurses trained there were all Tamil Christian females with a mixture of names ranging from McLelland to Annamutthu! The hospital was so popular and admissions so many that she called for and trained Dr. Helen Keyt, a product of the Colombo Medical College who became Dr. Curr's assistant. Dr. Young from America came in 1899 but left in 1904, before Dr. Curr did many years later. The medical doctors of the American Mission schools were appointed and with their departure doctors from South India filled the breach, first by Dr. Chacko and then by Dr. Gangamma who worked in this hospital for many years.

Lakshmi went back to her village a few weeks before the due date of delivery. Home deliveries were the order of those days, but Lakshmi's family could afford to send her to the private hospital. However, pregnant females would not wait for the onset of labour pains to rush to hospital. The mother to be was usually accompanied by her mother or maternal aunt together with another not so busy female and they arrived at the hospital ten days prior to delivery and confinement. Lakshmi with her relatives travelled by buggy cart. But her clothes, provisions and beddings were brought behind her in a bullock cart. Bundles of firewood too would have to be taken. We were impressed by the large buildings and even more so by Lakshmi's well ventilated room. There was a single bed - the helpers were expected to sleep on mats and pillows which had to be brought by them. A common kitchen was provided for every three rooms. Provisions and firewood were stored in them. Fireplaces were available but the pans, clay pots and tea pots had to be brought too. Food was not provided by the hospital. It seemed to the mother and to the

Dr. Curr and Nurses, circa 1916

hangers on that it was an enforced holiday. Nobody grumbled about it. The vegetables and fish could be bought from the women who set up their stalls close to the hospital. There was general harmony and gossip between relatives of the patients while they cooked, made cups of tea, or mostly coffee.

When we arrived there with an aunt, the baby boy was two days old. Much was made of him by my aunt, holding and caressing him. We younger ones were too nervous to even touch him, leave alone hold him. It was midday and most visitors had come from near and far. The morning visiting time made travel easier for the visitors. The garden of the hospital had as usual large, shady trees. Trees and plants grew luxuriantly in the red fertile soil of Inuvil. Roses grew well and most of them were potted and pruned but we were surprised to see, for the first time, two trees about five feet tall that bore rose blooms. One tree bore a bright yellow bloom and the other sunset pink blooms. Nobody believed us at home when we spoke with disbelief and awe about those rose trees.

The hospital was such a boon to the northerner and remained so for many years. Sadly, the last we heard of it was during the conflict between the rebels and the Indian army. Their artillery fire and mortar had shattered the buildings of this hospital. The hospital was so central, easy of access that the two gun toting groups would have rushed through the corridors, shooting each other and shattering the walls. The hospital would need a complete rebuilding and restoration.

The aunt who came to visit Lakshmi's baby had a great desire to pray at the Nallur temple. We had no interest in the religious part of the visit but were keen on an outing again. It was early evening, and as we walked towards the temple we could see the *gopurams*, the towers, and the colourful Hindu concrete icons sculpted into these towers.

The Nallur Kandasamy, alias Murugan alias Subramaniam alias Kathirgamar, was the most popular icon of the Tamil Hindus. This temple had a recorded history of its origin without recourse to legends, traditions and hearsay. The first Nallur temple was built by king Chakravathi of the Pandyan kingdom. He was the monarch of Jaffna in the thirteenth century. The kingdom of Jaffna of the thirteenth century had a series of Chola kings as its rulers. However, in 1450, King Sempaha Perumal alias Buvenekabahu alias Sapumal Kumara probably of mixed parentage, conquered Jaffna and made Nallur the capital. He built the shrine for Lord Skanda in it. Sempaha Perumal's name is mentioned with thanks and reverence in the chant of the Nallur Temple pooja. A large number of temples dedicated to the other deities came up in the same locality. Nallur became a historical city, as it was held in great reverence by the succeeding Hindu kings.

The Portuguese arrived, conquered Jaffna, dethroned King Sangili after many battles and sent him into exile to Goa. The Portuguese first took the valuable icons and jewels from the temple and razed it to the ground, supervised by Commander de Oliviera, in 1621. Fortunately, some of the smaller and lighter icons were taken away by the officiating priests and dropped into the temple well and later retrieved. The Dutch conquered Jaffna in 1733. Mapanna mudaliyar's family was the original custodian of the temple during Portuguese rule. In order to keep the status and the public service job of a mudaliyar, the latter would have to convert to a nominal Roman Catholic, which he must have done. He was given the title 'Dom' and referred to as Dom Mapanna Mudaliyar and to the Portuguese he was an apparent Roman Catholic. He reverted back to his original name and religion with the fall of the Portuguese. The Dutch were not coercive to baptize him to their Calvinistic Protestantism.

The Dutch gave him permission to build a small temple again. It was built not on the old premises which had absolutely no evidence of the old temple but at the present temple site. The temple was not very large when we visited it. It had a shed covering the front portion leading into the temple with its many niches and icons. The former site of the original temple, now discovered, became the site of the Anglican church St. James's built during British times.

While my aunt was busy praying, we enjoyed the bazaar outside the temple which sold every type of trinket a girl desires. In addition, there were the typical Jaffna sweets and savouries, the boiled, hardened palmyrah syrup and bundles of boiled palmyrah yams which were in season.

The festival of the temple was in the months of July and August. It was the most crowded as it was the most organized and colourful event with a great amount of piety in the worship of the main icons. Every night a particular processional icon would be brought out of the temple, placed on a particular chariot which may be in the form of a peacock or a decorated stage, and taken round the temple with much noise and devotion. The temple itself had a large tank as it was not near the sea or a river. The ancient hollowed out rectangular tank would have been lined by granite and granite steps had led down from all four sides to the waters of the tank. The newer tank had cemented walls and steps. The tank was only filled to three fourth of its height during the festival. The ceremonial immersion of the icons would finalize the ceremonies of the festival.

Then we trekked to the 'Sangili Thopu', probably a gateway to the palace. It had the name Sangili on it. King Pararajasekeram may have built it earlier during the Portuguese era as it had ornamental arches and narrow columns of Portuguese architecture. The arch had led to the Yamuna pond named after the Yamuna River in

India. The pond was built by king Pararajasekeram and its' first waters was brought from the Yamuna River. There had been a recreational park round that pond. The arch and the garden later became known as the 'Poothathamby Valavu' as it become the official quarters of Mudaliyar Poothathamby of the Dutch era. This diversionary trip made us late getting home, resulting in queries from mother for the delay.

Sangili Thopu as it was

It was just a few days before my eldest sister's marriage, the first in our family and in Jaffna. She was the eldest granddaughter of my paternal grandfather; my father was the eldest son of his many sons. If the marriage had been held in our village there would have been palpable joy, laughter, loud chatter which was on the verge of noise. There was music and colour. On the other hand it may not have been, as we were one of two families who were converts to Christianity in that *valavu*, the family compound. The colours may have been subdued, the noise of the music - of the drums and the *nathasuram*, the local clarinet, would have been absent. Colour and music were culled from Christianity as they were thought to be pagan.

These were thoughts that drifted by as we were now living in Jaffna. A few Hindu relatives were expected only on the wedding day. A stay overnight was inconvenient for them. Christian services were conducted in either Tamil or English in the church, mostly in the evening. A wedding lunch was easier to manage than a dinner and, if the latter, it was served early. Snacks and sweetmeats were not an option then. The wedding meal had to be substantial. Savouries and sweets were made in a small quantity to be served to the guests who came to accompany the bride to church. The guests themselves brought sweetmeats from the bridegroom's family. This followed the Hindu custom, but this custom too disappeared gradually from Christian weddings. Grandfather accompanied by his two nephews, their wives and children came on the morning of the wedding. He was quite upset at the absence of the coconut leaf decorations at the entrance to of the house and the mango leaves strung across the front door of our house. Far worse, there was no brass pot on a plantain leaf strewn with rice and no mango leaves surrounding a coconut placed on the neck of the pot. There was no brass lamp with burning wicks. He thought it was a pity as such auspicious and traditional symbolic things denoted illumination, happiness and fertility. The Roman Catholic Church tolerated all these traditional customs and even tolerated the loud music.

Maybe the influence of the Catholic female missionaries, mostly nuns, was absent in their homes.

My sister's jewellery and clothes were laid on the bed. She had no ceremonial bath with milk and 'sacred' grass but a quick one at the well. An aunt and a female missionary friend came to dress her, helped by mother.

However much the northerner appreciated the English education that they were fortunate to receive, they were never anglicized. The Christian males who worked for the British firms or attended church services wore a suit, even a three-piece one, but were equally comfortable in a *verti* and shawl. The dresses and long gowns, whether of the Portuguese, Dutch or British, were never accepted by the local females, as probably the heads of the families deemed these dresses immodest and not cultural.

My sister was ready to be dressed. A white silk sari worked with gold thread was her choice. The rather longer sleeved blouse was the idea of the missionary. She wore the sari differently. Instead of the end of the sari being thrown over the left shoulder to hang down, the end of the sari was lengthened and spread over the front of the body to show off the rich beautifully worked head piece. It suited her. However, when I looked at her feet, it gave me a start and I was amazed to see them in a pair of short-heeled court shoes and white stockings. The missionary was satisfied that something of the western Christian wedding was foisted on her. She should have worn gold slippers and silver anklets instead.

Her hair was in a coiffure at the nape of her neck with a garland of jasmines wound round it and not the long plait with jasmine and red flowers interwoven in it. The jewellery was watered down to the pearl throatlet, *atiyal*, with a *paddakkam* of pearls, emeralds and rubies, probably my mother's, and a longer pearl chain with a bigger pendant of the same stones. She had a brilliant diamond nose stud and bigger brilliant diamond earrings, without danglers. Her face and head were bereft of all other traditional jewellery. Her arms were covered with gold bangles, presents from relatives. A light pink powder, from a circular box, was taken on a flat powder puff and dabbed on her face. Finally, my mother and an aunt, who said a short prayer, laid the white nylon veil on her head and over her face, which was held down by another short jasmine garland clipped to the veil. The wearing of the head and face veils came from the west but was mid-eastern in origin.

We too dressed in the midst of all this excitement, darted in between dressing and peeped into the bride's room to see the progress of her grooming. When finally my sister the bride got up, I was surprised to see a long gold chain trailing from her neck to her knees. This must have had most of the gold sovereigns and was a part of a bride's regalia of Pandyan culture.

My older sister Nesam was in a pale pink sari, dressed with aplomb and elegance. She was the bridesmaid, an unheard of thing in our village where young girls were never seen in the bridal retinue in which there was only a matron of honour, who was usually a married sister of the groom.

Grandfather and brothers were dressed in their white silk and gold-bordered *vertis* and gold-edged shawls. Their wives were dressed in orange or scarlet coloured saris, the colours of the sun.

My grandfather was in shock when he saw my sister appear on the front verandah in her white sari. He whispered, but that was loud enough for all of us to hear, inquiring why she was in white and why she was going like a widow to get married! He also queried endlessly at the absence of the sun colours of the bridal sari.

My younger sister and I were too timid to answer but not Nesam, the garrulous sister. In that short time between the arrival of the bride on the verandah and her getting into the carriage, she gave a short history of the arrival of the Christian missionaries. She whispered loudly that Jesus, a brown-skinned man from the East in long robes, was taken to England and then was dressed in a three-piece suit, became white and was brought back to the East! In the West, the colour white for a bride denoted virginity. The missionaries foisted this colour on the brides of the converted Christians. My grandfather, still shocked, remonstrated that no young girl in his family or of the village had to prove her virginity. He said it was such a conservative and close society. He looked truly upset and sorry that our family had become Christians.

A short prayer was said by the missionary but there was no auspicious time for the bride to step out of her home. The day of the wedding had been found to be auspicious by the Hindu relatives, but this was not mentioned to the missionary, who would have been disappointed that such things were seen to. The conveyance to church had to be in a carriage with two horses. It was a status symbol. The Portuguese and Dutch bred horses in Delft as a source of income. Carriages were imported by them and added to by the Americans and then the British. The carriage was of an open landau type for marriages and a closed type for taking the dead to the cemetery, which was also a status symbol.

My sister was helped into the carriage. She lifted her sari and stockinged feet and got in. My father in his gold-bordered silk *verti* and shawl went with her in that decorated carriage. More carriages were hired for the close relatives. The saris, *vertis* and the carriages made an improbable and peculiar mixture of the East and West!

The groom was in his western suit and would not have dreamt of any other attire, since he began his career in a British private firm. The wedding service was in English. The tying of the *thalikodi*, the nuptial gold chain and solid gold pendant, was done during the service. However ardent the Christian convert was, the ceremony of tying the *thalikodi*, the most Hindu part of a wedding ceremony, was adhered to and included with the service itself. The registration of the marriage was in the church; the missionary was appointed by the Dutch and then the British as registrar of marriages in a church wedding.

The bride came down the aisle with Thurai. She looked a very pretty picture. Photographs taken at the church sufficed as formal photographs were taken in a studio few days after the wedding. She travelled back home in the carriage with Thurai. Then they were led to a colourful sari-covered settee, instead of a decorated throne, the *manavarai*. Thereafter the Tamil Hindu customs began. The *koorai*, the sari given by the groom, was taken around to be blessed by the guests who are married with children. The bride was presented with the sari by the groom and she left to dress in it. All the Christian attire of white sari, shoes and stockings were discarded and she returned wearing a red, rich, gold-worked silk sari, the colour which was considered the appropriate sun colour and a pair of gold slippers. Grandfather was happy and relieved to see this change.

The meal was mostly vegetarian, eaten on banana leaves. The guests sat on folded mats, just like in our village. A meat dish, usually chicken, was kept apart from the other dishes, so as to not hurt the sensitivity of the Hindu guests, especially relatives.

Thurai and my sister stayed with us for a few days and then my brother-in-law,

My sister's wedding photograph

now referred to as *Aththan*, went back to Colombo. If Thurai had been a marriageable cousin, he would have been referred to as *Machchan*.

I remembered the missionary coming after the wedding and inquiring from my mother about that part of the wedding held at home. Elizabeth was concerned about every event in our lives. To introduce part of their culture into our lives was not thought amiss by them. That may be the reason why we missed the pearl danglers from the ears studs that my sister wore at her wedding. Jewellery unless in moderation may have been thought pagan.

My sister, before she left for Colombo, wanted to build a house on the piece of land given to her as her dowry. The house was built in a very short time as my uncles were coming back from Malaya on retirement and needed their house in which we had lived for many years. The house that my sister built had a somewhat Dutch design, with its verandah and ventilated rooms, but was much smaller. We got used to the tooting of the train puffing into the Jaffna station, which was close to our home, every morning. The church, a hundred yards from our home, had a carillon bell that rang a melodious tune. It would play a quarter of the tune at quarter past the hour, half of its melody at the half hour, three quarters of it at three quarter hour, and the full melody at the hour. We never missed a wrist watch or hardly looked at the clock on the wall.

One difference in that house was that unlike in the Dutch houses the latrine, called the outhouse, was built far from the house. It reminded us of the village latrine, as it was built on the opposite side, far away from the kitchen and the deep but not very wide well. The kitchen, which was usually built a few feet from the house and close to the well, was now within the house. It was a large room which could hold the dining table and its' chairs. It also had enough room to cook in.

The latrine, however, brought memories of the same in our village home built at the furthest end of it, small, ugly and neglected. It had four walls, each stopping short of the roof for ventilation. It was built a few feet from the ground with steps leading to a narrow door. The name latrine came later, but in Tamil it had a long-winded name that meant the place where impurities were passed out. It was known as the outhouse to make it sound genteel. Whatever the name, it was claustrophobic. It never improved as the time spent within it was considered minimal. Nobody dreamt of taking papers or books into it as happened decades later in a toilet. Squatting on raised cemented blocks was considered the healthiest way to relieve oneself. The night soil was passed into a bucket which was removed by the *Parayan*, the lowest servile caste, through a gap in the rear wall. There were no sanitary services in the village. The coolie buried the night soil in a pit at the furthest end of the garden. The margosa trees that grew there flourished in that soil. The luxuriant growth of small leaves on large branches gave a insouciant murmur whenever a light breeze blew through them.

Ablution was always a hurried event and not to be dawdled over. The older males would smoke the Jaffna cigar while going to the outhouse to smother its smells with the smell of the smoked cigar. We hated to follow them to the outhouse as we could not decide whether the night soil or the cigar smoke had a more obnoxious smell.

My eldest sister, very particular in her habits, would rush to the outhouse following the departure of the coolie. When the Portuguese followed by the Dutch came to Jaffna they named the outhouse *kakkus*. This name was easier on the tongue. The British came and called it lavatory or the latrine and later named it the water closet. Whatever the name, it was not brought closer to the house or attached to it in Jaffna. The utensils used in the lavatory were never taken to the well, but water was brought to it in other pails. It took decades for it to be part of the main house, with its septic tank, cistern, toilet flushes and seating arrangement. The older generation were not happy with this arrangement and built a toilet with squatting facilities adjoining the house.

My married sister now felt that she should take charge of the family as my mother, though still energetic, spent more time helping with deliveries, confinements of various nieces or was an extra hand when needed. Father spent more time with my sick grandfather in Karainagar and when he did spend time with us picked quarrels with my mother on the most insignificant matter discussed, especially of the mollycoddling of my youngest brother. My eldest sister became bossy and dictated to us in the matters of our friends, visits to other homes, and who should be entertained in hers. My older sister was not going to be bullied. She did exactly what she liked to do, be it visiting or whatever her heart was set on but did it quietly, without creating much noise or starting quarrels within the home. It must have been an effort for her to have to curb her tongue.

My married sister was always more caste conscious than the younger ones. Caste had now taken a back seat in school activities and even in recreation and games outside the school but it was an ever important consideration in marriages and even in the listing of guests at a wedding. I remember the wedding of our second cousin's daughter and especially the lunch that followed the wedding ceremony. This cousin had a more advanced attitude towards caste and was tolerant of the lower caste people. When invited to lunch my sister noticed a family of lower social status than ours invited too. She abruptly left the room, having said a few words to the uncle and declined lunch. We meekly followed and dared not protest. We were so disappointed, as we looked back and saw the mouth-watering spread of food on the table. We were glad that Nesam was not with us. She was quite capable of giving a speech of the 'not too far off coming event' of equality of castes in society. She would not believe it herself when a marriage has to be arranged for her. It was very unlikely that she would consider a proposed groom of a lower caste. She was also aware that a lower-caste groom of her choice would not be accepted by the family.

My sister left to join her husband in Colombo after a few more months in Jaffna. Feelings were mixed. We missed her concern and care for us, which was much more than missing her domineering nature.

A wedding in the village was a far more enjoyable and exciting event than in Jaffna town. The one exception was the horse and carriage, with the horse all spruced up to take the bride to church and bring the couple back home. It was a sign of some wealth and prestige. These carriages became common after the first ones were brought by the Americans to Jaffna, and later by the British.

Hindu weddings were always held in the home of the bride. Temples hadn't become an alternate venue. The northerner was frugal with his money and even tight fisted if he thought the expense unnecessary. However he would spend almost lavishly for his eldest daughter's wedding, the funeral of a parent and the education of a son. Pushpam was the eldest and the marriage was remembered for days and months to come. Clothes and jewels to add to the family collection were bought. The only surprise was the *koorai* sari given by the bridegroom, who also had to give the *thalikodi*. In the future, there would be only a single *koorai*, but in those far off days at least three would be given as friends and family came for days to wish them and bless them. The bride showed off her many *koorais*, all rich and elaborate, given by the groom. The younger females of the family compared and contrasted their clothes and jewels, vying to be the best dressed.

Whatever the clothes, the criterion by which the wedding was judged was by the food served at it. The sweetmeats were done a few days before the wedding. The kitchens were small and smoky. The fireplaces of bricks were made under our large mango and margosa trees which made the exertion of cooking less hot. The prepared raw sweetmeats were fried in coconut oil in large brass woks. Sweetmeats were more than the spicy ones. There were the *chippi* of rice flour and sugar fried, then sweets of powdered green gram sugared, wrapped in rice flour and fried. The *murukku* of spiced rice flour which literally meant it was squeezed out through a mould, competed with the *vadai*, a flat and spicy eat made of lentils or *ulundu*, urid flour. The sweets of the culinary art of the Portuguese and the Dutch were great favourites in the north, but needed elaborate preparation and therefore were not made at weddings. Preparations of the sweets meant rushing repeatedly towards Pushpam's home and popping a few of these into our mouths. Nobody cared about sugars and fats in the body, even though every sweet and savoury item was fried in woks full of oil.

The main meal of the wedding was always vegetarian, which meant the cooking and chopping of vegetables the evening before the event. The cooking of vegetables was the culinary forte of any wedding lunch in the village. Each dish was so different to the other. I can still picture the dozen or so female aunts and older cousins, who would sit on the large verandah of my grandfather's home. They would each sit on a short bench with a sharp convex shaped knife at its end. They would sit facing each other and looked like as if they were steering miniature Viking ships going out to battle, but in this case it was the battle of cutting vegetables, potatoes and onions or scraping the coconut with an alternate serrated-edged knife. The cut vegetables whizzed into the containers, which was a reflection of the speed and dexterity of these females.

A Bride

Strangely, it was the *Koviyar* caste members who were entrusted with the preparation of the wedding meals. The *Koviyars* were the cooks and they would prepare these cut vegetables into white, not so hot and chili hot preparations. The women of the household were only tolerated by these cooks to supervise and not really cook. An auspicious day and time was chosen for the ceremonies. Mornings would be easier for relatives to come from further villages. They would come in bullock carts, some of which would have a more sophisticated seating arrangement of narrow parallel seats with a canvas awning. We also had a family coming in a conveyance which looked like a palanquin built on a cart. The sides were covered with canvas and there were coloured windows in the canvas too. Only the bulls replaced the palanquin bearers.

There was such hustle and bustle before the wedding. The whole house was mopped with water, easily done with a few pieces of furniture to be moved around. Saffron dissolved in water was then sprinkled. The young females with nimble fingers and great talent would draw *kolam* decorations, which entailed a free-hand drawing, using rice flour or coloured coconut refuse held between the fingers. Geometric designs, flowers and peacocks would appear on the cemented floor of the entrance to the wedding ceremony. They would be so beautiful and we would be reminded constantly that our feet should not touch them. The ceremonial arrangement of a brass pot brimming with water was laid on the head-end of a plantain leaf head strewn with rice. Saffron made pliable with water was made into symbolic god Ganesh. A cleaned coconut sat on the brass pot surrounded by a circlet of mango leaves. This arrangement was kept behind the *kolam*. Mango leaves strung on twine hung across doorways. A pair of uprooted plantain trees bearing ripe fruits were planted on either side of the gate. The washerman would stretch white *vertis* and sheets across and under the roof. Usually he would bring bundles of white sheets and *vertis* of the people he washed for! There would be no sophistication in his art, as the sheets would be fastened with rough nails hammered into the sides of the walls. The white cloth covering under the roof was essential for ritual ceremonies in a home.

The barber was sought after by the young and not so young males whose hair had to be spruced. The haircuts were done under a tree and each male took his turn for the haircut. Pushpam was in seclusion for a day before the dawn of her wedding.

On the day of the wedding all seemed to be rushing nowhere! The ceremonies were so long. The first part of the ceremony was like that of puberty. At puberty the female child becomes known as *periya pillai*, a big child. The maternal uncle was an important figure in the rituals. He poured some milk on the bride's head who in a silk sari, sat cross legged on the floor. All those with living spouses and children followed the same ritual. No widow or childless couple was ever seen near ceremonies or rituals. Pushpam was escorted to the well and water was poured on her, first by that uncle and then others eligible to do so. She returned to her room led by an older female who took over the dressing of the bride. The clothes used at this premarital ceremony and at the well were given to the washerman, with some cash and rice. Pushpam's saris would be one of the colours referred to as sun colours. Her *manavarai* first sari was less elaborate and lighter, the second the *koorai* had to be either gold, pink, red or orange or any of their shades. Blue, purple and green were taboo as colours for a bride. Her first sari was a pale pink sari and she was adorned with jewellery of gold and pearl necklaces and diamonds on her ears and nostril. Her forehead had a jewel, her hair on her head had jewels depicting the sun and moon, and her arms were full of gold bangles, some hers and some borrowed. She wore a gold plated *ottiyanam*, a girdle belt round her waist. Her hair was in a long braid, the whole length of it interwoven with Jasmines and red flowers. The braid itself was kept in place by a large elaborate ornament fastened to the back of the head. On her feet were silver anklets. The close relatives would then come and give her gold as gifts, mostly as bangles or sovereigns of gold. She wore neither face nor head veil.

The musicians played their music within the house in honour of the bride and very soon they were heard at the gate to welcome the groom. He came wearing a silk *verti* and shawl with a simple turban on his head and with unshod feet. The turban was made by the laundryman. He had a wonderful choice of shawls from that of the many householders he washed for! The groom had a retinue of females behind him, some carrying the sweetmeats they had prepared and another carried a brass tray in which was laid the gifts from the groom. On the tray was the *koorai*, the richer second sari, the *thalikodi*, a mirror, a comb and a garland of jasmines. This tray was carried by the maid of honour who was the groom's married sister. No bridesmaids were seen. Young girls were not allowed at the place of the ritual ceremonies.

There was a lot of noise of Chinese crackers and drums. The washerman was rushing with his clan spreading a length of white cloth, the *pavadai*, on which the groom walked on till he reached the bride's home. It was fun watching the washerman, picking up the trod-upon white cloth, bundling it and throwing it across to another, who spread it on the ground before the groom. It was like a relay. The whole scenery was one of colour. There were the very young, even the two year olds dressed in *pavadais*, the long skirt and a blouse that went over the waist. The younger ones would show a large span of midriff. The teenagers would be in *thavanis*. The *thavani* was a combination of a long skirt, sleeved blouse to the waist and another few yards of material tucked at one end into the skirt in the front, and the other end taken round the back brought forward and thrown over the left shoulder. Invariably the hair was in a long plaited braid and a garland of jasmines trailed from it. This attire was the prettiest dress of all as all three parts of it would be materials of the same colour or in contrasting but blending ones. The older females wore the bright coloured saris in the customary fashion, where the end of the sari was thrown over the left shoulder and its greater part draped over the left arm. However most of the older females lengthened the head end of the sari brought it round the waist in front folded it and then tucked it behind at the waist and the sari ended as a fan shaped tail. The males, whether young or old, wore a white cotton or preferably silk *verti* with a gold or coloured border, shirt and a shawl wrapped round their waist. Many of the male relatives in the course of the ceremony would make temporary turbans of their shawls. This was a prelude to the breaking of coconuts which occurred before an important ritual within the main ceremony.

 The Brahmin priest, seated a step below and in front of the sacred fire, began the ritualistic ceremonies for the groom, with chanting of Sanskrit verses. The groom left the *manavarai*, the throne, and the bride was brought to it from her room. Rituals were done for her. The main ceremony was done when both sat together. The bride was handed to the groom's parents with a gift of a sovereign of gold symbolizing her worth. Ceremonies that followed were symbolic of that of the gods and for a short time the couple were treated like gods and sat at higher level to the priest and the guests. The *koorai* and *thali* were blessed by the priest and the former taken round among the guests to be blessed. When it was brought back, the groom draped the rich, invariably red and gold sari over the shoulders of the bride and she returned to her room to change into it. She came back holding a garland and garlanded the groom, the *suyamvaram*. The names of the paternal generations were pronounced. The *thali* was then tied round the neck of the bride with loud sounds of crackers and even louder music. Rice and flowers were thrown over them. The ceremony of garlanding each other took place and this was followed by the circumambulation of the fire three times.

Various ceremonies then took place during these circumambulations. In one, the bride places her foot on a grinding stone to symbolize a firm marriage. In the next round they searched for a ring and bring it out from a decorated clay pot filled with water, the finder depicting the dominant figure of the marriage. The bride is then taken out into the garden and shown an imaginary star of Venus to remind her of constancy, like Venus. The groom does not promise anything.

The couple finally stood and held a tray of rice for a final ceremony where the parents first and then the family and friends, took a fistful of rice from the tray and showered it over their heads and shoulders. The Alathi, the circumbulation of the lighted wicks, stuck into three pieces of a cut plantain, placed on a tray, completed the ceremony. Everyone was hungry and ready for lunch where a certain protocol was practiced. The couple, males and children sat on the ground on mats folded lengthwise. The food was served on cleaned and warmed banana leaves. There should generally be more than ten vegetarian dishes. Meat was not missed by us. The meal was always followed by *payasam*, a fluid, sweet sago dessert with plums and cadjunuts. Fruits, curd, treacle, sweetmeats and a betel chew were also served. The older females were the last to sit for lunch.

The couple paid obeisance to their parents and then visited the groom's parents at their home and returned to the bride's home, which now would be the bride's, her dowry.

She received visitors for the next few days wearing the additional sun-coloured saris gifted by the groom. These visitors were those who could not come for the wedding and also the acquired relatives by marriage with their families. The relatives would stretch back to three or four generations. Visitors meant

Pavadai

Verti & Salvai 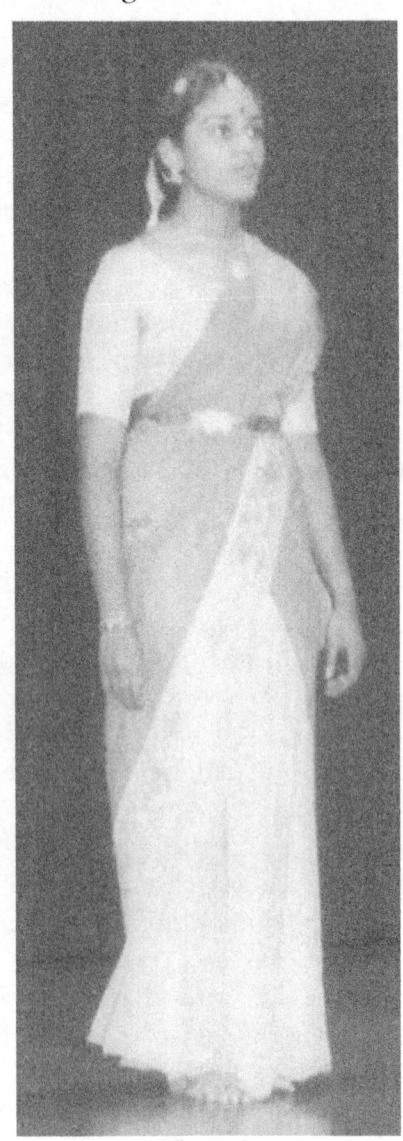   Thavani

Attires of Jaffna

more food and drinks, an added expense to the wedding. Going away on honeymoon was unheard of and the night of the wedding was at the bridal home. There was no demeaning custom of proving virginity with a stained cloth. After the legal registration of marriage and before the religious ceremony, the couple's behaviour was never questioned.

The Sari worn in many styles

Bustling Batticaloa was always, to us, a favourite destination to spend school holidays. There was the anticipation of travel by the seven ferries too.

The streets of that town were more crowded compared to Trinco. There was a stream of colourful heads; the colour was a part of the sari that covered the Muslim women's' heads. They too rushed around, like the rest of the people, bent on buying or selling their wares. A large number of the sellers were small-time traders, again mainly women, seated on the ground with heaps of fruits and vegetables in front of them. They looked mild in demeanour, but would argue garrulously and beat the buyers at the bargaining of prices. They reminded me of the women at the market in Karainagar physically, but they were different in their choice of dressing as they wore red or green handloom saris. They were not less vociferous than the women in our village. Handloom was a cottage industry in Batticaloa.

Batticaloa's added attractions were the numerous small lanes, each wide enough for a car to travel on, that branched from the main road. The houses were modest with cadjan fences enclosing a small neat garden. Like in Jaffna, hibiscus, jasmines and oleanders grew wild but literally overrunning them were the bougainvilleas that crept over shrubs and fences. Their bright colours of red, orange, white and many other shades of these colours vied with each other to look their best all through the year. The part of the town that enticed us was the coast with its sandy beaches, deep blue sea and rough waves. Adjacent to the coastline was the becalming scenery of the large and innumerable blue lagoons that seemed to appear on land and flow into the sea. The lagoons in turn were dotted with boats carrying fishermen and sightseers. The latter were plentiful in the late evenings, determined to hear or to say that they heard the 'singing fish.' Nobody was able to hum any note of it, even if they swore they had heard it.

The lagoon's harvest of crabs and prawns, absolutely the largest seen by us, became almost our staple diet during our stay there. The lagoons had their own sand bars built by the tides of the Bay of Bengal. The Dutch fort and church took second place to the natural beauty of the coast and lagoons. The most eye-catching landmark, however, was the broad and long Kallady Bridge, which went across what seemed to be the largest lagoon of Batticaloa and overlooked this lagoon to a great distance. At evening during sunset, which was mild in its glamour, we would stand at the pedestrian edge of that bridge and be mesmerized by the flow of the water beneath us. The boats whizzed past under us and a large amount of flotsam and jetsam sailed away under the bridge.

Past the bridge and along the coast was the Kallady village, which had a community of the remnants of the Portuguese Burghers. The Portuguese soldiers were never allowed to bring their wives at the time of their conquest of Ceylon, but were advised to live among the locals. They lived in towns and villages, marrying the local girls and later the girls from their own community. In a few generations they became so intermixed that they became dark in complexion. Their communities never gave up their Portuguese language or dress. The males donned their trousers and shirts and invariably walked barefoot. They found any excuse to sing with music played on guitars or mouth organs. They broke into Portuguese or English songs, and danced the *baila* brought by them. They were ardent Roman Catholics. They married within similar communities scattered in the Eastern Province, especially in Trinco where they lived in a specific locality in the town named 'Love Lane.'

Another community of the Portuguese lived in Puttalam too. They married into a community of Kaffir slaves brought from Africa by Governor North, the first governor of Ceylon. They retained their culture even there, but their dance intermingled with the dance of the Kaffirs and became the Kafrinja dance. These Portuguese spoke their language, Tamil and English the latter in a peculiar manner. They would say "on top of Almirah have" or "rounding the house" which were literal translation of spoken Tamil. Unlike the Tamils around them, they were quite content with a primary and sometimes a secondary education and then followed their fathers' occupations. They were experts at carpentry and were good cobblers. When required they worked as labourers at building sites. They were much appreciated by the locals. The people met them during Christmas time when groups of them dressed in their best clothes, wore shoes on their feet and instead of carolling, danced their baila on the front verandahs of many homes, collected money and then spent it on alcohol, which they were addicted to. Their motto of 'Eat, Drink and be Merry' always left them broke. When broke, they were willing to go to the ends of the district in search of work. In spite of their lifestyles, the locals would always give them work as they were so talented, hardworking and honest. They would be seen in their Sunday best in church, even when times were hard for them.

Lunch or dinner at my niece Pakiam's was a repast of every food of the sea and lagoon. This was invariably followed by cadju wrapped and hardened in sugary syrup, as dessert. Cadju trees grew in abundance in the sandy villages round Batticaloa.

My sister-in-law, who was called Aunt Victoria with affection by her numerous nieces, lived in Kattankudy, a Muslim village near Batticaloa. She had a large family of twelve. Her husband was the apothecary attached to a government dispensary. The children made haste to this mini hospital and saw again the liquid medicines in large flat glass containers which easily held ten bottles of a liquid. They were of various colours, done so for a purpose. It was thought that the uneducated patient recognized the exact coloured liquid medicine to be taken for each individual ailment. There was a psychological effect too in its varied colours. The patients left with smaller bottles containing these coloured liquids.

My sister-in-law was generous, thoughtful and very hospitable. Breakfast was made in excess of what she needed for the family including a few more boiled eggs in case "someone dropped by." She never stopped doing it as long as she was able to run her home. The village itself was a hot, dusty hamlet with groves of cadju plants. It was wonderful and something new to us as we walked between the trees and admired the plump yellow cadju fruits with their curved nut astride them. The owner herself gave us a few fruits. The taste was very tangy and needed salt to taste better. The cadju fruits when ripe were sold, but had few buyers. The cadju nuts themselves were carefully detached, roasted within a mound of hot sea sand, shelled and sold by the local Muslim women. They carried large capacious baskets of them, balanced perfectly on their heads. Raw cadju for curry was not a favourite dish in the east.

There was hardly anything of historical interest for the children to see, or be entertained by anything else there. In a couple of days we were back in Batticaloa. The Dutch conquest and stay was much in evidence in Batticaloa. Dutch architecture was evident in many houses and churches as in the north, as well as in other towns of the east. The population reflected the long stay and influence of the Dutch. Quite a large number of females were very attractive with a lighter skin, dark hair and were somewhat taller. The colour of their eyes also reflected foreign inheritance. Their eyes were a lighter brown than the deeper brown or black of the locals. From brown in some to greenish grey in others. The Dutch lived for a longer period in Batticaloa and the east, even during British rule. No vow of celibacy was enforced on the Dutch soldiers. They accepted paternity without fuss when they had relations with the local girls. The Dutch hoped that if the child was a female, she could be the future wife of a Dutch soldier, and if a male, a future soldier in the Dutch army. If the father had to get back to Holland, he realized his responsibilities and asked the local church to look after the needs of his child, leaving enough money with the church for their upbringing. The church looked after both males and females, and converted them to Christianity, the religion of their father. These light-skinned people never called themselves Aryan but teasingly and with great banter were called 'Indoor Aryans.'

With the arrival of the British, the administration which previously was separate and confined to each region, was centralized. Many young men in the north with their English education were, for the first time, sent to the south and east of the country for employment. The young men sent to the East saw and fell in love with these attractive girls and wished to marry them. The parents in the north vociferously objected to such plans and told all and sundry that their sons had been charmed by some love potion given by the girl, more likely by her mother, or charmed by some supernatural rites which were only found in the east!

The high caste in the east would be drawn down a peg or two, made lower than the equivalent caste in the north, because of the mixed parentage, and as a means of dissuading the sons finding brides far away. Many such alliances did take place, and were accepted in due course in the north. Thankfully these females had not inherited a bleeding disease that their Kandyan cousins did, a disease typical of European blood, and brought probably by the Dutch.

From Batticaloa, the southeastern coastline was a 'must visit' place. Passikudah Sea seemed so placid, like a large swimming pool next to the shore, as the water was contained in a secluded cove. Arugam Bay was more beautiful with its choppy blue sea. Huge, tall waves came rolling over as if to dash us to pieces or go over us when we waded into it. The children rushed to the shore when the waves broke with much noise and clamour.

Back in Batticaloa, we looked forward to see a drama called *naatukkoothu*, which literally meant a village drama with song, comedy in the spoken lines and dance. We saw a motley group of people trying to exhibit their acting talents. These were always done at a prominent street corner at twilight. The plays invariably had a king, a queen, his adviser, his subjects, and so forth. Costumes were elementary and any available material turned into one. The king had the most colourful or gaudy sari splashed with gold turned into a costume. Nobody dared dress better than him. The queen was less glamorously dressed and her role played by a young male. When the play began, the king seemed to stand higher than the others on the street stage. At every moment of the play he had to be on a higher level than the others. A little bench was carried around by a helper who rushed around with it and deftly put it down under the king wherever he desired to stand. Though a set dialogue was in place, the speeches may become impromptu, long, colloquial and even vulgar at times.

The popular ones were the dialogues from the *Ramayana*, *Savithri* and *Kannagi*. The king could say anything as long as the plot remained original. It was such fun to watch them and it was quite late when it finished. At times the play was so elaborate that only a couple of spectators were left to watch it to the end.

The Roman Catholic missionaries who saw these plays were inspired to dramatize the Passion of Christ in this form, and enacted it as a *koothu,* a true drama within the church premises. This form of drama was taken to Negombo which had a large Tamil Roman Catholic congregation. From there it was taken to the western coast to Sinhalese congregations and performed as Sinhala *naadagama.*

The eastern coastline became the path along which Hindu pilgrims walked to reach the Kathirgamam shrine in time for the annual festival. God Kadirgamar is the Dravidian aspect of God. Temples to him were only seen in South India and Ceylon. The pilgrims from the north and east travelled with great fervour and penance on this *nadai,* the walk. The walk was a penance, because the Tamil Hindus repented that they were not there to welcome Skanda when he arrived in the south. This pilgrimage was also much sought after by the South Indians. The pilgrimage would take a month to six weeks from its commencement at Mullaitivu. The pilgrims traversed the roads, foot paths, stopped at temples, and walked again along forest paths. They preferred to walk along the hot seashores and even over hot desert sands which removed the fear of confrontation with wild animals in the forest.

The pilgrims from our village never stopped talking about the *nadai.* The *nadai* was planned so that it would end at the commencement of the festival at the Kathirgamam temple. The pilgrims from the north and northeast trekked their separate routes and met at Selvasannidi temple, which was in the region of Vadaramarachi. This temple was a shrine to Kathirgaman. It was beside a picturesque river, the Thondamanaru. This Skanda temple followed the rituals of the Kadirgaman temple in the south. These pilgrims followed the religious rituals and started the journey with many shouts of "*Arohara*" meaning "God be praised." This was the cry whenever they resumed their journey from any temple they stayed at for the night. The pilgrims from the Vanni met the others in Mullaitivu at the Kannagi temple. The pilgrims from South India also joined the pilgrims from the northeast at Mullaitivu. The pilgrims appointed a leader who was well versed in the history of the pilgrimage, knew the paths and places traversed. He led them on this long *nadai*.

At Mullaitivu, as was the custom there, milk rice was prepared by the pilgrims and prayers offered for the safe arrival at the sylvan shrine. The pilgrims carried the minimum of things, a couple of changes of clothes, dry provisions and drinking water. They tied them in bundles and carried them on their heads. As they had a long trek, carrying by hand or slung on a shoulder was tiring.

The penance of this pilgrimage was also to walk with unshod feet. Each day's walk started long before the sun rose and always was accompanied by singing; the leader chanted or sang Hindu lyrics loudly and the others repeated whatever he said or sang. A pair of cymbals clanged and kept the momentum of the walk. If the crowd was large, small groups of them separated from the main one and walked at their own pace, but kept in sight of the others. Their main meal was at midday, and after a short rest, prayers were offered with fervour and they started again. They tried to reach a village or town to sleep on a temple corridor, where they stretched themselves out on the cold bare floor with no pillow or sheet. The people of that locality expected them and welcomed them as was done for years. It was considered great merit to give them a meal or two before the pilgrims left and the hosts provided them with cash and dry provisions too. The pilgrims preferred to walk along the beautiful eastern sea coast to reach Trinco. By this time many other pilgrims too had joined them. Rest and replenishment were repeated at any Skanda or Sivan temples of the town. However, a few of the pilgrims who wearied of the journey or those who had collected enough money, left the group, much to the pity and derision of the group.

It was a long trek to Batticaloa and even longer along the coastal roads to Passikudah, Arugam Bay, Thirukovil, Pottuvil, Panama and on to Okanda. Okanda had a shrine built for the goddess Pattini. The boat-shaped rock there was supposed to be the petrified boat in which King Gajabahu brought Pattini's anklet to Ceylon. This was the last stop for rest and cooked food, as the path after this was in the interior of the southeastern coast. Dry provisions were replenished and well water collected in plenty for the hazardous journey through the Yala sanctuary which its wild animals within it. They went in big groups mindful of the dreaded bear. The pilgrims were advised to lie face down to prevent mauling by the bear. By day and night, they sang loudly and beat their cymbals even more vigorously. Making much noise, they crossed the Kumbukkan Oya, the Menik Ganga and reached the boundary of the temple premises.

With great joy and a sense of accomplishment, they rushed across the suspension bridge, reached the Menik Ganga and dipped themselves thrice in the waters of it. They hastily changed and rushed to pay obeisance to Murugan and his consorts. They were so full of their journey and safe arrival that they were ready to tell their story to whoever listened. They forgot family and never spoke of them but said their return home was in the hands of God. They stayed all the days of festival and returned by road.

Relatives who went with the group described the beautiful sylvan shrine. Few walked the jungle paths, most walked along paths from the village of Tissamaharama to Kathirgamam. There were no roads or motor traffic. This path too led to the suspension bridge of the Menik Ganga and to Kathiragamam temple. Most pilgrims also went to Sellakatharagamam. Its surroundings were strewn with shrines to the many gods and a bigger temple to god Ganesh which was at the river's edge. Large trees, shrubs and groves almost hid the smallest shrines.

The legend at Kathirgamam was repeated endlessly. The name meant a place of ripe sheaves of cereals. Skanda met some hunters, probably the Veddahs and the Rodiyas, and they provided him with venison, cereals and honey. When he went to Sellakathirgamam, he met and fell in love with Valliamma, the dusky skinned daughter of a Veddah hunter and after many legendary escapades he won her, married her and lived with her on Kathiramalai and on which was the *vel*, the icon of Murugan. The hill was just across the main temple which was built later. By legend God Murugan had two wives, the spiritual or heavenly Theivanai and the worldly Valli. They are usually seen on either side of the Skanda icon, Valli with a darker Dravidian skin colour.

The temple to Skanda was a typical sylvan shrine with its entrance covered by branches and twigs. No icon of Skanda was seen; a painted curtain depicting Murugan and his consorts covered the sanctum and rituals were held behind it. Legend told of a sage who had a vision of god Murugan and he drew a mystic diagram on a gold plate, the Yantra, which is enshrined in the inner sanctum.

The first *pooja*, done by a Brahmin priest, started at the shrine of god Ganesh next door to the main temple. The Rodiya caste women were greatly honoured at the pooja main temple. Six of them started the *pooja* to Murugan by *alathi*, the circumbulation of small brass lamps with lighted wicks in front of the sanctum. Each woman did it separately and then together in a regular ceremonial pattern. The wicks for the brass lamps were dropped by the officiating lay priest, the Kapurala, on to the palms of these women. Their hands were never touched by the priest owing to caste discrepancies. During their *poojas* the priests, whether Brahmin or Kapurala, bound their mouths. During every pooja the priest walked to the entrance of his temple and held the lit lamp and the smoke from the incense towards Kathiramalai.

The temple to Valli was right opposite the main temple and is the main temple at festival time. The Theivanai temple was on the further side took a lesser part of the colourful festival. It was during the Nayakkar reign that non-Brahmin priests were sent to officiate in temples in the south. They were of the Pandaram caste. They not only stayed at Kathirgamam, but many of them migrated further south to the temple of Vishnu. The Vishnu temple was built on the ancient *Theneeswaran*, the Southern Sivan temple. It was on the southernmost promontory of the island and its gold plated pinnacle was a navigational guide to seafarers. It was one of the five Sivan temples, probably built in Chola times and with their architecture. The Portuguese destroyed it in 1578. The Sivan temple was never rebuilt. A Vishnu temple was later built in its place and called the Devinuwara temple, which also fell into ruins.

The Vishnu temple attracted the members of the *Pandaram* caste members too. The name Perumal with its many prefixes was popular with them. Perumal is the pure Tamil name of Vishnu. The Perumals never went back to their original birth places, but married within the southern population and left behind their names, with Tamil prefixes that describe Vishnu – like golden, young, lyrical, joyous, beautiful and great.

Skanda is considered a spiritual warrior who flies on a peacock to rush to wherever he was needed. He was also a warrior for the kingdoms in the south, and now a political warrior too.

Governor Brownrigg took office in 1812 following Maitland. He was most ambitious for the whole of Ceylon to be brought under the British crown. His ambition was fuelled by the fact that he was an army general.

Brownrigg looked closely at the Dutch law pertaining to the north, which recognized slavery of the lower castes to the higher Vellala caste. They were the lowest 'retainer caste' and a little higher 'servitude caste' of Koviyars, the latter still considered a low caste. He, like Governor North, condemned their services as slavery, but like North promoted a flourishing slave trade not of Kaffirs, like what North did, but of slaves from South India.

The parish schools revived by Maitland were continued by Brownrigg. The administration as well as the management of these schools was taken over by the missionaries. During Brownrigg's tenure the Methodist Mission set up the first vernacular and English schools. Their mission schools were not only in towns but every coastal village had a Methodist school attached to its church. They built girls and boys homes for orphans and for children not able to travel daily. Governor Brownrigg met the first American mission in 1816 and encouraged it to establish their mission in Jaffna. The school they founded gave the best of American education.

In 1818 the Anglican Church sent the Church Missionary Society. They established thirty schools but only a few in Jaffna. All the schools taught mainly in the vernacular.

Being a military man, Brownrigg dearly loved to conquer the Kandyan kingdom. It was made that much easier by the constant friction and suspicions between certain Kandyan chiefs and the King Sri Wickrama Rajasinghe. After the alienation of the chiefs from the king it was easy to forge a treaty with the disgruntled chiefs, who themselves eyed the throne.

The wily British with the help of John d'Oyly, an expert on Kandyan affairs, together with the help of the local and Indian troops, secured control of Kandy. The battle was made easy because some chiefs were in league with the British. In a month or so the battle was over, the king was captured and exiled to Vellore, India. Ehelepola, one of the surviving chiefs and an aide to the British, expected to be given the Kandyan throne. When he was refused he led another failed rebellion. He was captured and exiled to the island of Mauritius. Though the battle came to an end the majority of the people of the Kandyan kingdom but not all the chiefs were against the British.

The terms of the Kandyan Convention in 1815 gave concessions to the previous status of the chiefs. The Kandyan laws and their customs were retained and as promised so were the preservation of Buddhism with its worship in temples, its rites and priests. The convention was signed by the governor and the chiefs, with some of them signing in Tamil as they may have been of the Nayakkar dynasty, the same as that of the king or descendants of a South Indian dynasty like Pilimatalawa.

The isolation of Kandy ended and the British ruled over the whole of Ceylon by 1818.

Governor Brownrigg discouraged the Methodist Mission from setting up a mission station in Kandy for evangelization. He, like Maitland, prevented the civil servants from trading, but it did not extend to agriculture, a vague difference in the legislation. It was always Brownrigg's wish to reduce the status and power of the Kandyan chiefs and make them subordinate to the British. He left the status quo of castes in the north as it was during Maitland's time. Brownrigg's tenure ended in 1820.

Governor Barnes who wanted educational reform and reorganization started his governorship in 1824. He wanted to give wider scope to the schools and make them non-Christian institutions, a view not held by the bishops of that time. He wanted to reverse the trend of caste and poverty which were a bar to education and perpetuated the disadvantages of the female sex. He was considered a religious and good governor for his foresight in education. There was, however, great surprise when he refused permission to allow any more American missionaries to work in Jaffna.

The printing press had arrived in Jaffna. The printer, Reverend Jarret, was already on the high seas on the way to Jaffna when the order banning American missionaries was put into effect. On arrival his residency visa was refused. The many letters of pleadings and refusals that passed between Governor Barnes and the American Mission was of no avail and nothing changed Barnes' mind-set. The reason given for it was that Barnes had been an adjutant to General Wellington at the Battle of Waterloo, eight years before he came to Ceylon. He did not trust any foreigner and feared that the American influence might spread south with time and with more American missionary arrivals. The Methodist church was also refused permission to obtain a printing press. Only the Anglican mission was permitted a printing machine. Rev. Jarret returned home. The printing machine was sold to the Anglican mission in Jaffna. The American missionaries were refused entry for eleven years, almost the whole tenure of Barnes' governorship and a few more years after it.

Barnes disapproved of what he saw of education. He did not want to continue with parish schools nor Christianity to be taught to the children. The clergy and the bishops did not have the same view. He suggested that reading and writing in the native language were sufficient. The missionaries thought otherwise and went on to create denominational schools. These missionary schools did not falter even when economic sanctions were imposed and even when Barnes showed great favouritism to Anglican schools. Anglican denoted crown.

Trade till then was of the barter kind. The Jaffna peninsula exchanged tobacco, salt and cloth for arecanut and beeswax from the south. The British broke this internal barter trade to a market economy, even though the East India Company was much against it. The market economy was the stimulus for some sort of road network. This network at first was again like a broader bridle path. The original bridle paths were made by the Dutch and used by the British at the beginning of their rule. Travel was by horsemen travelling these paths to military forts. The biggest incentive to road building was the success of the coffee plantations. Governor Barnes thought that maintenance of the bridle paths was very expensive. The wages paid to the coolies, who carried the coffee in boxes on their heads and walked along these bridle paths, took a good part of the profits too. The journey itself took many months. The coffee had to be taken between harvest and ship loading, before the monsoon broke. It had to be pre-planned as the coffee seeds not only went to Colombo along these paths but were also sent from the hills to Batticaloa and Hambantota for shipment.

The overall construction of roads was under the civil engineer Major Skinner. This road was completed in 1823 for cart traffic. Ten thousand carters used this track, an annual average. The carters travelled in *thavalams*, a caravan of carts. Carters meant cart contractors. These contractors did not come from the Kandyan *Govigama* caste nor from any other castes of the hill country and they missed the opportunity to get rich. The contractors were of the Karava caste, business people of the low country and mostly from the western coast. The Kandyans preferred to be peasants rather than rich mudalalis. The contractors became rich, educated and political rivals of the *Govigama* caste who held sway in the social setup of that time.

Governor Barnes was the driving force behind the construction of roads in 1824. These envisaged carriage roads were at first only clearings in the jungles which became rough cart tracks. The newest roads built went to Kandy not only for trade but were of strategic importance for keeping an eye on the Kandyan kingdom. The locals became the backbone of construction and much later were supplemented by labour immigration from South India. Barnes was glad that the *uliyam*, compulsory service, was in vogue. Every male from the age of eighteen to fifty-five had to give six days labour for road building or pay cash in lieu of labour.

In 1812 it was the Dutch who tried to grow coffee in Colombo but it failed. Coffee was again experimentally planted in the maritime provinces together with cotton and hemp. There too the attempt at coffee growing was a great failure. Coffee was then grown in Peradeniya and later in the hill country and it flourished. The coffee berries were so abundant and luscious that the British sent these to Coorg, the hill country in South India. Coffee also flourished there.

The roads made the transport of coffee much easier and cheaper. Coffee prices soared and its revenue was used for more road building. The coffee planters clamoured for more roads. Branch roads, minor roads and estate roads made their appearance. With roads came the bridges, ferries and then a poll tax levied for their use.

The bridges and ferries were completed and opened by Governor Horton in February 1832, a year after his arrival. The first mail coach, the Royal Mail, probably the first in Asia, trundled along these cart tracks. He also sold land to enhance revenue. Governor Horton had a lucky break when he rejuvenated the pearl fishery in 1829. A wonderful harvest of pearl oysters was obtained from 1829 to 1836. *Uliyam* was seen in the tenures of all the governors, ultimately ending with Governor Torrington.

In 1863 there were two thousand miles of roads. These roads were gravelled and metalled during Governor Ward's time, still under the able skill of Skinner. The road was extended from Hambantota to Puttalam for trade, and then to Anuradhapura. Next was the road from Anuradhapura to Arippu, the centre of the pearl fisheries. It took a very long time for the Kandy to Anuradhapura road to be extended, first to Trincomalee and then to Jaffna in 1837, thus ending its isolation. The road to Jaffna fell into ruin and was rebuilt in 1873 by Governor Gregory. In 1929 there were sixteen thousand four hundred miles of roadways. Five thousand miles of these roads were metalled and the rest were broad bridle paths.

In 1855 it was Governor Ward who mooted the idea of the railways. The planters themselves agitated for it as they saw the success of the railway in the economy of India.

Coffee with its luxuriant growth since 1823, and the backbone of the economy, crashed in 1847 due to a leaf fungal disease and was completely destroyed in 1860. It was a pity this occurred when the Colombo harbour was ready and the Suez Canal was opened.

Tea, first grown and manufactured by James Taylor, re-placed coffee very successfully. It became the backbone of the economy. Then Governor Ward decided to build a railway. The Ceylon Railway Company, a private company, started it but the government took it over and completed the railway line from Colombo to Kandy, the construction of which was started in 1858.

The money for the railway was obtained by selling shares in London and from the revenue accumulated by the coffee sales. The shares became available first to the Burghers in Ceylon, and later were opened to the public. The railway to Kandy opened in 1867.

The railway gave employment to many, particularly the Burghers. The posts ranged from minor to managerial ones. The Malayan railways now in full steam employed a large number of Jaffna males, taken by the British for their fluency in English, as assistant or main station masters. A story related to us was that almost every railway station in a particular region of Malaya was manned by a Tamil. The midday meal to those who worked closer to the towns would be sent by a particular train which was nicknamed the *Sothy,* gravy train, and the station masters would ensure that the lunch sent in tiffin carriers would be put into the correct train.

The railway in Ceylon was extended to places economically viable like the hill stations. It was then extended to Badulla, Matale and to Dambulla. Next it was extended to the west to Puttalam and Chilaw for transport of coconuts grown in large acres of land. Still later it was extended to Kurunegala and the northwest, cutting off the isolation of these areas from the rest of the country. The railway was also the means of settling peasants in uninhabited places. The extension of the line to Talaimannar pier meant that goods for export were brought by the train to the boats and the Indian immigrant labour from India to work the tea estates was transported by that train to the hill country.

The north and the east, especially the north, had no viable economic produce for export and had the last extension of the railway. The extension first from Anuradhapura to Trincomalee and then to Jaffna and Kankesanthurai was opened in 1902 when West Ridgeway was governor. It had taken fifty years from its inception to reach Jaffna.

Much later, apart from the goods, the passenger traffic on this northern line gave enough revenue to the railway. The employment avenues in Malaya and then Africa were closed, and the northerner had to seek employment in the south, mostly in the clerical grades of government service. With their education they could even vie for the top grades of government service and the Civil Service, by competitive exams. The railway had these clerical hands rushing to Colombo on Sundays and returning to Jaffna on Fridays. This passenger revenue added greatly to the coffers of the government.

Roads and railways held sway equally to connect the interior and the main towns to Colombo. The railway still could not eliminate the cart *thavalams*, which transported goods till the end of the century. The Dutch canals also continued to transport indigenous goods along the northwest coast.

Of all these transport facilities, the railway never lost its fascination for us as children, since our first encounter with it. We were now living in Jaffna and in the newly built house of my married sister. Two absolutely different sounds impinged on our ears daily. One was the tolling of the church bell and the other sound was the ear splitting toots of the train at the station announcing its arrival and departure, the train being just a quarter mile away. For quite some time and thankfully, the tooting of the train was heard only twice a day.

My first encounter with the train was in 1916 and I was accompanied by my younger and more nervous sister. We went to the railway station and stood a few feet away from the tracks which

Jaffna Railway Station

lay at a great drop from the platform. There was a shrill toot and we craned our necks forward and still further forwards but still scared to look at the train. The train took the last curve of the track before the straight run to the station. It appeared to come rushing like an enormous black-headed monster that deliberately spat black dust and particles on us. Rushing behind it like a disproportionate tail was a string of brown boxes on wheels, the carriages. In it were hazy images of people sitting, standing and at the door ready to alight. In between the engine and the first carriage was a large black iron box that rushed along on larger iron wheels. In it were filthy blue clad men who were shovelling coal and throwing it into a red furnace. When that huge and ugly monster of an engine passed us, I had this great fear that it would topple and cause an earth bound 'Titanic' disaster. The real Titanic disaster of 1912 was still fresh in our minds.

The train stopped but it continued to wheeze like an asthmatic, reminding me of grandmother who had asthma. It hissed in between, with sharp bursts of steam that came out of its head. Finally the engine stopped, passengers rushed around and so did we to get back home as we had not told mother of our intended visit to see the train.

The monster was still in my eyes when we got back home. Our dresses were covered in soot and gritty coal debris clung to our hair which needed a quick wash at the well.

Even more thrilling to the northerner was arrival of the first motor car to Jaffna in 1905. The American missionaries had already got theirs quite a few years ago. The lorry came first for transport of goods and the buses a few years later. The Jaffna people had a great fascination for the British Austin cars. They were never discarded even after decades of their arrival even though newer and more modern cars of other makes made their appearance. The Austin cars were of little difference in style or shape from the initial Austin Thirty. The Forty and Fifty-Five models were equally popular. If one was purchased, it was kept for life. The Austin never saw death or destruction. It would somehow be resurrected by a clever mechanic (there were plenty of them in Jaffna), who may not have understood why and how things worked, but made the car roar into life. He cannibalised car parts. If a new part was unavailable, a new part was fashioned and fixed. For months an Austin would be supported on wooden blocks and then strangely would soon be on the roads again. When the Austin was too old it would be sold to be used as a taxi. The Jaffna station had a row of these Austins waiting for hires. During the civil war when no gasoline was available, the cars were propped up on strong wooden logs. Some smart owners of cars tried using kerosene oil and then vegetable oil for the engines. If the engine remained quiet with vegetable oil, a drop of eau de cologne was added to give the spirit of impetus to start the car, and off it went along but not for great distances. Gingelly oil, the thickest oil, would be used as grease to keep the nuts and bolts working. If nothing worked, the cars were treated as treasured relics in the garage. The modest and practical bicycle became the backbone of travel for the people in the north during the many years of war. The rich, the poor, the labourer, the professor, the students, housewives and the teachers all rode on them to reach their destination.

In those far away days, the Raleigh bicycle and the BSA motorcycle were like the Austin, firm favourites of the northerner, not to be discarded easily. The BSA motorcycle was the one on which cousin Soma visited us. He had innumerable tosses and scrapes falling from it. He was training to be a priest and at the same time trying to master the motorcycle. He was more successful in the former than on the BSA. He would come with the Amarans to visit us often. They were uncles by relationship but more like cousins by age. They visited us to play cards, draughts or simply chat and banter. It was a pity that the younger generation of youngsters never kept in touch with each other like we did with our cousins.

The other great attachment to things was to Johnson ceramic ware. They were thick, inelegant and came mostly in white or pastel shades. The more elegant ceramics took a long time to replace them. The Singer sewing machine was the accessory for every needle woman and each vied to be an expert in using it. Rarer was the Wilcox and Gibbs sewing machine. This was a bobbin-less machine, sewing chain stitch. It was brought into Jaffna by the Dutch Burghers who were fond of and accomplished on it. When using this machine, a knot needed to be tied at the end of the sewing or else the whole line of sewing would unwind. It was therefore not as popular as the Singer machine.

Most of these goods were British. They were found durable, and difficult to dislodge from one's use and mind. Then the not so pleasant addition was the denture. The northerners took a long time to consider wearing it. The women would goad their husbands with bad teeth or a few teeth to try it. It took them even a longer time to get used to the dentures. They removed them ever so often!

I remember a nephew in our village telling his uncle that though he was seated on the front verandah, his smile was at the well! However the uncle had not forgotten to clip his maroon and silver capped Parker '51 pen on his shirt. It was a status symbol. It was a far cry from the one we used. A pointed nib was fixed to a long piece of wood. The pen was dipped into a bottle of ink and we wrote with it until the ink dried. We took these pens with extra nibs and a bottle of ink to school. We were sometimes fortunate to have a ceramic ink well fixed in a hollow of the school desk, into which we poured the ink. Our school bags had many books, pens, pencils and a bottle of ink. Invariably our bags were stained with ink that had leaked because the cover of the bottle of ink could never be closed properly.

Sir Robert Horton, successor to Governor Barnes, removed the ban on American missionaries to work in Jaffna. This was done after eleven years of refusal to their entry by Governor Barnes. The American missionaries bought back the printing press from the Anglican Church. Scriptures, Christian literature and tickets for the hospital were printed. Governor Horton wanted and did set up an advisory council in 1831 but the ultimate authority rested with the governor.

Every governor since British rule commenced had absolute power. With power and with their personal idiosyncrasies they did whatever they wished. The Crown, realizing this, sent a commission, one of many to come, which became a regular feature of its rule. The Cameron-Colebrooke Commission came to suppress the power of the governor for the development of Ceylon and to scrutinize the recurrent deficit in finances.

The Dutch pattern of economics was seen in early British rule with their state monopoly and *uliyam*, the compulsory service of males to the state. Entrenchment of the caste system was hard to retrench as much as to retrench Hindu and Buddhist practices. The decision of King Keerthi Sri Rajasinghe to restrict the Buddhist clergy to the highest caste was not debatable as much as it was to dislodge the Brahmin from the Hindu temple. The commission's most valuable contribution was to give a liberal form of government.

In place of the Advisory Council, two councils were proposed, executive and legislative, to diminish the power of the governor and to be a greater source of information and whistle blowing to Whitehall and the Crown. From 1833 the Legislative Council was looked upon as the local parliament. Cameron's contribution was in the judicial system, but it was not rooted in the local laws. However, it laid the foundation of the modern judicial system. The Kandyan kingdom too came within this legislative unification. The Dutch pattern of economics was changed. The British civil servants had no sympathy with these reforms, including the abolishment of compulsory service, the *uliyam*.

The economy depended on the plantations run exclusively by British planters in the mid-nineteenth century, and they did have a say in the legislature. The government's policy was determined by numbers. The Legislative Council commenced with nine officials and six non-officials appointed by the governor. Of the six non-officials three were Europeans, and one each came from the Sinhalese, Tamil and Burgher communities. There were no Muslim or Kandyan representatives. The Ceylonese were from the elite, educated and Christian families. This council became the first instance of racial representation. It had no power but was only an advisory body.

Colebrooke recommended that locals be included in what was solely a European Civil Service. The first civil servants appointed were Simon Casie Chetty and Frederick de Livera of the judiciary. Simon Casie Chetty was a well-known writer. He published a series of articles on Tamil culture, the history of Jaffna and a catalogue of Tamil books based on the seventeenth-century chronicles. He later categorized the caste system of Jaffna.

Colebrooke was keen on propagating English education in government schools which he encouraged to be set up, both in the north and east as well as in the south. By now the denominational schools flourished in all parts of Ceylon but gave an education that made only the elite educated. State schools made their appearance and it was encouraged by Colebrooke.

The stage coach had come into existence, and shares in it enabled even the headman to purchase one, and this elevated one's status. Colebrooke unified the country by this legislative Council. A Muslim and a Kandyan were appointed to the Legislative Council many years later. Bills could only be introduced by the governor. Overall, the Crown dictated terms, a policy in which Executive Council members and the Europeans appointed in the Legislative Council were of adequate numbers, and always voted with the Crown to pass any bill, overriding any veto of the Ceylonese members.

The bureaucracy went on with just a number changes in the Legislative Council, keeping it just right for the Crown. Commerce and the plantations thrived. The elite, educated Ceylonese became politically conscious. Payment for defence came out of the revenue of plantations. 'No taxation without representation,' was the cry of the non-officials. In 1863 the Ceylon National League was formed and demanded a non-official majority. As this was taking place, the members of the Ceylon League disagreed among themselves, and the league was dominated by the low-country Sinhalese.

The Civil Service, the highest in status in government jobs, was only for Europeans who were nominated by the Crown. However, even they had to sit the examination for that service from 1856. The exam was of a lower standard compared to that held in London, but from 1870 they had to sit the London examination. Ceylonese were excluded from the higher bureaucracy; the ratio of officers was nine Europeans to one Ceylonese. Invariably the latter was a Burgher, most often from the judiciary. In the early twentieth century the Medical, Education and Works departments offered remunerative posts to the Ceylonese.

The administration in Ceylon from the early era of British rule had only two administrative divisions, the Kandyan and the maritime administration. More political power was given in the eighteen sixties to the locals by Governor Sir Henry Ward, and later by Governor Robinson. Governor Gregory, succeeding them, was instrumental in the opening up of irrigation tanks and their repairs. He set up an irrigation fund to do so, but the Europeans in the Legislative Council were much against it. Governor Gordon, who came later, set up a fund for irrigation works from grain taxes. The greatest impact of irrigation works was in Batticaloa and the Eastern Province – the former was the granary of the east.

Jaffna was not dependent on these irrigation tanks as its' wells were sunk into limestone that soaked the rain water. The peasants, industrious and resourceful, knew how much water to draw daily to prevent saltwater surfacing. Heavy manuring was done and yields were great. Rotation of crops was practised and tobacco grown in many parts of Jaffna. However, whether in the north or northeast, malaria was rampant and a scourge.

Politically, there was no sustained agitation for reform, both from the south and from the Jaffna Association. The cry for more local representation was made when Sir Henry McCallum took office in 1903. This cry was taken up more by the educated elite of the Karava caste of the south. It was refused, but Durbars, an old Indian practice, were held by governors Gordon and then Gregory. Governor Gregory had a Durbar in Jaffna in 1903. It was held as a facilitator of a united Ceylon, and the term Ceylonese nation was mooted there. However, no concessions were made politically.

In 1910 reform proposals were announced. The secretary of state gave a limited form of election, and franchise was given only to the English-educated elite. The Buddhists protested as education in Sinhalese was not recognized. The reforms agitated for included a larger council and territorial representation.

McCallum gave communal representation rather than territorial representation. He increased the Legislative Council to twenty-one, with ten non-officials. The low-country Sinhalese and Tamils had two seats each, with one for Muslims and another for the Kandyans. However, by appointing two Europeans and one Burgher as members, he was sure three non-officials would vote with him. James Pieris proposed that an unofficial member be elected on a territorial basis and many others be elected to the Legislative and Executive councils to curb the power of the government. McCallum would have none of it. The secretary of state, however, agreed, and four seats were elected on the restricted franchise. Only one of them was for an educated Ceylonese, the others comprised two Europeans and one Burgher.

In the north, there was more political agitation, and the Jaffna youth became more vociferous. The Jaffna Youth League was formed in 1905. One of the earliest leaders was Handy Perinpanayagam. The youth who completed their education up to university level had no local universities to go to. They went to the university colleges of the Madras Presidency. In fact, many youth for decades got their academic degrees from Madras University colleges. The early graduates came under the great influence of Indian politics, especially of Mahatma Gandhi and with it the cry for Swaraj – self-rule.

In the election of 1912 for the educated Ceylonese seat, Ponnambalam Ramanathan, a Vellala and equally well educated,

Dr. Marcus Fernando, a Karava, were the contestants. Restricted franchise made the number of voters just three thousand out of a population of almost five million. Ramanathan won it. It was surmised that voting surprisingly went on a caste basis rather than a communal one, since more than half the voters were Sinhalese. Ramanathan became the first educated elected member to the legislature.

It was only in the first decade of the twentieth century that the Civil Service opened to the Ceylonese. They were chosen by open competition at an exacting written examination. Ponnambalam Arunachalam, Ramanathan's brother, won a government scholarship to Cambridge. On his return he was the first to pass the entrance examination of the Civil Service. He became a solicitor and then the attorney general. Having political ambitions, he retired from the Civil Service in 1913 and founded the Social Reform League.

The educated elite drifted to Colombo and made their homes in Cinnamon Gardens, a former Dutch possession. A disproportionate number of Jaffna Tamils too built their homes in the same locality.

In 1915, an unfortunate riot started between Buddhists and Muslims, as a sequel to a Buddhist *perahera* accompanied by load music and noise going past a mosque in Gampola, which abutted the road. There was mayhem from then on, with riots against the businesses of the coastal Moor community who had settled in Gampola. At the same time there was deep-seated anger of the educated Sinhalese lower-caste Buddhists against the Sinhalese Govigama Christian elite. Anti-British feelings were high too as the revenue of Ceylon was depleted after financing the First World War that had just ended. The pride of the island's glorious past was remembered. The clamour of self-rule increased. The temperance movement was also active and loud. When the case concerning participation in the riots was heard, the district judge ruled in favour of the Buddhists but the Supreme Court overturned the verdict. Prominent Buddhists were imprisoned with death sentences hanging over some.

The riot spread from Gampola to Kandy with greater destruction of property. It took a month for the riots to subside. Ponnambalam Ramanathan spoke against the verdict and made an appeal to the Privy Council. He was sent to London, and he pleaded the prisoners' case and won. Chalmers, who was the governor at this time, was recalled. When Ramanathan got back, the Ceylonese were so overjoyed and thankful that the horses of the carriage he rode in were removed and a few Sinhalese men pulled the carriage to his home in Ward Place. It was all forgotten soon, and Ponnambalam realized rather late that he had lost the sympathy of the Muslims and the Sinhalese did not even want to remember it. Only a painting depicting that incident of his return went back to Jaffna, to his ancestral home.

He still had the gift of oratory though, and in 1917 he was re-elected to the legislature with more votes than the Sinhalese Govigama candidate contesting him. The early twentieth century saw the Ponnambalam brothers spearheading political change. Even the anglicized politician Alwis did not speak for the Buddhists but Ramanathan did so, even getting the British to regard Vesak as a holiday. He played a leading role in the abolition of the grain tax. More was expected of him but his Achilles heel was his caste consciousness, barring the lower castes to temple entry and he was, like the latter day Senanayake and Sunderalingam, against franchise for the Indian immigrant workers. Sunderalingam became most vociferous against temple entry of the low castes. Ramanathan was considered more a great intellectual politician than a statesman. He died in 1930.

In the early twentieth century ethnicity became a greater factor in politics, more so than rivalry between the Kandyans and the low-country Sinhalese. The Social Reform League, founded by Arunachalam, together with the Ceylon Workers' League, became the Ceylon National Congress in 1919 of which he was the president. To Arunachalam's despair, the CNC never became a turning point in the politics of the government. The leaders wanted it to be more an elitist association than a broad based political party. The birth of the Ceylon National Congress coincided with the arrival of the shrewd William Manning as governor in 1919. The CNC was fired up with reforms and recommendations and proposed a compromise between communal and territorial elections.

James Pieris assured the Tamils that they could get a larger Tamil representation territorially, a promise that was not implemented and was seen as a bluff made by a Sinhalese politician. Governor Manning saw the harmony of Sinhalese and Tamils within the CNC and regarded it as a great challenge. This harmony was only there for the first two decades of the twentieth century. In 1921 the shadow of things to come was seen when only Sinhalese members were appointed to the Colombo and low-country constituencies. In 1922 the congress instead of being the voice of national unity became the voice of a Sinhalese majority and a Tamil minority, which has continued until now. The CNC was in disharmony.

This suited the wily Governor Manning. The congress wanted a government of Ceylonese on constitutional grounds. Goonesinha of the Labour Union and the younger people of the Young Lanka League agitated for Swaraj, like in India. The older Congressmen were too conservative for this. Manning was happy that the Kandyans wanted to claim their political rights with their representatives. This was promoted by Manning.

He did make reforms. The Manning Minute introduced reform by making the Legislative Council of thirty-seven, with twenty-three non-officials and fourteen officials. Of the non-officials, eleven were to be territorially elected. He gave more seats disproportionately to the north, citing their educational status. The official members were of European, British, Kandyan, Muslim, and Indian communities. These eight officials were of benefit to him.

Eight special nominees made a mockery of the non-official majority as the officials would have to vote with the government, and some issues could only be voted on by these nominees. The franchise was extended to all English-educated men and those earning fifty rupees or more per month. Elections to this reformed legislature took place in 1921. Arunachalam, still the president of the congress, sent his nomination for a territorial seat and was quite sure he would not be contested. Strangely, James Pieris, who initiated the idea of unofficial members for territorial seats, contested him. Arunachalam was taken aback but was wise to see the shadow of things to come and withdrew his name and resigned from the congress.

This was ideal for Manning and he was overjoyed to see the detachment of Tamils from the Congress, and with it their association with the low-country Sinhalese. The Legislative Council had thirteen Sinhalese to three Tamils, whereas they were almost equal in number to the Sinhalese as unofficial members.

James Pieris started the divisive communal politics but feared the agitation of the Jaffna associations for proportional representation to the Crown. Pieris promised again a special seat for the Tamils in the Western Province at the next elections, an arrangement that was kept, to get the Jaffna Association to support the congress. Manning was happy with his resourcefulness and the recurrent blunders of the Ceylon politicians which only benefitted him.

Arunachalam left as he felt betrayed. The written undertaking to give a Tamil seat in the Western Province was made by Pieris in 1918 long before the elections.

Lessons in politics were never learnt by the Tamils. Arunachalam went back to academic work for which he was best suited. He joined the Royal Asiatic Society and became a president of it. He founded many Hindu societies and with his brother Coomaraswamy were the moving figures in the establishment of the University of Ceylon, giving its own degree. This university was to be built in the salubrious environment of Peradeniya but was ultimately built in Colombo. Arunachalam encouraged *swabasha* as the medium of instruction in schools. He was knighted and was truly considered a statesman. He died young leaving a void among the Tamils.

Governor Manning, seeing the disunity, increased the Legislative Council to forty-nine with thirty-seven non-officials. After 1921 the Ceylon National Congress had split into the Sinhala Maha Sabha and Tamil Maha Sabha. The low-country Sinhalese formed People's Councils. The Workers League left the congress and became the Ceylon Labour Union in 1922.

The non-officials of the new council would be eleven territorially elected members and eleven communally elected ones, with one seat for Tamils in the Western Province.

Elections were held. The elected members, mostly those of the Ceylon National Congress, clashed with the British heads of departments.

The situation worsened after Governor Sir Hugh Clifford came in 1925. He was against all the political reforms given and wrote a thesis of many pages against the previous commission. He was diagnosed as being paranoid and was recalled. The story goes that Noel Coward, after getting to know all these unfortunate incidents, was inspired to write his song "Mad Dogs and Englishmen."

The Legislative Council now turned its attention to education, which was still done by missionary denominational schools, producing the anglicized elite. More Sinhalese and Tamil schools with English as a subject were suggested. Education became highly politicized thereafter.

In August 1927 the secretary of state appointed a special commission led by the Earl of Donoughmore to report on the existing constitution and suggest further reforms. This was not a Royal one nor had it any Ceylonese representatives, so plenty of criticism was thrown at it. The commission met and received complaints from all and sundry. The complaints ranged from caste discrimination, to the educated *Karavas* demanding more say in politics. Complaints came from the plantation workers and requests for minority representation.

Mahatma Gandhi made an impassioned speech at Jaffna College in 1927 which became memorable. The Youth League became more powerful than the Jaffna Association, founded at the same time by the older conservative, educated Tamils, especially school teachers.

The commission proposed reforms for minority rights with a Bill of Rights for a wider franchise. When it was implemented it proved to only increase the power of the Sinhalese elite, and restrict the votes of the plantation Tamils. The reforms were passed with a small majority when Governor Stanley was in power.

Elections for the first State Council were held in 1931. Four Tamil districts boycotted it. The Youth Association, greatly influenced by Indian politician Kamaladevi Chattopadhyaya, had a stronger voice and overrode the conservative Jaffna Association which had many educated elite, mostly teachers. Ponnambalam was missed by the conservative group to argue and reverse the decision. The boycott was a mistake, gaining nothing. The State Council had fifty elected members, eight nominated members of the minorities and three British officers. The latter were in charge of finance, defence, law and justice. The Board of Ministers that included D.S. Senanayake, C.W.W. Kanangara and Baron Jayatilleke, were in-charge of the ministries of agriculture, education and home affairs, respectively. Committees to represent regions and ethnic interests were absolutely non-efficient. The Committee of Ministers did their own projects and programmes with no coordination. However, social welfare, education, cooperatives and village expansion increased. Senanayake still had his 'Indian labour complex' and wanted to reduce their representation further. The first State Council had to battle the malaria epidemic, the world economic depression, and the labour leader Goonesinha could do very little for labour. Income tax as a source of income reared its head.

A Tamil conference that was held in 1933 condemned the boycott of the Youth League, which relented rather late, and an appeal was made to the Colonial Office to hold an election. Elections were held and four more seats were added to the State Council in 1935, four years after the first election.

Senanayake pressed for colonization of peasants in the dry zone at a cost for irrigation, incentives and infrastructure. With it came the deep suspicion of the Tamils of a competition with original settlers in the Vanni and the boundaries of the area. Later concerns about the changes in demography raised its head. However, colonization went on.

Though the State Council provided democratic politics and an anticipation of independence, many opposed it as an unnecessary step to self-government and independence. In fact, elected and nominated members had been reduced; the Kandyans too became a minority, especially by integration into the Ceylon National Congress, which was now an association of low-country Sinhalese. So again, the ruling of the council was by low-country Sinhalese. With time the demand for self-government, already given to other colonies, became louder. The minorities and the Kandyans opposed it. The Kandyan National Association pressed for a federal political structure, not even thought of at that time by the Tamil members who preferred a national government.

Ethnicity was exploited by the Sinhalese politicians among the ordinary Sinhalese. The Tamils were blamed for taking the clerical jobs in the south, although this was due to their competence in English. It became an ever-growing cry by the politicians of favouritism, a divide and rule policy bequeathed by the British.

The British stopped the civil servants coming from London. Economics was at a low ebb, and this was again blamed on the Tamils for their domination of banks and loans of money. This was far from the truth. The British did not lend money directly. There were money lenders called the *Nattukotai Chettiars* from South India. They were not the Chetties who settled down in Ceylon, but were recent newcomers from a place called Nattukotai in South India. At the same time, Afghans, Sindhis, Borahs and Memons made their appearance and dominated trading, pawn-broking and money lending.

British banks loaned money to the Chettiars who reloaned it to the Ceylonese at a higher interest rate. These Chettiars became rich and took their money back to India to build fortress like homes in Nattukotai. They were so trustworthy in finance that they became shroffs at banks, long before the Tamils did. They were all foreigners, but unfortunately the Tamils from Jaffna were also considered foreigners, as they took jobs in the south. This appeased the Sinhalese feeling of inadequacy.

The State Council established a State Mortgage Bank and a Central Bank, all under British supervision, in 1934, so that Ceylonese were able to buy land. Legislation was passed to prevent foreigners having a stake in land ownership, rice cultivation and gemming. Politicians kept reminding the people of their past glory and past kingdoms. They ignored the fact that there was a kingdom in the north, looking after its own people.

The next election was in 1936. This saw the beginning of political parties, the first being the Lanka Equal Society Party led by Gunawardena and N.M. Perera. The Sinhalese state councillors dominated all the committees and it became a pan-Sinhalese government. This was, they said, to be able to unite to bargain with the British for more reform. Mr. Bandaranaike, who had just entered politics, was made a minister.

Governor Andrew Caldecott took office at this time. He promised but opposed communal representation and a Cabinet to replace the Executive Council. The vote of the people was the cry of even the anglicized elite. Only a few favoured English as an official language so as to be the language for law, finance and international links. Those educated in the national languages, especially Sinhala, would overrun the advantage of the English educated. The type of Sinhala to be used also became a debating point.

The first workers' strike was in 1939 and led by N.M. Perera. The police held no discussion with the ministers on the matter and opened fire. Senanayake protested but nothing came of it. The ultranationalists, either born or converted to Christianity, changed their religion to fit the situation. The first to do so was C.W.W.Kannangara, the minister of Education in both State Councils. In 1939 he removed the control of schools from the Mission Board to the Executive Council. He founded English-medium schools in many districts, encouraging the learning of Sinhala and Tamil as second languages. Both languages were encouraged to be used by government departments. The ultranationalists, looking back to the past, wanted a Sinhala Buddhist utopia with nobody else around. That meant they wanted the abolition of Christian schools and English to disappear. This was not disapproved of, even by anglicized Buddhist politicians, as Sinhala Buddhist votes counted a great deal at winning elections. The ultranationalists even wanted classical Sinhala language to be used and Sanskrit words to be replaced by new words.

Disunity was sown among the ethnic groups from British times and never let up. Senanayake again restricted the Indian labour vote and encouraged emigration. India prohibited new immigration. However, when the Second World War broke out, Indians were brought for war work.

G.G. Ponnambalam, elected to the State Council, saw a pan-Sinhalese Board of Ministers and requested the Crown for a balanced representation. This was cunningly changed by the ultranationalists as asking for 'fifty-fifty' by the Tamils. Then came negotiations for self-rule between Caldecott and the Board of Ministers.

The future was debated. All parties were represented and rulings asked for regarding language and education. The ultra-Sinhala Buddhists were most vociferous.

Emily Gnanam was so alert in mind but physically used a Zimmer frame to propel herself from room to room, and even to step down to the garden. She did it so smartly and speedily, her slim body, which had not changed for decades, helped her to do so. She was ninety and still loved to be a teacher and a storyteller. She loved to teach children and young adults. She was so keen to impart her knowledge of English and mathematics to anyone who would give an ear to her. Those who were close to her were indifferent as they were domestic helps. Her knowledgeable chatter was blown away in the wind.

She loved to talk of her childhood, her teenage years in school. Memories flitted across the years with no sequence. At the age of ninety, dementia was creeping in. She said, "I remember Karainagar, my paternal village." Then she looked around to see whether her siblings, most of them long dead, were seated with her and called them by name. Her senile dementia was typical, recalling places, images and voices of infancy. Her immediate family seemed of no concern to her.

Karainagar was an island off mainland Jaffna on its west. "You should have seen it," she explained. "Acres of green paddy fields, colourful vegetable plots inland - all surrounded by arid sandy plains next to the seashore. I loved my grandfather. I was one of the younger siblings, quite ignored by the older ones. My memory goes back to the time I was four years old, and my little world revolved round him." She was childish and childlike. At their respective ages both had enjoyed the same mushy food – *puttu*, milk, plantain fruit and brown sugar mixed in all sorts of combinations. Brown sugar was the only sugar available. If not sugar, palmyrah jaggery was used. The jaggery came enclosed in cute little cases made of dried strips of palmyrah leaf or larger and more cumbersome cases of the same type. "While stripping the cases we took so many licks of the jaggery within them," she recalled.

She said again, "My grandfather was very rich in lands, paddy fields and livestock. He was tall, broad shouldered and light complexioned." Then she smiled and said, "The light skin in the north reflected the intrusion of the Portuguese and Dutch blood, though nobody dared say that in the village." Then she made a peculiar noise between a giggle and a snigger when she was amused by reminiscences. This peculiar noise interrupted her memories very often. Her grandfather was very proud of his caste. His schooling in the village school, and mostly his stature in the village, made everybody who knew him look up to him. He never had to work for his living because of his lands and fields. He told Emily Gnanam that the people of equal caste on the mainland were not as equal or high as his! The mainland people had the same idea about the islanders! Insults were hurled across the strip of sea between them. Thankfully the verbosity would dissipate in the trade winds blowing across this water. There would be minute differences in the same caste depending on the compass points of the village where one lived. The east better than the west, so it was said.

Emily Gnanam said, "Why this fuss, when the Vellala caste belongs to the sudras!" They were not considered the high caste like that of Brahmins, Kings, Warriors, and Chetties, the latter were the merchants. The sudras were people of earth and water and had to touch and dabble in them for their living. "The high caste did not contaminate their hands with earth or water." Then she made the peculiar sound and said, "The Vellala made themselves higher within the Sudra caste because they owned the land they worked on." In Karainagar, nobody forgot or was allowed to forget his or her caste.

Then she digressed from this topic to something quite different. She said, "The coastline of Karainagar has such an ascetic beauty. It was a sandy plain of a few hundred meters. The palmyrah stuck out singly and in clumps. Suddenly a flamboyant tree with its sun-scorched orange clusters of flowers interrupted the sombre dark brown trunks and fronds of the palmyrah. Greenery of shrubs and small trees were absent even during the monsoon rains. The monsoon rains which came down with a vengeance smothered the hot windy dry climate of the island. The palmyrah tree got fresh fronds, the flamboyant looked rain drenched and the sandy soil became wet and soft. The only things which became green were the reappearance of the Ipomoea runners on the ground, which became a great treat for the odd hare that appeared. The noisy leathery sound heard constantly could only come from the rubbing together of the palmyrah fronds. Nothing else could imitate that sound."

Every part of the island's interior was cultivable, so Karainagar was prosperous and self-sufficient. The northeast monsoon rains only came for four months in the latter part of the year and ending with very cold misty weather before the sun scorched the island again. The farmers couldn't depend solely on the rain. Deep broad wells were a common sight. Each *valavu*, the compound, was the land in which the house or houses stood with its garden of flowers, fruit trees, coconuts and palmyrah. The paddy fields were at the end of it separated by the bunds. The well in each *valavu* was a symbol of the prosperity of the villagers and its size was a status symbol. The size of the *valavu* was prestigious. Each family had a *valavu* whether small or large.

Emily Gnanam's mind flitted again to the memory of her grandfather. "My grandfather's name was Sarvanamuttupillai, a mouthful of Sanskrit and Tamil. I always wondered why I was given the name Emily Gnanam till I understood when I was a little older. My immediate family was the early convert to Christianity. My English name was a symbol of conversion. Though it was my mother's family who converted to Christianity, my father who went to a Christian school became a Christian too. My grandfather, though rigid in his Hindu practices, was very tolerant. We lived with him for a long time. However, when he took me to the well for the morning ablutions I came back with holy ash daubed prominently on my forehead and arms, but my parents just ignored it."

The extended family members lived a stone's throw from each other and the majority were orthodox conservative Hindus. As she grew up she always wondered why the missionaries gave her an English name as a symbol of Christianity. Probably, they remembered their families back home, and felt most at home with their names around them. The name Emily was not even found in the Bible. Thankfully she said her children were given eastern names, though practicing Christians. This conversion made her branch of the family 'lesser people,' as Christianity was equated with eating beef. She vehemently said, "We never ate beef, it was a die-hard tradition not to eat beef and was followed by everybody, both Hindus and Christians." A sigh of past events remembered was heard, and Emily Gnanam dozed off.

My mother's birth heralded the naming of Christian children at baptism with both Tamil and English or biblical names. The English and biblical names were those of the much admired missionaries who worked tirelessly in schools and hospitals in the north. My grandmother who studied in Uduvil named my mother after her principal at Uduvil. She was given the names Liza Agnes Rasammah, a mouthful of names. This mouthful of names wasn't commented on as the Hindu names of her companions were even longer!

She studied in Uduvil School till the eighth standard. As in Jaffna College, the girls in the sister school of Uduvil were taught a string of subjects. English, Tamil language and literature were stressed on. Maths, science, health and even astronomy were part of the curriculum. No further education was considered for a female and she left school to be groomed to be a wife and mother.

She was the only sister to five male siblings, and

School Girls of Uduvil 1880

she was expected to do the housework with her mother, learn to be a good cook and a wonderful seamstress, which she was. After two years at home, she was ready for marriage.

My father, Vethanayagampillai, had his education at Jaffna College. After his First in Arts qualification, he was considered able to teach in the American Mission schools found in the many villages of every island. The islands lay like a wrapped chain on the west of the peninsula. My father, who was physically like my grandfather, broad shouldered, tall and light of complexion, was stern in his manner, unlike his father who was gentle and amiable. My father wanted a say in the marriage proposal brought for him. He wanted to see the bride well before marriage. In Jaffna it was either a temple or church where these unseen glances and glimpsing of people could be done. It was at the Uduvil church, where my mother attended services, that he saw her. He was pleased with her appearance and said many years later that her black wavy hair tied in a large *konde*, coiffured knot, at the nape of her neck made her very attractive.

The mother-in-law to be also wanted to approve her before the marriage arrangements. She came without warning or invitation to my grandmother's place. The latter was a widow by now. She was pleased to see Rasammah busy at work! She was squeezing out the pulp of the ripe palmyrah fruits into containers and then pouring the pulp onto new mats spread out in the sun to dry. She was making *pinatu*, a rubbery, sweet or spicy toffee-like substance made from the pulp of the palmyrah fruit. The mother-in-law, wasn't she pleased! She thought that the young girl was very industrious, a much admired feature in a wife to be. Her dowry was cash to build a house. My father had the land given to him by my paternal grandfather. However, it was my grandfather who built the house for my father and family as he could afford it. My mother never told me the details of the wedding. It must have been simple, as my father was a first-generation Christian and many of the colourful ceremonies were left out. They were thought pagan!

Soon after marriage, mother accompanied my father to his island school. The teacher was left to do the formal teaching and the wives were expected to teach the girls to sew and cook. My mother's needlework was much admired as she was a good seamstress. She was given material by the American Mission to sew blouses for the girls who came topless to school. In fact, she took to sewing in her spare time to make some extra cash, to help her many brothers with their educational necessities.

Once, when I was quite young, my mother took me to my father's school where I was made much of. Suddenly the joy and pride of being pampered was shattered by a boy's scream, and I was shocked to see a young boy being caned. My smile turned to sobbing and whimpering and I was rushed home.

In those early twentieth-century days of any school, the wrong doings of the students even at home were carried by the parents to the school master, who was expected to give them suitable punishment even corporal. They were never corrected at home!

My father was a hard taskmaster and his punishments could even border on cruelty when caning boys or punishing any of us at home. He and other such masters were dreaded.

The teachers and their wives were expected to find work for the school leavers. They even helped in arranging the ex-students' marriages, as they knew the community, in which they lived, very well. They were expected to attend weddings, help in the confinement of the wives, be a comfort at their sick beds and then attend funerals! In short, they were a ready source of help to the islanders and help was expected of the teachers with a smile and a sense of duty.

My parents' lives were not easy, though they were given much respect. They had to uproot themselves ever so often when transferred from island to island each time when father had to take a new teaching post. They and their meagre belongings were taken by boat on these travels and travails.

Then my father, who found his salary was too small to look after the seven of us, decided to follow his brothers who had by then settled in Malaya. He went to Singapore for a clerical job. My mother then settled down in Jaffna town in the old Dutch house. It was easier to send my brothers to Central College, the premier Methodist boys' school. Father's salary was just enough for basics, and my mother gladly took up her sewing again to sew blouses for her friends and relatives. The cash from this was a much needed addition to my father's pay. Mother's five brothers were very fond of her and repaid her financial help and kindness to them by educating two of her sons, when they themselves settled down in Malaya and Singapore.

My grandmother, Jane Augusta, lived with us. In the wet and dewy monsoonal months of the year her asthma was much worse. She was lucky in that she could pack her bags and sail to Malaya to her sons. One of her sons met her in Singapore and another in Kuala Lumpur. Her travels were on the decks of cargo ships. She would make herself useful abroad too by helping in relatives' and friends' confinements and was only too willing to arrange marriages between males of Kuala Lumpur for brides from Jaffna. She had got all her sons married to brides from Jaffna, all of whom she approved of.

She would be back in Jaffna during the *cholan* season, when a hot dry breeze blew from the north. This weather made her asthma disappear!

My mother was very keen on family prayers, usually said before dinner. Jane Augusta being a catechist's daughter was even more keen on it. We would say our prayers kneeling near a chair and would bend our heads over the seat of the chair, a convenient posture for sleeping when prayers, invariably long, were said by my grandmother. We would note who had nodded off to sleep and had to be woken after prayers and there was much teasing of any sibling who had done so. I remember the time when I fell asleep in the same position and had to be woken up and then teased. I remember telling my grandmother, "How can God give you all those innumerable requests you make. You must ask a little at a time and you will be given them. Your prayers and requests are too long."

They were happy times even when father could be harsh when dealing with us. We and our cousins were quite scared of him.

Water was precious in the peninsula and so too in Karainagar. The water was brackish and visitors to Jaffna found it difficult to get used to it. Plants, which had no choice, thrived in that brackish water. Our compound was full of trees. Margosa grew in abundance, even if not wanted, in a particular place. It suddenly appeared there. Mango, jak and plantain trees of all varieties were planted, watered and nurtured by us. The northerners loved their fruits, even a daily plantain would do. The vegetarians, among us, would be quick to spot a fruit on a tree!

We were totally dependent on the rainfall which replenished the deep wells of Jaffna. No one spoke of the average rainfall; they didn't think there was such a thing. Rains came with the northeast monsoon between October and January, giving fifty inches of rain. It poured bucketsful on a parched earth creating floods, pools, ponds and even small tanks in what were deep hollows in the ground. These vanished with the hot sun of the other months. After that we expected no rains. Light showers came only occasionally. However, the weather was always the safe opening topic of a conversation. It was an agrarian society and a sudden change in the weather was disastrous. We were totally dependent on our wells and that northeast monsoon rain.

My grandmother told me a story of how the villagers asked the weather god Indran for rain in between. The God heard their plea for rain and he let down a rope to earth, and said that if anyone wanted rain, the rope should be pulled. It caused a lot of problems. When the farmer attempted to pull the rope, the washerman stopped him as he had spread the clothes to dry. When the latter pulled the rope, the farmer stopped him as he was drying the paddy. Finally, the people themselves asked god Indran to pull up the rope. The weather was predictable and repetitive. The Dutch called the northeast monsoon the good one as the southwest monsoon gave no rain to us. The rains that poured onto Jaffna soaked the coral and porous limestone of the soil. They acted like a sponge and absorbed water to a depth of sixty feet or more. This was the water table. Below this layer lay the brackish and saltier water. The fresh water literally sat on the salt water. The water in the wells would rise so high and to us younger ones, frighteningly so. Water was used carefully to retain the fresh groundwater.

My uncle near Inuvil was lucky. They had the best soil, the red earth. The wells in this soil had a supply of fresh water which was abundant and hardly decreased in hot weather. The farmers living near the coast were the worst off. The fresh water after the rains was about twenty feet, and the wells would run dry of fresh water even at the beginning of the hot weather.

My grandfather's prosperity was reflected in the three wells he had in the compound. The watering of the paddy fields in the hot weather, keeping his vegetable and cereal plant plots green and alive, depended on these wells. The well closest to the house was the smallest compared to the other two. The water in this well was brought up by a pulley rope and bucket. A large trough with an outlet, closed when necessary, was on the cemented skirt of the well. This would be filled with water drawn by an able male of the family. The females used that water for washing themselves and their clothes. It was not given to the washerman even though he lived at the end of the compound.

The second well was deeper and much further away. Water from this well was drawn down by a larger pulley, thicker rope and bigger bucket. There was a small well sweep too at this well and it could be drawn down by the older members of the family. The water from this well was poured into a coral-stoned channel that led the water to almost the end of the garden, where the retainer castes lived. They would take the flowing water from this channel to a sunk-in coral-stoned trough. They were never allowed to draw water from any well in the garden. Water would be drawn for them quite willingly, as they worked as daily labourers when not occupied with washing clothes or cutting the hair of their customers.

The third, the largest, thirty-feet deep well, which I remembered from childhood, was between the paddy fields and the vegetable plots. I was not allowed to go close to it. I myself preferred not to do so as I saw its size and the frightening cannon-shaped well sweep the *Thula* pointing to the sky. Later I thought of them as picturesque in that flat land of ours. The well sweep was a twenty-foot palmyrah trunk shaved smooth by a carpenter. It narrowed a little at one end, the butt end of the sweep. The sweep had a handhold or, when made, buttresses were left on the sides which made narrow steps for the sweep walker. The sweep swung like a see-saw on a fulcrum, also a part of a palmyrah trunk, lashed between two trees,

The Well Sweep

after going over the notched trunks of the palmyrah sweep. Grandfather had his fulcrum and sweep made of timber. These two trees gave the only shade to the labourers working the sweep.

The butt end of the sweep had a thick rope tied round it and a twenty-gallon basket, woven out of the palmyrah fronds, attached to the end of the rope. Four labourers worked the well sweep, two in the very early morning and two in the evening. The two working in the morning were Sivan and Kanthan who lived in our compound. They started at four in the morning when the village was still asleep. I would see them at six in the morning, when they would be almost stepping out from the sweep. They appeared dark, scorched and sweaty, dressed in a *verti* taken between their legs and tucked at the back, and the head turbaned to keep out the sun. Sivan walked down the well sweep. The butt end of the sweep with its rope and basket dipped into the well. Sivan turned round and walked back on the buttress to the broader end. The basket, brimming with water, would rise to the surface. Kanthan lifted the basket and poured the water into the trough which led the water into a broad channel. This channel led the water to the paddy fields which needed the most amount of water for paddy to stand in it. Smaller channels led from the larger one to water the vegetable plot or gingelly plants. The channels were opened and closed temporarily by mud walls.

To get maximum water to one plot I saw Kanthan rushing around, opening and closing the channels in turn. About three hundred trips were done on the sweep leaving them tired and hungry. My grandmother would give them soured rice and lentils, a great favourite of theirs as rice always filled their stomachs. They were paid well too as it was hard work.

This whole procedure was repeated in the cool of the evening - such was the rate of evaporation of water from that soil. The well sweep was again worked for two hours, from half past four in the evening.

Maniam had more cattle on his land. The bulls were made to pull up the baskets of water from the well by a chain which ran over a pulley. This was another system of irrigation, the Persian wheel, but no one in our village had it.

Meena was my friend. She lived at the bottom of the garden. We played in the garden but she was not allowed to come to our home. She was different, so said my grandfather. Later I knew why. She was called the *Nalavar* girl because her father climbed the

The Well Sweep and the Water Pump

coconut and palmyrah trees. Meena and her mother would come to the well to fetch drinking water, which was drawn for them. They were considered different, but I enjoyed the company of Meena. Meena's parents had no land to have their own well. Subha, living in another house, was able to draw water from our well, but still was not one of us, I was told. She was a Koviyar.

Wells were always protected by a four-foot bund, and I would lean over it to see the water when I got over the fear of the well.

This leisurely way of life and the well sweep did not last very long. Along came the ubiquitous oil pump to get the water out. Nothing was easier. Sivan put it on and forgot about it for two hours. The pump pulled out the fresh table water in gallons. The fresh water was suddenly replaced by the salt water beneath it, and Sivan realized that the water had been pumped out too rapidly and for too long. The laborious well sweep was much kinder to the well.

It was in our late teens that we ventured further out from Jaffna, to see smaller rural towns and villages. After much planning, we visited Mullaitivu and travelled over the harsh terrain of the Northeast. Mullaitivu was truly the most verdant part of the northeast scenery. It was a great place of pilgrimage for the Hindus. The first impression was a blanket of tall satinwood and mahogany trees that leant towards each other and vying for space with the spreading and wider girthed tamarind trees. All these were not growing wild, but were within live-fenced or palmyrah-fenced gardens. The drumstick trees would raise themselves much higher to vie for the sunlight which poured on us too with its heat similar to that in Jaffna, but its humidity was mellowed by the breeze between the verdure. The ever-present palmyrah stuck out tall at the edges of habitation.

At a sudden bend of the road there lay before us the paddy fields, each with its perfectly square bunds and the fields which seemed to stretch for acres and ended with a modest sized house. It was humorously surmised that the farmer armed with a tape measure made these perfectly square bunds. Though the species of trees, fruits and flowers were similar to those of Jaffna, Mullaitivu was more agrarian. If not farming, the rest depended on the bounty of the sea.

There were the young, not so young and the old busy in the fields. So very unlike in Jaffna, there was no great ambition for the young for academic prowess. The sons of farmers who finished the Senior Cambridge level, and some not even that, were content to work their lands. Only a couple of sons in a large family would embrace a professional lifestyle. The majority loved and appreciated their fields and gardens, the harvest of which made them as rich as academics or even more. Each family branded their cattle used for ploughing and for milk .The majority of them were vegetarians. The non-vegetarians loved to hunt their meat. They would set out with their shot guns and invariably bagged deer, elk or wild boar and made the tastiest curries with them. The migrating Siberian duck and the inelegant birds with stick like legs, 'the roaming road runners' were also considered good for the pot. They nurtured the tall mahogany and teak trees at the edges of their fields. The agrarian scene was pretty, but lovelier by far was the *Nandi kadal*, the sea and the broad beach. The *Nandi kadal* lagoons dotted the seashore beyond. The fishermen had packed their colourful boats on the shore and were drawing their nets ashore with much chatter or they sang the songs of the sea and drew their nets with their catchy choruses.

The structure starkly visible on the shore of *Vattapalai, Mullaitivu* was the temple of Kannagi. Kannagi was immortalized in the Tamil classic *Silapadikaram*. She was deified and worshipped by the Hindu world and revered as an incarnation of Siva's consort Parvati, commonly called Amman, the mother god. Kannagi was made divine by her purity and single-minded chastity.

There was no evidence of any royal patronage with regard to the beginnings of this Amman temple. The temple was also called Rajarajeswari temple. Kannagi's tale began in Madurai, a southern city in India. She was the rich and ever-faithful wife of Kovalan, who was not. He dallied with a courtesan Madhavi and led a prodigal life, spending his and Kannagi's wealth. When he became a pauper, he with great regret went back to Kannagi and she took him back. Their poverty forced her to ask Kovalan to sell one of a pair of her silver anklets which had a ruby within it. A jeweller bought it from Kovalan. Unfortunately on that same day, the queen of Madurai had lost an anklet of a pair similar to Kannagi's in design. Kovalan was accused of having sold the queen's lost anklet. The king in his fury executed Kovalan without trial.

The grieving and the furious Kannagi accosted the king, and blamed him for a miscarriage of justice and her widowhood. She broke her remaining anklet and showed the ruby in it. She asked that the queen's anklet too be broken. When broken it showed a pearl within it. The king begged for forgiveness but Kannagi was unrelenting and as an act of revenge immolated herself by cutting off her left breast and threw it into the city, cursing fire on it. The whole of Madurai burnt. Her burning of this city gave her the name 'Pathini.'

Legend recalled that she travelled south as a mendicant seeking solace and tranquillity. She stepped on the shores of 'Nandi Kadal,' the sea at Mullaitivu. She appeared as an old woman to a few boys who were herding their goats. She sat on a discarded plough made of margosa wood. She seemed exhausted hungry and incessantly scratched her head. The young boys offered her their prepared milk rice to appease her hunger. As darkness set in she asked them to light their clay lamp. There was no oil available and she requested them to fill the lamp with salt water and light it. The lamp burned brightly. They in turn requested to see her head and the reason for her continuous scratching. They were amazed to see a large number of eyes on her head. She then disappeared.

Nobody in the village, at first, believed the boys' story and her request to make milk rice annually at the spot of her apparition. What time the hallowed spot became a shrine. The people of Mullaitivu and the adjacent communities flocked there in the month of May. They prepared the milk rice and lit the lamps, adding salt water to them. The shrine grew into a temple and housed a statue of a rare and beautiful Kannagi. The temple festival in May saw a mass of people of the agrarian community from every nook and corner of Mullaitivu, and even further away, gathered at the temple. At the ceremony preceding the boiling of milk rice and at an auspicious time, a temple dignitary carried a new pot on his head, waded into the Nandi sea. He dipped thrice to fill the pot with seawater. This was used in place of oil in the brass lamps of the temple. They were placed in a row right up to the holiest sanctum. Three clay pots covered with elaborate patterns of white thread were used to make the milk rice. The ground round the temple would be a mass of bent heads over similar pots in which, the devotees too, made the rice. Rituals and ceremonies followed. The devotees at the end of the day, believing in the grace of Kannagi, walked on hot coals with great faith.

The story of Kannagi spread all over the north and the rest of Ceylon and in India too. King Gajabahu II visited the Chera kingdom and heard the story of Pattini and was enamoured by it. A replica of the anklet was made and brought back by him to Ceylon. It was placed on a beautifully decorated chariot that went in a procession to many parts of the island. Wherever the anklet was taken, a shrine was built in her honour.

The worshipping of Pattini in the south became a cult with legends, poetry and song. It lost its connection to the story of Kannagi. The largest number of Kannagi temples was in the east rather than in the north, especially in the district of Batticaloa. These shrines opened to devotees only during the time of the annual festival. At other times devotees prayed and praised her in front of the closed door of the temple. In some temples the legend was enacted in dramas and sung in lyrics.

The temple at Mullaitivu got its name *Vattappallai*, as Kannagi had appeared in many places and Mullaitivu was the tenth place of her apparition. It was referred to as *Pathampalai*, meaning (in Tamil) the tenth place. With time, the place became Vattappallai. The Vattappallai temple also became the venue for the pilgrims of the north and the Vanni to meet for the commencement of the '*Nadai*' the pilgrimage on foot to Kathirgamam. The pilgrims would make the milk rice, request the blessings of Kannagi, and then commence their journey.

The Board of Ministers in 1944 drafted a constitution with the aid of Sir Ivor Jennings, the vice-chancellor of the University of Ceylon. The board insisted on meeting the Soulbury Commission without minority representation. This seemed to be so out of tune with the democracy preached by the British. The Constitution was legalized in 1946. The lack of minority participation undermined its worth and opposition to it went on for years till it was changed in 1972. Senanayake convinced the Colonial Office that he would protect the rights of minorities - a political bluff. He went to Jaffna to reassure the population there. He came to the east too on this visit, and a lunch was given to him and his retinue at our home where he met prominent citizens. I remember the preparations of putting the house shipshape and organizing the cooking at home. D.S. Senanayake was a charming man with his broad smile under a bristling moustache and heavy eyebrows above it. While in the north he promised parity of status to Sinhala and Tamil. Like typical politicians of short memory he conveniently forgot his promise when he returned to Colombo.

The young politicians Jayewardene and Bandaranaike followed the leadership of Senanayake and convinced the Ceylon National Congress, now pan-Sinhala, to accept the terms of transfer of power to the Ceylonese. The Ceylon National Congress was created in 1946 under D.S. Senanayake's leadership.

Independence was given, literally on a scroll, on February 4, 1948. There was not a shot fired nor was there a violent death for freedom. Unity against a common foe was never seen. J.R. Jayewardene as early as 1943 strongly wanted to include Tamil as an official language in the Tamil-speaking areas, but Dudley, the ever reluctant crown prince, opposed it as he feared that the numerous Tamil-speaking South Indians may swallow Ceylon. Communalism had already reared its head in the second State Council of 1936, which ended with a pan-Sinhala government. From that time only a few Tamils ventured into the lion's den, even so today. The Sinhala Buddhist votes would determine the results of any election and the policies. The politicians painted a picture of going back two thousand years to the kingdom which had a perfect society, a utopia. This made the Sinhala Buddhists think they replaced the British. No leader had a vision of a true and fair pluralistic society. It was only a dream of the minorities for the last forty years.

The first parliamentary election was in 1947. A large number of Tamils joined the UNP, which won the election, trailed by the leftists with a quarter of the seats. The leftists found fault with the way the conservatives gained power and the economic plunge. Senanayake continued with his government which included the 'yes' men of the Tamil Congress. The socialist party was the opposition led by N.M. Perera.

In 1951 the Ceylon Workers' Congress came into being under Thondaman. The Indian Workers' Congress was the previous Ceylon Indian Congress. The CWC looked after the interests of the plantation workers, many of whom had become stateless with the loss of citizenship following their inability to prove origin by descent in Ceylon.

Philip Gunawardena left the merger of the socialists, and Chelvanayagam broke away from the Tamil Congress and formed the ITAK alias Federal Party in 1951. The Tamil Congress of Ponnambalam stayed on with Senanayake. Then Bandaranaike with a following of five left the UNP. He had played a minor role in the government. He knew he would not succeed Senanayake, as along as his son Dudley and his relatives Kotelawala and Jayewardene were on the scene. Bandaranaike was ambitious.

During the tenure of this government the economy took a plunge. The money left by the British had to be spent mostly on welfare schemes. Tea did not bring in the expected revenue as the patronage of the British was missing. Many non-viable industries were started and closed with loss. Rubber was not much in demand after the war and the amount tapped was little, as most trees had been tapped dry till they died. Only rice production increased due to the colonization of the dry zones by Sinhalese peasants, which became, again, a grievance to the Tamils. Unemployment reared its head. The LSSP started innumerable strikes. Dudley Senanayake was now at the helm after his father died in an accident during his regular horse ride. Though he controlled the required two-third majority in parliament, he resigned unable to cope with the dissidents. John Kotelawala, a cousin of Dudley, succeeded him. He was westernized, impetuous, garrulous and intolerant of minorities, and promptly removed Ponnambalam from the Cabinet; the latter was a greater threat than his replacement, Vaithianathan.

Dudley had been to Jaffna in 1954 and in his ebullience promised parity of Sinhala and Tamil, and a change of constitution. In parliament, he reneged on it, another bluff in political history. He was as hard as D.S. Senanayake on the rights of Indian workers and intolerant of non-Govigama Sinhalese as well. Kotelawala, in his exuberance and in spite of low export prices and unemployment, called for elections in February 1956, fifteen months earlier than necessary. Bandaranaike came forward as his opponent and became the leader of the MEP, a coalition of Sri Lanka Freedom Party and the socialist parties. Bandaranaike was the 'Man for all Seasons.' He was a Christian, educated in the best Anglican school of that time, and a graduate of an even better university, Oxford. He had great oratorical skill and had made a name for himself in it. He returned and was ambitious to enter politics. He changed himself in every way to fit the political situation. He threw off his three-piece suit and donned new attire. It was a sarong, a compliment to the Muslims, and a *verti*, shirt with a high collar. This combination became the national costume. To the people in the north, it did not seem to be new. He threw out his Christianity of birth, invited Buddhism into his life and introduced the Buddhist clergy into politics. "The Sangha is the voice of the Sinhalese," was the cry of Rev. Rahula. Hostility to Christianity became a part of their thinking. Bandaranaike wed a Kandyan to increase his vote base. He went with the wind that swayed the people and politics.

Three main parties contested the elections and Bandaranaike won it as the leader of the MEP, getting fifty percent of the seats. The Federal Party got ten seats and the UNP only eight. Almost every politician in the south of that time and of the future looked at the northeast with a jaundiced eye and a mind-set that never could be moved.

As he took office, his first bill was the 'Sinhala Only' Bill, amidst jubilation in the south. In the north, the students who had willingly learnt Sinhala from 1949 threw away or burnt the Sinhala books and said 'goodbye' to their teachers, who returned south. The UNP followed suit. Ukwatte Jayasundara proclaimed 'Sinhala Only' louder.

Almost every Tamil UNPer resigned from the party. This was followed by the Federal Party organizing demonstrations and hartals in Tamil-majority areas and in Colombo near Parliament. This was meant to be a nonviolent hartal on Galle Face Green. Non-violent protests were never known in Ceylon, and it probably died with Gandhi in India. The only nonviolent entity was the seated Buddha at the street corner. The hartal was forcibly stopped, the participants beaten and the clothes stripped off the members of the Federal Party. They experienced the indignity of running almost nude to the nearest hotel.

Bandaranaike delayed the enforcement of 'Sinhala Only' and tried to appease the Tamil politicians by promises that could not be kept. The Federal Party at a convention in the east put forward a few demands including federalism, parity of Sinhala and Tamil, and gave the government one year to decide. No goodwill was however to be seen in Bandaranaike's first Cabinet which included Muslims, Christians and non-Govigama Sinhalese, but not a single Tamil.

In 1957 Chelvanayakam and Bandaranaike put forward a compromise solution of regional councils with substantial powers in place of federalism. The Bandaranaike-Chelvanayagam pact was born in early 1957. This would have been the best solution. It however died in its infancy. The Sinhala extremists, the opposition and opportunists like Jayewardene and strangely Ponnambalam opposed it, though many moderate Sinhalese accepted it.

The bill was torn apart by Jayewardene, now the leader of the UNP, and the Sinhala Buddhist extremists on that famous march to Kandy on October 1957. Bandaranaike was morally too weak to resuscitate it. In the discrimination of the Tamils, 'Sinhala only' was stressed for employment in the public service, a service that had many Tamils with their English proficiency. 'Sinhala only' debarred Ethiraweerasingham being made the captain of the national athletic team, even though he was the only gold medallist at the Asian Games. The diaspora that started with students seeking education abroad shot up with seekers of employment too.

The UNP and the SLFP tried to beat each other as to who was more Sinhalese! In 1958 the first communal riot was instigated. Bandaranaike blamed it on the Tamils for effacing the 'Sri' on cars in Jaffna. Communal politics became the backbone of every government together with unabated colonization of the east.

After the violence subsided, a 'Special Provisions Bill for the Use of Tamil' was mooted by Bandaranaike but the pro-Buddhist faction in his government opposed it, and was unhappy that more pro-Sinhala Buddhist policies were not implemented. The coalition too was falling apart and Bandaranaike's short, ambitious political life ended with his assassination by a Buddhist monk in 1959. As he could not be buried in his father's grave, the Samadhi in Horagolla made its appearance.

The UNP won the election in March 1960 with Dudley Senanayake again at its helm. He now had the support of the leftists and the Federal Party. He increased the rice subsidy but did not act on the Tamil language issue, though he was supported by the Federal Party. The government lasted only a few months and elections were called again in July of the same year. Sirimavo, very popular, as she was the grieving widow of Bandaranaike, was at the helm of the SLFP. She had little political acumen and depended on her relatives for that acumen. She first wooed the LSSP with a no-contest pact. She wooed the Federal Party too with promises of Tamil as a regional language. She thought she might need them to form a government. She won the elections with a large majority. She did not need the Federal Party for its support. She was ambitious and turned out to be politically ruthless to the Tamils.

To the Tamils she appeared now as the 'avatar' of goddess Kali, the goddess of vengeance. She walked from the kitchen to the Cabinet room and while doing so she looked through the members of the Federal Party as if she had never seen them. She pulled out her pen instead of the sword and made Sinhala the only official language of the country, which included the work of the judiciary. The latter was a new concept.

A civil disobedience campaign in 1961 came to nothing. Some of the Tamil members now sat pretty in Colombo and had a policy of 'wait and see.' They believed that the government would do something but 'something' never did happen then, or ever after. The small voice of militancy which started in 1956 now grew louder. Words of 'Separate State' and 'Eelam' had their beginnings at the meetings of the youth league in Jaffna. The diaspora increased. Direct action was contemplated but was stopped by the dictatorial emergency declaration. In 1961 the nationalization of schools took place. Jaffna felt it most. Over two hundred private schools under private religious management that depended on government funding were nationalized. Just a handful of Christian schools of the Anglican Church and of the American Mission remained fee levying. It was sad to hear that Vembadi, my school of fifty years ago, went under the nationalization hammer.

A new elite of Sinhala Buddhists who were to displace the English-educated elite did not materialize as English was essential for the plum jobs of the private sector and other international careers. The trade unions had nothing to lose and backed the government. The police and the army had only Sinhalese recruits. Sepala tried very hard to get our son, who wished it, recruited to the army but Sirimavo insisted on that ruling. Hoping to reverse the political situation, a coup d'état was planned by some police and military officers, but it failed even before it started.

It was time for elections. The UNP was led again by Dudley Senanayake. The Federal Party led by Chelvanayagam joined the UNP in 1965 to form a national government to give a necessary majority. Dudley wanted to implement the Tamil Language Special Provision Bill of 1958, which would make Tamil the language of administration, records and judiciary. He promised to give lands to the landless Tamils of the dry zone by decreasing colonization. A draft of the bill became the Dudley-Chelvanayagam Pact. As usual it found its opposition with the Sinhala Buddhists who now had a fixed backbone, the Sangha.

The UNP government refused to allow the non-nationalized Catholic schools, now dependent on facility fees and contributions, to levy fees again but funded transportation to schoolchildren. Sirimavo was at the helm of the SLFP.

The elections of 1970 saw a coalition of the SLFP and the socialist parties, including the Communist Party, swept into power. It was called the United Front coalition. The Federal Party had no place and no political say with this government. Education was free from grade one through university. The second university, Peradeniya University, added to the number of graduates who vied for employment that wasn't there. A large number of these unemployed youth became the nucleus of the JVP in 1965 led by Wijeweera. It supported the United Front at the elections but was anti-imperialist, anti-Christian, anti-elite and anti-Tamil, and they shouted the socialist state slogans. The JVP then turned against the state and started an armed rebellion against it. To counteract it, the police force was increased in numbers. The JVP spread its violence even up to Jaffna, but failed there, and most of the leaders were imprisoned in Jaffna itself. In 1971 Wijeweera was arrested and imprisoned. The movement was brutally suppressed and a state of emergency came into force and is still with us.

The government was made stronger by increasing the armed forces with help from the ever-ready India, Russia and the United States, the latter not wanting to be left behind.

Sirimavo now thought that the problem of the JVP was due to the Jaffna youth who were too educated and were employed disproportionately. In 1972 she again took the avatar of Kali, again looked across to the north, saw the educational facilities there and decided that the marks obtained at the Advanced Level examination should be standardized. She, her Muslim Minister Mohamed and the 'yes' man Kumarasuriar made the required average percent of the three communities to be eighty-five, seventy and sixty, if the student was Tamil, Sinhalese or the favoured Muslim, respectively. Thus the Sinhalese had to get an average of fifteen percent less than the Tamil. The Tamil student who got "A"s in all four subjects he sat at the Advanced Level Examination was relegated to his second choice of academic discipline. If

Sirimavo thought that this would uneducate the north, she was mistaken. The pen wrote the standardization of marks but her sword went through the educational heart of the north. The north could not and would not be uneducated as education was the lifeblood and livelihood of the Tamils. This was the turning point of the diaspora. Those who could afford to or now had expatriate relatives who were willing to finance them, went abroad for education. If not for education, then they went for employment. Quite a few educated, disappointed and angry youth joined the militants and trained in an armed struggle.

Then the irascible politician Professor Sunderalingam appeared on the scene. He had given up a lucrative Civil Service job and was a member of the first UNP government. He, with the militants, talked of Eelam and even drew a map of it!

The Tamil politicians themselves advocated separation in their speech at Vaddukodai and asked India for assistance, which it never gave. 'Sri' was added to Lanka, to make it more Aryan. The politics of the United Front government created more militant groups and more repressive measures were foisted on the Tamils. Into this scenery, Prabhakaran came as the founder member of the Tamil Students' Federation. This body started the unfortunate and unnecessary formation of many militant groups from 1972.

Sympathy for the groups came in 1974 when, during a Tamil conference in Jaffna, Sirimavo for no apparent reason objected and encouraged the police to fire into a crowd of fifty thousand. Power lines came down - a few got electrocuted in addition to many others who were injured. She did not condemn this, but promoted further violence, as she had unlimited power.

The Tamils were in a dilemma, more so as the Tamil politicians were unwilling to countenance the militants, but wanted a democratic solution. In 1976 Tamil politicians met at Vaddukodai to demand a separate, free, sovereign and secular state. This was opposed by the Tamil Congress.

Prabhakaran, from Valvettithurai, a son of a government servant, had dreams of Eelam since his teen years. He left school early, had enough charisma, and many youth followed him with implicit faith. In 1976 the most active militant group called itself the Liberation Tigers of Tamil Eelam, LTTE. It became powerful and during the next years decimated other militants, even travelling to South India to do so. The LTTE became ruthless for supreme power among the militant groups. Remnants of other militant groups straggled behind it.

Sirimavo struggled with the economy. She drastically reduced the foreign exchange allowed to two pounds sterling for anyone travelling abroad. She refused to give any foreign exchange for graduate studies abroad. Her whole family, however, studied abroad in prestigious universities.

The elections that should have been held in 1975 were postponed by Sirimavo. Dudley Senanayake who was the leader of the UNP died in 1973. R. Premadasa organized a Citizen's Front for power and Jayewardene organized a protest against Sirimavo, citing the takeover of Lake House newspapers and food shortages that saw the locals eating manioc and green gram for their meals. The protest was also against the prolongation of her government and the alleged coup of the Bandaranaike family itself. Jayewardene resigned his seat in parliament. The leadership of the UNP created rivalry between Premadasa and Jayewardene. The latter with his higher caste, his education and oratory consolidated his position as the successor to Senanayake. At the elections in 1977 he won handsomely, and with a new constitution he authored he became the president. Premadasa was made the prime minister. Jayewardene was seventy-seven years old.

The TULF, the Tamil United Liberation Front, too came in with a sweeping majority to become the opposition. Jayewardene tried to find a negotiated solution with the TULF. He promised to make Tamil an official language and formulated elected district councils. It was tiger bait that held no attraction to the Tigers' appetite. In 1980 Jayewardene removed the civic rights of Sirimavo. There was just a whimper heard and then it died down.

The district council elections were held in the northeast. The DCs were a sham, having no autonomy, no power, nor money given for any development process. They were toothless. Jayewardene formulated a new amendment to the constitution regarding the crossover of a member of parliament from one party to another. The policy was that a member must vacate his seat and face re-election, but not so anymore. He removed that clause so that Rajadurai, a TULF member, crossed over to the UNP. Crossing over became a habit.

The violence of the Tigers increased, mostly against police officers and civilian informers to the security forces. An emergency was declared in 1979 and the Prevention of Terrorism Act became law that year.

The security forces, now mainly Sinhala Buddhists, were given wide powers. Indiscipline was rife. Extra judicial killings, disappearances, arbitrary arrests and many other abuses against Tamil civilians occurred. In 1981 the UNP candidate for the Jaffna Development Council was fatally shot. The police rioted, vandalized places, broke monuments and found an excuse to burn the Jaffna Public Library, instigated by a minister. This was a symbolic gesture against the love of books of the northern people and was the second only to the burning of the library at Alexandria.

The Tigers were never far behind in violence. A few weeks later, Sinhalese hoodlums assassinated Indian labourers on a tea plantation and burnt their homes. It was unfortunate that this happened to them as neither they nor their leaders had ever endorsed or assisted in Tamil politics. Many of these refugees found a new life in Tamil-majority districts.

With the additional minority votes, Jayewardene had received a five-sixth majority at the 1977 elections. He had the votes and the goodwill of all the communities but never rose to the occasion to settle the communal problem. He only removed the standardization of marks. He preferred to win over the west with his policies of investment. This economic liberation was the trump card to extend his term of office. A referendum was held which he won and having a majority in parliament he extended his term to 1989. The opposition was in disarray and lost its sting after the demise of its leader N.M. Perera. There was a lack of another charismatic leader.

The TULF participated in the 1977 elections. It had no faith in the UNP or the JVP, whose leaders were released from imprisonment. The response of the Tamils to all these crooked policies was determined by the radical militants rather than the TULF. The separatist groups became more violent with a similar response by the state security forces. The TULF was torn between democracy and separation. Jayewardene's elections and referendum were suspect and democracy was ever so much weaker with the retention of the emergency.

The culmination of armed violence was the killing of thirteen soldiers in Jaffna. Eighteen Tamil civilians were killed in revenge in Jaffna but this was not made public. The government flew the bodies of the soldiers to Colombo and collected the victims' families for a mass funeral at Kanatte. Some members of the government goaded the crowd to violence against the civilian Tamils, which started from Kanatte on that black day of July 1983.

Jayewardene wanted to teach the Tamils a lesson once and for all. The violence of communal rights since 1958 was not enough for him. He was the modern Dutugemunu, who believed that killing Elara's wife and children was as good as killing Elara himself. The violence, that included the burning of hundreds of homes of Tamils in Colombo, went on for days and spread to adjacent towns. Jayewardene not only failed to control the situation, but lay low, fiddling more days than Nero ever did. He appeared on the state television four days later, portrayed himself and his government as blameless and referred to a past history of communal feuds. His misrule made the blackest mark in the Tamil psyche. The separatist Tigers and the call for Eelam were banned.

The diaspora from Ceylon now numbered in the thousands. Homes, money and visas had been given by western nations. The TULF left parliament and the militants took control to establish Eelam. Many in the diaspora, who had been at the butt end of communal politics and violence since 1956, supported the Tigers with monetary generosity.

The Tigers could not win over the smaller militant groups and decimated them. The LTTE had, however, attracted youngsters from all castes and made a dent in the caste system. The Tigers had a fixed aim to win Eelam in any way possible. Anyone not with them was against them was their cry. No rationalization was condoned. The violence of the Tigers was matched equally by the violence of the state security forces. This saw the callous death of hundreds of civilians in the north and south. The state tried to involve the Muslims against the LTTE by shooting a few in the east and blaming it on the Tigers. That policy did not hold for long.

An eight-month truce followed, but the Tigers did not stop recruiting young men, and later children, to their cause. An All Party Conference with the help of the Indian Prime Minister Rajiv Gandhi was held. The extremists as usual objected. Gandhi did not want separation, and his envoy Parthasarathy brought the idea of regional councils, to have the powers of 'law and order,' administration and justice, and many more clauses. The Thimpu Conference was held, but no agreement was reached. To show disapproval the Indian Air Force dropped parcels of food on the northern terrain. The Ceylon Air Force then bombed Point Pedro, which was followed by an economic blockade in 1987. The electricity and water supply were cut off. This created a mass exodus of refugees to South India. In 1986 Jayewardene then proposed elected provincial councils.

The Indo-Sri Lanka Accord was signed in 1987. One of the clauses provided for an interim administration for a merged northeast. Rajiv Gandhi escaped death at the hands of a state soldier just after the accord was signed, but died in a bomb blast in south India at the hands of the Tigers in 1991. That was the greatest mistake made by the LTTE, which lost the sympathy of the Indian government.

Elections were held in 1988. The UNP with Prime Minister Premadasa at the helm won seven provinces. The EPRLF with Varatharaja Perumal won all the seats in the north and half of the seats in the east. The LTTE was never interested in the ballot but only the bullet, and hostilities between it and the government resumed in 1990; the LTTE shifted its operations from Tamil Nadu to Jaffna.

Under the peace accord with India, six thousand troops in the Indian Peace Keeping Force (IPKF) were sent to Jaffna to disarm the LTTE. Within months, and for some unknown reason, seventeen armed and captured LTTE cadres were ordered to Colombo, but they staged a mass suicide in which twelve died. The LTTE went on a rampage, massacring Sinhalese villagers. The IPKF launched a major offensive against the Tigers. The RAW made its appearance too.

There was a saying in Tamil that the northerners to the north of us were like their symbol the cobra, backboneless and fork-tongued. We had no experience of it in our private lives. There was hardly a marriage arranged or condoned between South India and Jaffna. There were more marriages between the northerners and southerners of Ceylon.

The IPKF showed its two faces, one in the east, the other in the north. They hardly met the Tigers in the east. The officers of the IPKF used my home as their headquarters and looked after it well. The IPKF marched by day on the roads of the east with their guns ready to shoot a 'Tiger'. The Tigers sauntered by night with their tails up and extracted what they needed in food and money from the civilians. There was hardly a battle. The Jawans, the foot soldiers, had been brought from parts of India that had no link language with the north of Ceylon, neither Tamil or English.

In Jaffna it was different. They were frustrated by the land itself. The lay of the lanes and the fences frustrated them in their chase of the Tigers. The cadjan and palmyrah fences suddenly rose out of the ground and blocked them. The numbers captured were fewer than they desired. They were on edge and wantonly killed civilians, even middle-aged ones. The latter put up their hands in surrender or held a white flag, which was conveniently ignored by the Jawans. Lawyers, doctors, nurses, teachers and ordinary civilians lost their lives, and their numbers were added to the total amount of Tigers killed by the IPKF. The northern civilians sorely missed General Kobbekaduwa, who had controlled his soldiers better. When things got worse with the Tigers, the IPKF resorted to looting. There was no discrimination in what they took. Households of things were taken away in trucks and probably taken to India. Saris that came from Tamil Nadu went to Madya Pradesh via Jaffna. Women begged for a few saris to wear. Jewellery was a great temptation. Minesweepers swept over hearth, home and compound to look for that gold, the officers no less keen than the soldiers. *Thalikodis* were simply given to them when asked for, as there was always a gun behind the request.

My niece recalled an event long afterwards with humour, though at the time of its occurrence it was not funny at all. A Jawan roamed her compound looking for egg-laying hens and took them easily. Then he asked her for husband. She lied to be safe, not knowing his intentions, and was relieved when he wanted the husband of the hen!

The Tigers' violence knew no end. The IPKF was equal in its response but their morale diminished. Premadasa had two problems on his hands now. The JVP opposed the accord with India and started its campaign of violence, sabotage and assassinations. Premadasa became autocratic and suspicious of the members of his party and the opposition. He sent back the IPKF and tried for a political solution with a northeast merger. Extreme opposition to him saw the end to it. Premadasa of all prime ministers was not communal minded, as he grew up in a mixed milieu of communities, but many upcoming southern politicians were assassinated during his tenure, and the Tigers were convenient scapegoats.

The violence between the Tigers and the army began with greater gunfire. The army bombed anything that looked suspicious to them. At first Sepala prevented my house from being bombed. My son's house was. Later, my house was bombed to rubble as Sepala was not in authority any more. Premadasa was assassinated by the Tigers in 1993. The violence of the Tigers especially against civilians became mindless, immoral and soulless. Who knows, they may be destroyed within and without, by the proverbial sword mentioned in the Bible.

The battle may finally end with the help of the cobra that will, when inconvenient, flop onto its back, and the six-starred and the multi-starred opportunists. The 'doe eyed' men may make their appearance at this time too.

Small insignificant things and mundane events make up sharp memories. A Saturday or a holiday seemed to drag slowly, like the rope sent through the nostrils of the bull which went reluctantly with that grazing bull.

The holiday, like every other day, started early for the females of the household. We would get up much later, but still early enough and heard the familiar and numerous noises of nature and people. The sharp and loved chirps of the sparrows were everywhere. Sparrows, like the crows, were numerous, and every household would try and attract the sparrows to build their nests in deep clay pots on the walls of their homes. The mouths of the pots were gripped by a strong and long nail hammered securely on an outer wall under the eaves. Large holes made on the rounded bottoms of the pots ensured easy access and flights out for the sparrows. Sparrows were considered lucky for a home and many clay pots stuck out from the wall. Their chirps woke us long before the noise of the mynahs and screeches of the parrots.

Somewhere between the bird noises came the plaintive notes of the flute, plaintive as only a young boy practicing on the flute can make it. Every parent in the north was ambitious to make their offspring clever in studies and versatile in Carnatic music. The flute and *miruthangam*, the drum, were learnt by the males, the *veena* by the females, and vocal music by both. The violin was introduced from the west to Carnatic music and taken up with the same enthusiasm. The little boy with the flute would stutter and stammer on his flute though he practised daily and faithfully. The wrong notes played were interrupted by many loud and impatient disapprovals by a better artiste of the family. If there was a silence it meant a twist to his ear or a knock on his head. It was harder for a female vocalist to hit a high note without it becoming nasal. The drum would be easier to tolerate even when drummed wrong. To cap all noises was the loud monotonous repetition of the multiplication table. This table from numbers two to twelve had to be memorized by the young ones and answers spat out for every combination of multiplication asked for. We heard the reluctant voice that repeated 'two times one makes two, two times two makes four, two times three makes six,' and so on. A mistake, a loud reprimand from a parent, then a second or even third repetition of the table. It was not surprising that many of these students became wizards of mathematics. A theory that went around in the village was that the brain took a mathematical turn if more fish was eaten than meat!

We preferred to study in the morning from five thirty till it was time to trot off to school. The sun would come flooding in to light up the tables and the books on it. Evening study meant hurricane lamps, candles, and much later gas lamps. If we studied, especially during the month of Christmas, we had waves of insects swirling round these lamps. They were similar to the dragonfly in shape, but had mini bodies and larger gossamer wings. We named them Christmas flies. They would be so attracted to the light that we would spend half the study time keeping bowls of water to which they were attracted. When everything failed to stop the insects coming, we gladly turned off the flames and were relieved to see an end to our studies. The next morning we would see the discarded gossamer wings of those dead flies on the ground, the table, even stuck to our books and worse on pages of the books we forgot to close.

It was always a cooked meal of hoppers, stringhoppers or *puttu* for breakfast. Then the whole day stretched before us and we had to amuse ourselves. Radio and television were of the far future. The cooler part of the morning was spent playing 'hide and seek,' marbles or hopscotch. These games had our male siblings and cousins playing with us. The big difference in the game of marbles was seeing the brothers and male cousins flaunting their prowess in playing it but we would beat them at hopscotch. We, however, would covet the marbles they flaunted. They carried their marbles in bottles and boxes. The marbles were coloured and transparent or opaque, with rings of colour round them. We girls would have a handful of them and knew we would lose almost all of them in the morning. Our garden was pockmarked with numerous little pits as many played in groups and pairs. The game was to roll a marble along the ground to hit another marble that was rolled on to it by another player. If the marble was hit, it was bagged. The game went along the ground in a similar fashion till the home of a little pit was reached. There would be arguments of cheating, tears on losing, marbles thrown at each other in anger and we lost the few marbles we had. The boys would add these marbles too to their collection and we would beg from them the marbles we thought were ours to be returned.

Hopscotch meant that we drew, with our big toes, rectangles and squares in a pattern on the dusty ground. Then a smooth stone, individually treasured, would be thrown into the spaces in a particular way, retrieved, then thrown overhead to bag a square which was crossed, belonged to us and was not in the game anymore. While the game was on, the boys would have drifted away, as they were not good at it. Then we would be called to play the game *kitti*. A small stick laid across a shallow pit was lifted up and swung out with a longer stick. The winner was the one who achieved the greatest added sum of the distances travelled by the small stick, over a few rounds of the game. After a short time we would be bored of each game. We rushed then to the *oonchal*, tied to a sturdy branch of a mango tree. We sat decorously on the seat of the swing and persuaded our brothers to swing us on it. At times we threw off caution and shyness and stood on the seat, bent and stretched our knees alternately, went higher and higher and held on to our skirts for modesty's sake. Grandfather had a theory that the vibrations of swinging from a mango tree made it bear more fruit. Now I see my grandchildren are poring over playing cards and the Monopoly board seated at the table. Marbles, swings, hopscotch, unknown to them.

It was a different kind of enthusiasm and anticipation when the mangoes ripened on their trees. We had four varieties of which the Karuthakolomban was the best, and the next the white variety. The branches of the mango trees spread across, while the margosa grew straight, taller and then branched out. No villager ever stopped talking of the harvest of his mango trees – the greater the variety, the greater the boast.

When the months of June and July came around everyone in our compound looked up to see the first yellow tinge on the green fruit. This upward glance was repeated every morning till the yellow tint was seen, which meant it was time to pluck the mangoes. However keen our eyes were, the parakeets and the squirrels beat us to the first fruits.

A labourer, versatile in climbing and plucking mangoes, was hired. He came along with two other urchins and they carried two gunny bags and a long stick with a piece of iron bent like a hook at one end. With a bound or two of his stretched legs the labourer, carrying a gunny bag, climbed and reached the sturdier branches. He plucked and dropped the mangoes into the bag on his shoulder. He next stretched the hooked stick and broke the stems bearing mangoes on the further branches. The urchins who were all eyes, looked at the man, ran in his direction and each holding an end of the other gunny bag held it directly under the falling mangoes. They seemed to fly hither and thither, with the sack, and our eyes too flew in those directions. Each mango falling on the sack would be gently rolled onto the ground to prevent it being bruised. The plucker teased the younger ones by pulling the branches further away from him so that the mangoes fell even further away and smiled at the speed of the little boys who caught those mangoes on their sacks.

We as children would be enthralled by their activity and cheer when a mango landed safely in the sack. Later we appreciated their labour of nimble legs and felt sorry for the urchins who were rushed around by the bullying plucker. The workers were paid in cash and mangoes.

The mangoes were gathered and spread on old mats in the storeroom, to ripen. My siblings, cousins and I made numerous and sometimes unnecessary trips to see the progress of ripening and many times pilfer them when they were not quite ripe. It was many years later I saw my granddaughter do the same to the mangoes gathered from my garden. When young it was fun to eat them sour with salt and chilli. The plantain trees, in contrast, were humdrum and would bear their fruits right throughout the year and their fruits were invariably served as dessert after a meal. In fact, when grandfather returned from the temple holding half a coconut in which he had a plantain, the coconut smeared with holy ash, sandalwood and *kumkumam*, a scarlet powder, a Hindu cousin prised open grandfather's hand and took the plantain. By now we Christians were debarred from taking it as it came from the temple.

Sometimes in the morning, when it was too hot in the house, the oldest female inmate of the compound would be carried out on a mat from her daughter's home. She was affectionately called *Pethamma*, which gave no indication of how many generations ahead of us she was and what generation she belonged to. The name literally meant a mother who had borne children. The pallet with her on it would be set in a shady spot under a margosa tree, which was believed to have healing and disinfectant powers that it gave to the air around it. She looked around to see us. She was covered with dappled shadows of the beautiful margosa leaves. She had a permanent smile on her face and it revealed her toothless gums. She was tiny and made childlike noises. To us she was only a soul without a body. She would lie there absorbing the sun and the air. When tired she made high pitched noises to be taken in. She was accepted as part of old age and was affectionately cared for by her family. Her son-in-law, who took her out and then in, would be remembered for introducing a proverb into every sentence of his. It seemed he knew thousands of them and his favourite proverb for us was that of the mouse who not knowing his way out was dragging the *ekel* broom too behind him. He would say this when shouting instructions to anyone who had no idea about the direction he was going.

The sultry and humid afternoons saw us playing games seated on the verandah. Three or four of us girls would sit cross legged on the cool cemented floor to play *kokkan*. This game entailed playing with stones. We would take five or seven stones, keep them on the palm, throw them up and catch them on the back of the hand, then throw them up again and catch them again on the palm. The stones that fell on the ground were counted against the player. The other game was to place red, round seeds in a wooden slat, with holes in it, in a particular way that was predetermined. We would play till we were bored. The happiest way we spent the hot afternoon was practicing our dances learnt at school and danced under a shady tree.

There was the dance of *kummi*. A circle of girls standing facing each other was made. We would lustily sing the appropriate song, clap our hands with our bodies bent and then again with our bodies straightened. We struck our palms on others' palms. There were elaborate patterns and movements within the same dance and more songs sung. Then we danced the *kollatam*, a dance with cylindrical strong sticks. All of us had a pair, a compulsory item to be taken to school. Instead of the palms of our hands, the sticks were struck against one's own or the other dancers' sticks. There would be complicated patterns made with sticks and all accompanied by loud singing and rhythmic movement of the dancers. The louder we sang and hit the sticks, the happier we were. The boys not to be outdone sat as in an imaginary boat and sang songs of legend, history or a comedy. This was called the *villupaatu* and a popular extracurricular activity of their school.

Evenings came in fast and when grandfather was alive he would call the grandchildren to say their short prayers. We too would trot behind them as Christian prayers at home were at a later hour. Their main prayers were in the mornings. There were rituals, prayers and singing of lyrics. The shrine room was the smaller room opening onto the courtyard complex and was adjacent to the front door leading in from the outer verandah. The room had only a long table on which were arranged the icons of brass and bronze. Holy pictures hung on the wall above the table. The icons were arranged in an order of importance.

The previous day's flowers had been taken away, so too the burnt wicks. The old oil in the brass lamps that held five wicks, or an odd number of them were removed and replaced with fresh oil and wicks. Flowers and garlands were a must for prayers. Flowering plants had to be truly nurtured to get a few flowers every day. Only certain flowers are considered auspicious, hibiscus and jasmine were just two of them that could be grown on that sandy stretch between the gate and the verandah. Numerous jasmine plants were coaxed to trail over walls and run on wire meshes to get the best harvest of flowers. Each jasmine with its sweet strong smell would be nipped with care.

The oleander that grew easily and luxuriously was inauspicious for the shrine room. The younger females with their nimble fingers would make garlands of the jasmine. Each icon would have a garland of flowers round them. Incense was burnt, joss sticks lit, wicks lit and lyrics sung. My brother saw these rituals and thought it not amiss to make the sign of the cross before leaving! The smell of incense and jasmines would linger long after worship and the lighted wicks would be left to burn themselves out.

The quietness of a morning was shattered by the music coming from the adjoining temple. These musicians were of the *Nattuvar* caste, a middle caste in the hierarchy of castes. The music would be purely Carnatic. The main instrument, the *Nathasuram*, a long clarinet like instrument, held sway with the drums of various tones. The *thavil* was the drum of the lowest Carnatic note. The learning of these instruments would be transferred and guarded from father to son, guarded jealously within their caste. Grandfather related to me that a young lad of that caste who was not even able to carry the instrument was coaxed to support it on a half wall of the temple and learn it. If he played the wrong notes on it, his father's knuckles came down and gave him a hard knock on his head as well as admonition. These *nathasuram* players with many years of blowing their instruments had very prominent chests. *Devadasis* who in ancient times did the Bharatha Natyam in the bigger temples were hired by the smaller ones. The reputation of the dancers as temple servers did not make the dance popular. It came into vogue with the disappearance of *Devadasis* in temples and it took a longer time for the dance to become popular in schools. The temple musicians were wealthy. A group of them was attached usually to a temple. The musicians were compulsory hired invitees for all ritual ceremonies especially weddings.

Occasionally the younger females would play 'doll's wedding.' Five cents in our hands would be enough for the wedding feast. Half a cent for sweets, another half for savouries, another two cents for a bottle of sweet aerated drink. The drink came in a beautiful bottle, which when empty, had to be returned to the shop. The beauty of the bottle lay in the large coloured marble that was the stopper. The drink could be poured out only when this marble was pushed in. However much we turned and twisted the bottle, the marble could not be taken out. We looked at it longingly and vainly. The dolls used for the wedding were celluloid or made of any rough material. The wedding was only an excuse to the feasting. The young males would drift by for the feasting, but it was great fun.

The happiest days of the holidays were the season of the *Cholam* wind. It blew strong, scattered the dried leaves all day long, lifted the clothes off the clothes line and bathed us in dust. This wind was the harbinger of the kite season. The kites were simple, made of tissue paper, bent *ekels* sticks and twine. The boys monopolized the making of kites and flying them. They were so gaudy but looked colourful in the sky. The kites in the sky always made a humming noise. The kites were not made flat but with a belly in it by curving the *ekel* sticks. A little palmyrah fibre was attached to the middle of the belly of the kite and when it flew it vibrated in the wind and hummed. It was a typical noise of a 'humming' kite that flew in the northern skies.

We would beg to hold the kite's line, but it was refused. After quite a time of flying, we would be allowed to hold the string and then we felt the wonderful tug of the string in the wind. There was no competition for kites to be hacked and brought down by sharp bits of metal attached to the strings. When dusk came, the kites were lowered and many got entangled in the branches of trees and tore. Some young male cousins who thought of the advantage of height already gained by the kite would tie it to a sturdy branch of a tree. The *Cholam* wind would rip it into shreds and we would be amused and thought it served them right!

Then there was the season of the butterflies. Thousands of beautiful golden ones swept across our village. A golden splash of colour suddenly appeared between the green trees and the brown earth of our garden. Within a few minutes they were seen across the paddy field and then they disappeared from view. There were intermittent arrivals and departures of these lovely butterflies. We regretted their short stays. They did not stay long as the belief was that they were on their way to Adam's Peak.

The dawn of the year in our village was not the first of January, but most often the fourteenth of that month. January first was celebrated only by the Christians – just a few of us, in our village. The fourteenth, sometimes a day earlier or later, marked on the Hindu almanac, was the calculated date in which the sun moved into the Phase of Capricorn, astrologically a pre-Galilean concept of the sun moving and not the planets.

The sun's entry into Capricorn meant that it would travel north and back to its zenith. The warm rays of the sun ensured the ripening of the paddy and our wish for a plentiful harvest. This auspicious day was *Thai Pongal* and was considered the first day of the New Year. Pongal literally meant the boiling over of milk. The calendar at home marked the western dates with the Hindu dates below it. The calendar also had the day divided into auspicious hours, which was taken great note of for auspicious events. The next day, the *Maatu Pongal*, the cattle pongal, was done as a thanksgiving to the cattle that played an indispensable role in an agrarian society.

Pongal was a thanksgiving for the previous year's harvest and the harvest to be.

As in most festivals, this meant a thorough cleaning of the house. The evening before the Pongal the females of each household squatted on their haunches and mopped the floors with water in which a generous amount of saffron had been dissolved. Pongal was prepared in the open in front of the house, early the next morning prior to the rising of the sun, whose first rays we hoped would see the boiling over of milk.

Grandfather made the biggest Pongal and every member of the family would partake of it. The younger families too made it in their homes. Widowed members did it in their kitchens. There was so much to be done before the actual cooking of rice. Mango leaves were strung on top and across the front door. The boiling of the milk was done in the garden in front of it. Like in any festival and sometimes on auspicious days too a decoration, the *kolam*, was drawn on the cemented front verandah and in front of the fireplace to be.

A married female, bathed and dressed in a colourful sari, drew a square on the ground in front of the house with rice flour, drew another decorative *kolam* within it and arranged a fireplace facing east. There would be the ceremonial brass pot of brimming water and its accompaniments of a coconut and mango leaves. The pot was placed on a banana leaf strewn with rice. A lamp with five lighted wicks was on one side of it. A new large clay pot had been purchased, and cleaned and washed mango leaves tied round its neck with a few stems of sugar cane among them. It was filled with sufficient milk to boil over, placed on the fireplace and the fire was lit with wood chippings and camphor. The milk seemed as if it took ages to boil over and it became the proverbial 'watched pot.' The boiling over of the milk was anticipated mostly by the children. It was believed a good omen if the milk boiled over the rim that faced the east. There was a little cheating with the pot tilted slightly to the east prior to the boiling. This was overlooked as being on the safe side. Finally, the milk boiled over accompanied with loud vocal salutations to the sun that came over the east, and louder prayers for a good harvest expected in a couple of months. All these vocalizations were drowned by the noise of the fire crackers and the general melee of noisy joy.

Grandfather would bring a few measures of rice which had been cleaned and kept with care from the last harvest. He put in a handful or three handfuls, as numbers should be of the odds, into the boiled milk. This ritual was followed by other married members of the family. The milk in excess of that needed for cooking the rice was removed from the pot.

There seemed much more to do to make the rice palatable and sweet. Green gram was added, and when the rice and the green gram were cooked, palmyrah jaggery, raisins and split cadju nuts were added to the pot. Usually a senior aunt would take charge of the final cooking with much bossing.

Finally it was announced that it was ready. The head end of banana leaves and smaller rectangles cut from other banana leaves came in thick and fast. Three ladles full of the Pongal were placed on the large banana leaf and placed on the ground. Circumbulation of this with prayers was done by the Hindu relatives. All of us had a small portion of the sweet milk rice with the added sweetmeats and savouries to complete the meal. The older members of my family did not partake of this as it was thought to be a Hindu ritual, and we were now Christians.

Grandfather would query as to why we did not celebrate the harvest in like manner and thank our God in a similar fashion. My older sister, having an answer to every query, would explain why not to grandfather. She explained to him, in what seemed to me long sentences, that the missionaries who brought Christianity to us, brought Christianity with certain of their more cultural western customs included in it. She was proud to say that we had a harvest festival offering fruits and flowers in our church in the month of October. He was amused and amazed that we celebrated harvest in the month of torrential monsoonal rains and remarked that it could not possibly be a thanksgiving for any crop. For every query about Christianity, my sister had a ready answer. Her final repartee was to tell him that Christianity and its missionaries made a dent in the caste system by educating all castes. She added that all castes were equal on the playing field and in the social events of a Christian school. She reminded grandfather that he had not even improved the status of his household castes.

The Roman Catholics were more progressive and amenable to introduce cultural backgrounds into their faith. Pongal, on its day, was made at the entrance of their church. The ceremonial brass pot of water, its additions and the lighted brass lamps were kept there too. The cooking of the rice was followed by a thanksgiving mass in the church. They introduced more cultural accompaniments in the wedding ceremony too, including the loud *natheeswaram*, the local classical music.

Years later we regretted that the Protestant missionaries failed to introduce Christianity within the cultural environment. They could have won more souls by doing this.

Pongal was always followed by many in our family attending the local temple for the *pooja* of thanksgiving which was accompanied by music, especially of the deep bass *thavil* drum and the local clarinets. This type of music was always a part of temple worship. Invariably a devotee got into a religious frenzied dance. The devotee in this state was said to prophesy and declare oracles. The truth was never verified. The frenzied dance would be stopped by sprinkling or even pouring water on the frenzied dancer!

Pongal was still not over. The cattle were honoured the following day. They had been allowed to range freely the previous day. The cattle shed was cleaned thoroughly, the hearth prepared near it and the milk, rice, jaggery in plenty and more green gram was cooked ceremoniously. The cattle were washed, the bulls' horns were coloured with crayons, garlands of hibiscus flowers and bells strung round their necks and holy ash applied on their foreheads. A prayer for the gift of cattle was said. The cooked rice was placed on banana leaves with other fodder, plantains and fed to the cattle. The cattle were not worked for a couple of days. Grandfather and the women folk who milked the cows would make much of them, stroking them and embracing their calves. The local cattle were brown and much smaller than the bigger white Sindh cattle brought from India. A cow was never sent for slaughter, however old. The bull would be taken away after it had ceased to be a stud or could no longer be worked by the household.

No sooner Pongal was over the Tamil New Year would be looked forward to, which was in mid-April, a couple of months away. The date was again determined astrologically pertaining to planet Mesha and the sun, the almanac giving the exact time of its dawn.

This again was the time of spring cleaning. Sweetmeats were prepared well in time and rice cooked like Pongal, but within the house. Family reunions took centre stage in the New Year. Times for various rituals were not strictly adhered to by grandfather or his family. A well bath was taken, after the application on the head of a fragrant liquid in which a number of small leaves and herbs were seen. This was usually prepared by the Brahmin priest and brought from the temple. The application of this liquid on the heads of the family members was done by an elder of the family.

Dressed in new clothes, most of the men and fewer women would rush to the temple. They wanted to be in God's presence at the exact time of the dawn of the New Year and start the year right with him. They leisurely strolled back home. Their hands held half a coconut from which peeped a little bit of milk rice given by the priest. They were in time to partake of milk rice and a vegetarian meal. The auspicious event was to get a few silver coins from grandfather's hand and he was generous to all who held out their hands for these bright coins.

Visiting the relatives was the done thing for the day. Many relatives had gathered from the same village or from the neighbouring town. The only obstacle to a visit was when the New Year fell on a Thursday. For ages, visiting for the New Year or any first visit was never done on a Thursday, and some even stretched it to a Tuesday. It foretold of quarrels if visits took place on these days.

It was an opportune time for entertaining marriage proposals and for looking around for eligible males for their marriageable daughters among the visitors. New Year holidays were long enough to cement arrangements already spoken of.

The garden was full of noise made by us, the younger ones, by the barking of the roaming mongrel dogs who seemed to have more adopted an owner than vice versa, and crows that never failed to appear, festival or not. Then there was also the cry of the *kooyil*, the local cuckoo. The male would start this mating call long before New Year. The first call of the male cuckoo of the year was pleasant with a sweet vocal beginning, the trill in the middle that ended with another high note, but the last note heard was not quite as melodious as the first. These cuckoo calls became so numerous and loud that we would be awake earlier than we wanted to. It came to such a peak of noise that we would have liked to smother those birds, but were only able to smother our heads with our pillows. Sometimes just one male went on plaintively calling for a mate, even after the New Year, probably crying of defeat in his quest of a female.

Games on New Year's day were played with great gusto by the males with much cheating and shouting. The girls in their brightly coloured and gold bordered long *pavadais*, would compete for the *oonchal*, tied to a sturdy branch of the mango tree. We would swing higher and higher whilst standing on it, and the wind would blow the skirt wide and high to oblige our wish to show off our clothes. As children we loved to try the swing within grand uncle's house next to the inner courtyard. The swing had a metal crossbar fixed firmly to the floor by a pair of long metal rods. A pair of brass chains hung from the ends of this cross bar and held between them a broad, strong and long wooden seat. The seat was three feet from the ground. It did not swing much but we thought it prestigious to spend some time on it. Grand uncle and aunt would be found seated on the swing chewing betel, discussing household matters while gently swayed by their movements on it. Young couples were permitted to sit and sway on this swing if they were betrothed, but it was taboo for a young male and female to sit together on it.

Our village was famous for the racing of bulls in the afternoon of the New Year. This was held in the open space that was in the middle of the village. There were a few bullock cart races, but majority of races were when bare bodied young men with *vertis* tucked up, sat astride these ferocious looking beasts racing each other. These races, of which there were a couple or more, were keenly contested and handsome cash prizes were donated to the winners. More cash exchanged hands with the betting on the riders.

The introduction of a three year old preschool child to write the first letters of the Tamil alphabet was a ceremony. Held at home, it was done on the day devoted to Saraswathi the goddess of knowledge. An erudite older member of the family did the honours. He sat cross-legged on the floor in front of a shallow brass tray covered with red raw rice and a five wicked lit lamp on its side. With the child on his lap he took the child's forefinger of the right hand and guided it to print the first or even a couple of letters on the rice with shouts of encouragement from the female relatives who hovered around ready to serve sweetmeats and coffee to complete the ceremony. Minor ceremonies with specific sweetmeats accompanied the piercing of a female infant's ears and the appearance of the first tooth in an infant. No less important than all these festivals was the annual festival of the village temple – the festival being in the first quarter of the year like most temple festivals. The festival in the first quarter meant that the devotees were free to give of their best in worship and spend maximum time there. This was the period after sowing and before reaping. Many temples had the festival mid-year, when harvest was over and the villagers had ample time to devote to their temples. The northerners though prosaic became active, proud and jealous of their temples. Auspicious days and times for the commencement of the festival were strictly kept. This festival commenced with great pomp with the hoisting of the temple flag, which had a figure of a bull if it was a Sivan temple, or cockbird if it was a temple to Skanda.

Families were proud and jealously guarded the privilege of having a day of the festival given to them. This privilege was passed on to generations of that family. Grandfather was given a day too in that festival of fourteen days. He had to be in charge of all non-priestly preparations for the day including the midday meal. This meant money to purchase the many things for the main *pooja* of the day, payment to the priests and to the musicians numbering about six for playing their music at the temple for that day. The musicians demanded much and got whatever they asked for, as musicians came from a particular caste family and were not numerous enough for grandfather to be choosy. In contrast to the Carnatic classical music we heard, we would remember the noise of the 'paramelam' beaten by the lowest caste members. The drum gave no rhythm to sort the music but produced only a harsh noise when it's leather diaphragms were beaten with a couple of strong sticks and the drummer beat it with great gusto. He was heard in the village even before the colonial rulers. He was the town or village crier giving news and information that was given to him and relayed to all. A crowd gathered round him whenever they heard the loud drumming. He stopped drumming and shouted out the appropriate messages he was expected to deliver. Of all the notices of coming events the best, to us as youngsters, was the coming change in the bioscope that was shown within a canvas tent in the adjoining village of Vaddukodai!

The young and especially the older males would be at the temple from morning until the last ceremony at night. There was no time consciousness in temple festivals. Music and processions got dragged on till midnight to be resumed early the next day. The night processions had the icons taken by palanquins or by chariots round the outer courtyard of the temple. On the last day of the festival the icons were taken along the main roads of the village accompanied by loud noise and louder music. In addition to the temple noises there would be heard the voices of the domineering devotees who would shout and herd the worshippers, who would ultimately get irritated and shout back at them. In the village, this was a time of vegetarian meals for the full duration of the festival. The traders of eggs and fish would feel the economic pinch as their goods would have to be sold at drastically low prices, more so the meat. Our vegetable seller would increase her prices drastically, in spite of our protests, to make a quick profit in her income.

When the festival of the village temple was over many would trek to more distant temples for their festivals. The grandest would be at the largest temple with the greatest number of devotees.

Every festival ended with the ceremony of immersion of the processional icons in a tank brimful of water, or in the sea if it was close by. As immersion took place, the devotees would rush down the steps of the tank or the seashore and immerse themselves too in the now considered sacred water.

The joys of these festivals were somewhat diminished by the birth of a new arrival in that large household. We would know that a son had arrived when the father distributed sugar candy to us. If a girl, sweeter brown palmyrah jaggery would be given.

Festival time with its long languorous days provided ample time at the temple for social life too. It would also be used to discuss money, land transactions and invariably marriage proposals, all of which were spoken of in a little louder voice to drown the noise of the drums, the chatter and the chanting.

In our village the present temple was smaller than the original one. The large granite blocks of the temple, which were destroyed by both the Portuguese and the Dutch, were used to build edifices of their own faith. The months of July and August were also the season for festivals of the Hindu temples in the south of Ceylon. Grandfather would say that the Hindu priests from the peninsula, who officiated in various temples in addition to their own, would travel south and officiate in temples there to earn more money.

They had gone to Kandy and officiated at the Hindu temples situated within the perimeter of the Temple of the Tooth. Kirthi Sri Rajasinghe, the Nayakkar king, revived Buddhism, its art and architecture in the latter part of the eighteenth century. Being a Hindu, he did not think it amiss to conduct daily Hindu rituals in the worship of the Tooth relic, which was considered as another icon. Hindu rites were performed by both the king and the Buddhist priests. Rituals of ablution, food offerings at set times - all accompanied by music - were performed. The king introduced the Buddhist tooth relic as a symbol into the traditional annual festival of the four gods of Natha, also called Sivan, Vishnu, Skanda and Pattini, whose temples became a part of the palace complex. These processional icons were taken round daily on elephants accompanied with music but there were no dancers. The

A Religious Procession

immersion of the icons was in a tributary of the Mahaweli River. This ceremony was later called the water cutting ceremony and this took place on the last day of the festival.

When the Buddhist clergy of Siam on a visit to Kandy in the early nineteenth century saw this procession they were shocked to see that the homage paid to the Hindu deities dominated the Buddhist worship. Thereafter the procession of Hindu deities literally took a back seat and the tooth relic procession became more prominent and more colourful. With years the festival, now the *perahera*, became spectacular with many elephants, music and a host of dancers in the procession.

The Hindu festival of Deepavali in our village meant mainly new clothes and visiting the temple. The house and surroundings were illuminated by a large number of lighted clay lamps which brought out the essence of Deepavali, as light conquering darkness of the soul of man.

When my family moved to Jaffna I was still young, and the school and the church became the centre of my life. Christianity seemed easier and simpler to follow than the ceremonies and rituals of the Hindu temple. God's presence was a visual experience in the temple while it was an auditory one in the church. The altar was bereft of all icons, burning lamps, incense and the loud beats of the drums. It was by reading the Bible and listening to what was read that we learnt to concentrate. The vociferous singing of hymns, Tamil lyrics and the repetitive choruses became a favourite part of that worship. The village temple and the worship seen there became lost in memory. We were reminded of it when we visited grandfather, which became infrequent. With his death, contact with our village was lost.

A journey to Mannar, an island on the northwest coast, from the east coast was a trip through the driest and monotonous regions of the island and over the ruttiest roads of the country. It took eight hours with a break in Anuradhapura with time to stop and stare at the ruins. The road then went through the arid lands of Vanni, which was pleasantly interrupted by luxuriant green paddy fields. This road ended at the two-kilometres-long causeway. The sea lapped its shore and went over it during the monsoonal rains. We crossed it and reached the mainland. We spent a few days with my brother Seeva who was the district medical officer of Mannar. My brother and his wife Kanmani were wonderful hosts to friends and relatives visiting them, in spite of his large family of children and their adopted nephews and nieces who were part of that household. It was a large sprawling Dutch house similar to others given to the senior government servants in the northeast.

Mannar had vast plains of sand bereft of small trees and shrubs that were in the north. Mannar got its name from the Tamil word for sand river but the river was salty and looked like a strip of a lagoon. Mannar and the salty river could be walked across in about five hours, if one had a mind to it despite the heat. It was hot, as Mannar lay just a few degrees above the equator. The sand of the lagoon, or river as it was called, seemed to have been thrown all over Mannar and bare feet could sizzle on it.

When Pastor Baldeus of the Dutch regime saw it, Mannar was impoverished but still showed stately buildings, monasteries and a church of a bygone prosperous era. Decay was a sequel to the absence of the pearl fishery that flourished ten years before the Dutch conquest. The Dutch restarted it. There was a good harvest in 1666 and then it dwindled.

Every type of Roman Catholic mission visited Mannar. The Franciscans were followed by Jesuits with an aim to educate the locals. They were followed by the Dominicans, then by Augustinians and finally Paulists, and Mannar had a very Roman Catholic ambience to it. With these missions came conversions and many churches in Mannar and its surrounding areas, including the

The Fort of Mannar

islands northwest of it. Mannar itself had seven churches of Portuguese architecture with their rich ornamental altars. The population of that area became as fluent in Portuguese as in Tamil. Rev. Baldeus very wisely introduced a Calvinist Protestantism in the language of the people.

Mannar had a fort built by the Portuguese. It was a four-sided granite building, the entrance of which faced the river. The granite for the walls had come from the destroyed huge temple at *Thiruketheeswaram*. The canal in front of the fort had only a depth of five feet and allowed navigation of light craft. The Dutch fortified and deepened the canal to enable larger vessels to bring in trade and to station a naval force. Both the Portuguese and the Dutch had engraved their dates of arrival on the wall of the fort. Trade was brought to Mannar; the goods had been unloaded at Mantota in Mannar, a well-known harbour of ancient days. This was across the river and its name was mentioned and was famous in the Naga era too. Mantota was best known for the pearl trade. The Arabs monopolized the pearl trade as at that time they were the best seafaring traders of the East. The Arabs brought the donkeys too to Mannar. The donkeys must have been the ideal transport for Arabs, on the sandy desert like environment which they were familiar with. The Arabs left but the donkeys stayed behind to be seen by us and probably by future generations. They were there in their braying hundreds.

The trees that took root in Mannar were the thorny acacias that were able to retain water. They were not eaten by animals too. The tree that we were enthusiastic to see was the Boabab tree. It was surrounded by a crumbling short wall and was right in the centre of the town. This tree was brought and planted by the Arab traders for shade. It was a souvenir of that time. It stood about seventeen feet tall and fifty feet in circumference, and the locals called it *perukka* tree. It must have been brought from Africa or from one of the Arabian lands, where it flourished and gave shade. The water stored in it was used by survivors of their tribal feuds who were dying of thirst in the desert. It was also called the 'upside down' tree as the girth was larger than its height. The Roman Catholics called it the 'Judas' tree, as its pod had thirty seeds in it, the price of betrayal of thirty pieces of silver. The bark and leaves were used in the treatment of malaria; it probably brought down the fever.

There was such a variety of seashells, not only on the beach but along the causeway as well. The seashells were cone shaped, flat, typical shell shaped of many sizes and even nail shaped. These were seen on the northeast shores too. We would collect bags full of them. This harvest of shells lasted only till they were washed away with the high tide.

The Boabab Tree

Inside view of the Fort of Mannar

The sea beach was the centre of attraction of our holiday. The vast stretch of sand was ideal for any type of game the children played. The fishermen drawing in the nets, the sea gulls screeching and diving in to steal a few fish and Brahminy Kites spotted in the midst of the gulls was a constant phenomenon.

Mannar was in the direct path of the Coromandel shore and its wind drifts made it a birds' paradise. Not only were the local birds seen but the migratory ones in their season. Mannar was eclipsed by the teeming migratory birds in Arippu. It was a bird's sanctuary in the early months of the year. The seashore and the collection of monsoonal rain water in ponds and lagoons made it so.

We travelled north along the coast past Erukalampitti and Pesalai, the larger villages, and we went past more villages and reached Talaimannar, which literally meant the 'head of Mannar.' The pier suddenly came into view and a crowd of people were on it to board the ferry and sail to Rameshwaran, in India. Legend has it that the Sivan temple at Rameshwaran was built by Prince Rama when he travelled back to India after defeating Ravanan. This was an act of contrition by Rama for having killed Ravanan, a great devotee of Siva. The sea of Rameshwaran, with time, was to the Hindus a place where the ashes of their dead relatives were immersed. The lighthouse in Talaimannar stood sentinel to all these activities.

In that stretch of sea between Mannar and the Jaffna mainland was a string of islands. Our knowledge of them would have been very little but for the Portuguese and the Dutch. They were enamoured with these islands, changed their names and described them in great detail. The closest to Mannar is the island of Nedunthivu, which meant long island. The British mispronounced it as Ninduntiva. The Portuguese named it Ilha das Vacas, the cow island. Cows were imported into this island. They were much smaller than the Jaffna ones. The island had many cliffs and rocks with small inlets into which the sea rolled in making them caves of water. The people were very poor and the island was hardly visited. It was also called Middleburgh. The Portuguese introduced horses into the island. They increased so much that groups of sixty to hundreds were seen. The horses were taken to Jaffna for trade.

The Dutch sustained them and called the island Delft, and it remained so. When the British came, they stopped the trade in horses and stationed a garrison there with a lieutenant in charge. With time not only the ponies were left behind, but blue eyed and lighter skinned foals among the human population! The British lieutenant was believed to be responsible for them. With time, the eyes remained blue but the skin became darker as that of the present generation. This combination of features was incongruous but striking. The people of the island depended on a fishing economy and were still poor. Most of the houses in Delft had strong walls of coral. The coral stones were from the ruined walls of the fort or even from the retaining walls of the paddocks of the horses bred there. Delft also boasted a Boabab tree. Adjacent to Delft were two uninhabited islands called the 'twin brothers,' which in Portuguese was Twee Gebroede.

The island further to it and towards Jaffna was the island of Nainativu. The Portuguese promptly named it Braemines. Its name derived from the jackals that were in plenty. It became famous with the Hindu temple built there. This was destroyed by the Portuguese and rebuilt later. The island's fame spread with the legendary visit of the Lord Buddha. The island is called Nagadipa as the Naga tribes had inhabited it. Annalaitivu was a smaller island below it. It was well known for the abundance of oysters in its seabed. Again, the Portuguese promptly renamed it Don Clara in honour of a female noble called the lady of the island. It was said that she was so corpulent and heavy and used a chair that could sit two, and this chair was exhibited for a long time.

Parallel to this island was Punguduthivu. It was renamed island Deferta. It had a large number of peacocks, hares and very tall people. Fishing was the source of their income.

The Portuguese always feared the arrival of other conquerors and built forts – one of the furthest forts from Jaffna was in the isle of the twin brothers. These isles had a large number of goats. The hard masses found in the stomachs of these goats were called the *bezoar* stones, a word of Persian origin. This stone was considered an antidote to poison. Horses were introduced to these isles too, but their import stopped as water was very scarce. The

The ruins of Delft Fort

only fresh water produced was by thunderbolts striking the rocky surfaces.

Then came the two largest islands, habitable and appreciated as defence against intruders. One was Urukuthurai. It was the port from which elephants were exported to the Coromandel Coast and Bengal. It was renamed Kayts by the Portuguese, which meant the Elephant quay but was Velanai to the Tamils. They also named that part of the island where the fort was built Olim. The Dutch came along and called it Leyden. Velanai was the stronghold of the Portuguese who built the first fort there. The churches on the island were built with the conversion of the Hindus to Roman Catholicism. The largest number of Roman Catholics was found here.

The island of Karaitivu or later Karainagar came next to it and closest to Jaffna. The Dutch renamed it Amsterdam. Between these two large islands was the Fort of Cays built by the Portuguese, which was renamed Hammenheil by the Dutch. This fort was built as the first defence of the Portuguese to safeguard Jaffna, but the Dutch conquered Jaffna by land and not by sea. During British times when the American Mission came to Jaffna, they set up schools in the islands and Karainagar too came under its influence but most of its people remained Hindu.

Islands off Jaffna

Hammenheil Fort

Most of these islands had particularly good soil for the Chaya dye plants, especially of the dye indigo. It was a source of revenue for the islands as the raw cotton material was woven and dyed here by the weavers, a caste on the islands. The Dutch enforced a strict supervision of the indigo dye, to send it to Batavia for the dying of cotton there.

These islands were just names to us. They were hardly visited. Kayts was the most populous of the islands. Nainativu was visited often by the Hindus, as every newborn in a family was taken to the Nagapooshani temple to be blessed.

There were many small islands further north that appeared and disappeared with the tides. When it was visible fishermen stood on them and fished with their rods and lines. These islands formed a bridge, the Adam's bridge. Adam when banished from paradise was supposed to have had crossed this bridge to reach Ceylon, the second paradise, and then travelled south and reached Adam's peak. The legend of Ramayana also related the story of the bridge built by Hanuman, the monkey god, across the small strip of sea the Sethusamudram to enable prince Rama to cross over to Lanka to battle Ravanan. The guardian deity of Sethusamudram was Sethukavalar, another name for Siva.

Mannar became neglected when Mantota harbour lost its prestige with the arrival of the steam ship. When sailing vessels of various types were in use, the trade winds played a major role in the trade from west to east and vice versa. The trade winds were prevalent for many months of the year. The winds blowing in the direction of Ceylon brought the boats from the west to Mantota. The goods were unloaded and the boats reloaded with goods of Lanka. When the winds blew away from Mantota these boats set sail to their own lands. The name Mantota was changed many times, and now it is known as Manthai rather than Mantota.

The road back from Mannar to the east coast seemed dustier than before. The trip back was more leisurely and it was customary to divert from the main road to the road to Thiruketheeswaran temple. This temple was close to the Palavi River, which is a tributary of the Aruvi River and is also known as Malwathu Oya. The temple was, as the crow flies, very close to Mantota.

It was initially a shrine called Ketheeswaran, the abode of Siva. The Chola kings who ruled Ceylon in the eleventh century built two temples on that site, one in place of the shrine which they named Rajarajeswaran in honour of one of the scions of the Chola dynasty. Only one of these temples remained.

In the sixteenth century the Portuguese destroyed the surviving temple and with it the carved Tamil hymns on its walls. Most of the broken granite stones were used to build the fort in Mannar, and also to build a church in a part of the temple premises. The only thing that escaped destruction was the large granite seated bull, an emblem of Siva. The place was left desolate with no temple or church.

In the nineteenth century, the British governor auctioned the land. The Indian *Nattukotai Chettiyars,* the wealthy money lenders of that era, bought the land. The ancient lingam together with other statues and the granite *Nandhi* the bull were found and a temple built. It took almost fifty years to build the temple and cast the bronzes of the icons.

We saw the temple stand out large and beautiful in that bleak environment sans trees and shrubs. If it was a day in the month of February, we would not have been able to visit it. The Sivarathri day in February was the holiest and the most crowded day at the temple. The annual festival ends with the icons immersed in the Aruvi river. This temple was praised in Tamil poetry by the saints Sambanthar and Sunderar, who described its location, the port of Mantota and the roar of the ocean near it. The poems described the temple, the *gopuram,* and mainly the beauty of its icons. With these poems the fame of the temple became widespread.

On the same trip we took another smaller sandy road to the Madhu church. The Madhu church was a beckoning shrine to people of all religions. On the approach road, a small white, painted church sprang into view amidst a grove of the tall and thickly branched trees. This gave the impression of a jungle shrine. It was a Marian shrine and the holiest shrine for many Roman Catholics of the whole island and particularly to the northern Roman Catholics. For most of the year there would be the regular worshippers of that church as well as visitors from far and near. In

August, the place would be overrun by devotees and piety, as it was the festival of the church, coinciding with the assumption of Mary.

The festival of the Roman Catholic Church here was much like that of the Hindu temple. The Hindu converts made it so. There were many masses like the *pooja*s and ceremonial processions in which the icon of Mary was taken round the church. A flag too was raised at the commencement of the festival. The history of this church was legendary. It was at first a shrine of Pattini that followed the cult of her anklet brought by King Gajabahu. He may have built the shrine to be away from Anuradhapura, the Buddhist capital of that time. It became a temple known as the Amman temple, as Pattini was regarded as a mother, an avatar of Siva's consort Parvati. The tank built next to the temple was always called *kovil kulam* in Tamil, meaning the temple tank. This temple survived till the Portuguese era and then lay in ruins.

The Madhu statue of Mary was originally in Manthai in the Mannar District, patronized by the Portuguese and the local Roman Catholics. Mary of this statue was called the 'Lady of Good Health.' With the Dutch invasion and persecution of the Roman Catholics, the statue was taken by a few Jesuit Priest and Roman Catholic families of Mannar to Madhu. It was installed at the site of the destroyed temple and among its ruins.

A shrine was built. A larger number of devotees followed suit and settled in Madhu, a thickly forested area of the Vanni. With the end of persecution and the revival of Roman Catholicism under British rule, Jesuit authority ceased. A small church was built only in 1872, with a facade, presbytery, a chapel with a wooden altar and a grotto to the 'Lady of Lourdes.' In 1920 a special ceremony of crowning the statue took place.

In 1944 the present church was built. The wooden altar was replaced by marble. The sanctuary wall was replaced with blue and white marble. The church had a stark white beauty standing in contrast to the surrounding green trees. Devotees sat on the cemented floor with a couple of pews only at the back of the church. Devotees flocked there whenever they were in need of healing or when they prayed for the healing of others.

It was a quiet few hours that we stayed in the church's precincts, and then proceeded back to the east through thick jungle and arid plains with shrub vegetation.

Our first journey by train to Colombo in the nineteen twenties was memorable. It was not many years since the railway was extended to Jaffna. There was just a day train plying between Jaffna and Colombo.

There was such excitement and anticipation of the journey. Even the clothes we were to take became a hot topic, undecided whether the length of our dresses would be in fashion in Colombo.

We boarded the train at the Jaffna station in the early hours of the day. Excitement turned to trepidation as we wondered whether we would have seats in any compartment as the train had started from Kankesanthurai. My brother had jumped in and stretched himself on two seats. Seats we did have and the journey gave us a couple of hours' enjoyment. Then it became tedious and tiring. The hot air blew in through the windows and was laden with the grit of the coal. There was the screeching noise of metal wheels on metal rails and the banging of the cylindrical steel connections between compartments. Then there was this great push forwards of our bodies when the train stopped at a station. If I remember, it stopped at twenty stations at least. At every station there was a high-pitched tooting of the train, a hissing of steam and the train started off again. There was a repeat performance of all these at every station.

We arrived at Maradana and it was not the pleasantest part of Colombo to arrive at. The poorer people of Colombo seemed to have gathered there. There was a cacophony of cycle bells and rickshaw bells which competed with hawkers shouting their wares. Rickshaws were the conveyance of the Europeans and the locals alike. Only a couple of British-made cars were seen at the station. We looked anxiously around and spotted Thurai with a smile on his usually stern face. He literally packed all of us, including himself, in two rickshaws. The rickshaw pullers seemed to match each other in physical features and in the rhythm of their movements. They all seemed tall, gaunt and were from the immigrant workers from South India and had a typical accent in their spoken Tamil. Their feet were in old worn leather slippers and flip flopped in time with the rhythm of their feet as they ran pulling their rickshaws. The rickshaws turned into narrow roads and the city now seemed to us so green and quiet. This made an impression on my sister, who had commented nonstop on the dirt and noise of Colombo.

There was then no pang of conscience about using these rickshaws, one human pulling another. It was many years later that we thought it amiss to ride such a vehicle. The rickshaw made of a small leather seat and a thick cloth cover that could be pulled over to shield the passenger from the hot sun or the rain. The seat was astride a shaft that had, to our young eyes, two enormous wheels and two long shafts jutting out in front that were gripped by the rickshaw man as he pulled us along.

Travelling first through broad and then narrow streets, we arrived in Kotahena at my brother-in-law's home. There was such a rich mix of people living in the area. The Sinhalese, Burghers, Tamils and Muslims jostled each other for space. In religious belief, the majority of them were Roman Catholics and the Kotahena cathedral was the centre of their lives. The Tamils from Jaffna made their homes there when their husbands were employed mostly in the middle-grade clerical jobs of the government service, or in the private sector. Kotahena was considered the best residential area and, in fact, was recalled as the first Cinnamon Gardens of Colombo. The rich bought lands, built houses of Dutch architecture and settled in them for many generations. It was many years later that the cinnamon gardens of the Dutch were cleared, still verdant with trees, and became the popular Cinnamon Gardens of Colombo seven. Politicians of all races bought a few acres in this locality and built palatial homes on that land.

Kotahena being close to the harbour was a Portuguese enclave with its churches and the converts to Roman Catholicism. The Dutch too made it their domain, and converted the churches and the houses to Dutch architectural designs. The house my sister lived in had a small walled-in garden that abutted the road and was so similar to our Dutch house in Jaffna. A narrow but elongated flight of steps led to the verandah. The house was separated from the neighbour's by a common wall and there was hardly any space between the house and this wall. The richer households had horse carriages and walked the horses through the house from the stables at the rear. The horse keeper, always named Muthu, walked behind the horse with a pail held at its rear end to collect the horse's dung, in case it dropped, within the house.

The Chetty population, the merchants originally from South India, had trickled down the western coast to Negombo and then further down to Colombo. Many of them put down their roots in Kotahena. The majority of them converted to Roman Catholicism. With conversion, they took on Portuguese names but added the Tamil word *pillai*, which became *pulle*. *Pillai* denoted their high-caste origins. Chetty too became Chitty, and Venderkoon, meaning in Tamil 'king of kings,' became Vanderkoen and sounded Dutch too. However some clung to their original and pure Hindu Chetty names, like Casichetty and Perumal.

The large and elaborate Roman Catholic cathedral was not only the focus of worship to all the Roman Catholics of this area but to those outside it. The deep toll of the church bell of this church was such a contrast to the melody of a carillon of the church near our home in Jaffna. A Sunday saw the worshippers walking down our road, the females in light-coloured Sunday best. A white veil would be over their heads and a rosary in their hands entwined between fingers. I remember the middle-aged man in a white suit who walked our road daily on his way to work. Every Roman Catholic home down the road had either an icon of Jesus or Mary within an ornate wood and glass case in their drawing room. The statue was seen easily through the large Dutch windows of that room. It was also seen from a window of my sister's house. This gentleman would doff his hat whenever and wherever he saw an icon. We saw him doing this through our window. There were so many Roman Catholic homes adjacent to ours this resulting in walking with his hat held aloft while he went past all these houses. This scene enacted daily kept us in fits of giggles, but we did admire his religious fervour.

There was much bonhomie among all communities living in Kotahena. The chatter was over walls and most of it was about customs and culinary adventures in making different kinds of food of the other communities, especially trying out a variety of the favourite Dutch sweets.

My young nieces were attending the Dutch Reformed church and the school attached to it. These nieces were the first to refer to us, the younger three sisters of their mother, as *Sinnammah* - the small mother, *Seeniammah* - the sugar mother and *Assaiammah* - the love mother. These pet names were also carried on by the nieces of my older sister.

The Calvinist church my sister and family attended was architecturally more ornate than the ones in Jaffna. It probably was rebuilt from the partly destroyed Portuguese Roman Catholic church. It had a high roof which looked like a high steeple. The roof too was also circular in parts, triangular in parts and double storeyed in parts. The name of this church was Wolfendhal, which seemed to be a mixture of names. Probably the Portuguese church that stood there may have been one of the Lady of Guadalupe churches found in Ceylon. The Madonnas that were in these churches was a favourite icon of the southern European nations. There was no river or valley at the site of the church in Kotahena, as in the original Church but the site was beautiful, with crowded trees and beautiful gardens. For posterity the Dutch may have retained the 'Loupe' of the Spanish name for wolf, and changed the valley and river to 'Dhal,' a garden in Dutch. The Wolfendhal church became a landmark in Kotahena. The school of that church was known for its discipline and the Christianity that we listened to in that church was Calvinist.

Kotahena later became crowded. The infrastructure though remained the same. There was plenty of land in the south of Colombo. The Tamils of Kotahena, mostly the Hindus, bought large extents of land in Wellawatte and moved out of Kotahena. Houses and temples came up in Wellawatte and more families moved into that locality. My sister moved too.

Subsequent train journeys from Jaffna ended at the Fort Station which was noisier but more spacious. Anxiety at arrival ceased when we saw Thurai, and our trip by rickshaw was to Wellawatte. My sister and family lived in a small house within a large garden in High Street. The house, which was rented, never changed its appearance nor did the garden flourish as the landlord made it remain so. Fifty years later, it stood there as before, and may remain so for ever.

It was in Colombo that we met the *thorombelkaraya*. He trundled into the garden ringing the bell of his cycle loudly. He had a large box on his cycle which contained every type of trinket a girl desired and in addition he sold practical things like pins, needles, buttons and beautiful laces. We had only the Chinese traders in Jaffna. They carried bundles of materials ranging from cotton to gorgeous silks, neatly arranged wrapped in brown khaki cloths and carried on their shoulders. The trader would unwrap the bundle on the verandah of our home and painstakingly display every material he had. Invariably we did buy something from him. Quite a few Chinese families lived in a particular interior village in Jaffna. In addition there were a few local people who had brought back to Jaffna their adopted Chinese daughters from Malaya, when they fled back home during the war.

The House in Wellawatte as seen in 2012

The train journeys back to Jaffna always seemed an anticlimax to the journey to Colombo. Life was busier and bustling than the quiet conservative life in Jaffna. The Jaffna railway station itself had a rural look to it. On getting back to Jaffna we rushed to the well to wash the dust and grit off the clothes, a constant feature of train travel. Washing and bathing were at the well. The well was not half as deep or broad as the wells in our village. The water was drawn using a bucket and pulley. The *thula*, the well sweep, became an object of the distant past. There was no dawdling at the well as before. Soap became the fashion to keep body as well as head and hair clean. Bathing at the well had been an experience to the younger ones, an adventure in our village.

In the village Saturday was the day of washing the hair thoroughly with a homemade shampoo. It was years later that shampoo came in bottles. The making of this decoction took time, so it became a communal affair and many females chipped in to make it and then used it. The shampoo was made in a clay pot. Ugly, hard, herbal black pods with seeds, the *siyakai*, bought from a shop were soaked in a pot of water and placed on a temporary fireplace made in the garden. The fire was kept alight with many sticks and dry leaves from the garden and it took an age for the hard pods to soften. Limes, preferably the overripe ones, were cut and added to the pot together with a fistful of fenugreek seeds. When well-done the pods became a soggy mess with a pungent smell. Each female took a bowlful of this, further mashed it, took handfuls of it and massaged it through her hair. It was not unusual to see the males too using this shampoo. The females trekked to the well wrapped in dark coloured and floral printed cloth that covered the bosoms and torsos. The cloths prevented their figures being silhouetted by the sun or outlined by the water poured on them.

My sister had hair that reached her knees and she would need help to rub the shampoo in and it was left on the head for about half an hour. Many buckets of water were needed to pour on their heads to wash away the debris of the shampoo, shreds of the pods, lime and dill seeds from their heads. The hair was left lustrous, and more than this was the feeling of utter cleanliness of body and head. My sister would take the longest time at the well and I with my short hair the shortest. The unwritten rule was that the cemented portion of the well, the apron, should be left spotlessly clean for other members of the extended family. Between Saturdays, there would be 'cat washes' and body washes, but not the long-winded shampoo baths. My sister's hair would stay lustrous till the next shampoo day. I remember sitting on a rough stone on the apron of the well, usually used for beating the clothes on, and watching the scene of the bathers.

Trincomalee as I remember it was truly beautiful and nature made it so. The waters of the Bay of Bengal lipped or lapped the edges of almost every part of town. The land was dry and unyielding to the growth of green trees unless nurtured by the people. The people in the east were not as industrious or hard working as the people of the north, who made the same type of soil fertile.

Of the waters collected around this town, the most beautiful was the harbour. It was not symmetrical. It had two picturesque headlands which protected it from the monsoonal onslaught. These headlands gave a hidden enclosure called the inner harbour. This became a haven for ships. The British naval ships which were anchored there were not seen from the outer harbour, but were seen from the sky and were bombed by the Japanese during the Second World War.

Verdant islands dotted this calm water; the most familiar to us was Sober Island, with its shore covered with vegetation. It had a beautiful avenue within. It was maintained by the British naval

Approach to the Harbour

Avenue of Sober Island

establishment stationed in Trinco for many years. We would see, on our many motor launch trips in the harbour, the elephants followed by their babies, swimming to Sober island from an adjacent island to relish the vegetation there. In its season the blue whales made their home in the outer harbour and there were shoals of them. They soared out of the water and slipped back with beauty and grace. We watched them for hours from a naval motor launch and never tired of these outings.

The naval establishment, well protected by metal fencing, was easy to visit with the permission from the navy. The British conquered Ceylon in 1798, and this was their first establishment. They were there till a few years after independence. Within it was the beautiful and spacious Admiralty House, the home of the chief of the British navy.

At one end of the harbour were the ruins of Fort Ostenburg, built by the Dutch who were the previous rulers. Hills could be seen beyond the harbour and in the distance. To the north of the harbour was a horseshoe-shaped bay. One side of the bay was a hill named Dutch Point. On it stood a typical sprawling Dutch designed house. This became the official residence of the government agent of the British and later of the officers belonging to the elite Ceylon Civil Service. On the other side was another promontory on which stood Fort Frederick, so named by the

British who captured it from the Dutch. The latter claimed it after their conquest from the Portuguese.

An island in the Trincomalee Harbour

Swami Rock, Trincomalee

Fort Frederick was actually a peninsula with a narrow isthmus and a wide, bold front of sheer precipitous rock jutting out a mile to sea. This crag rose from the sea, probably due to volcanic action, to a height of over a thousand feet. Its sheerness was broken by a ledge very close to its summit. The town of Trincomalee lay at the bend of the bay beyond the rock. This promontory was called Swami Rock by the British, but it once had a grand Hindu temple called the Temple of a Thousand Pillars. The Chinese spotted it on their travels and called it a pagoda, as they referred to every temple they saw in the East whether it was a Buddhist or a Hindu temple.

There was no writing about a kingdom in the north till the thirteenth century. It was a fiefdom of chiefs or there were tribes and their chiefs. It was during this time and many years after that history mixed with legends began. One of these was associated with Ravanan, the king of ancient Lanka. Ravanan had been a great devotee of god Siva and built a shrine to him on the promontory of Swami Rock. He, with his mother Kaikeyi were ardent worshippers here. Ravanan was at this rock when he heard of Kaikeyi's death which had occurred many miles away. The funeral rituals and where they were to be done by Ravanan was the beginning of the legend associated with the Kanniya hot springs.

Ravanan very foolishly abducted Sita, the wife of prince Rama, when they were in the forest to which they were exiled from their royal kingdom. Ravanan abducted Sita in revenge for the mutilation of his sister Surpanahaika's nose and ears by Lakshmanan, the brother of prince Rama, who was also in exile. Ravanan fled with Sita in his airborne chariot and hid her in various parts of Lanka. Finally he hid her in a beautiful garden in the central hills of the island. The first place he hid her was thought to have been at Swami Rock. He had cut a huge cleft on a side of its promontory and hidden her in it. This cleft was named Ravanan's Cut. Worshippers who walked up the rock would see it on the side of the promontory, not far from the start of theirs climb. It was hard to imagine Sita hiding in it, unless there was a dry ledge above the water. The constant waves of the Bay of

Bengal that whooshed in and out of the cleft with such great force would have drowned Sita.

Ravanan was known to be an accomplished musician and sang lyrics in praise of god Siva, which is still remembered in Tamil poetry. King Mahasen was supposed to have destroyed the shrine in the sixth century. It was rebuilt as a small temple. It was, however, the Chola conquest of the north in the tenth century that saw the building of the temple on a massive scale. The Chola conquest of South India and Lanka saw a renaissance of Hinduism and Tamil culture, as they brought with them the architecture, music and dance related to Dravidian Hinduism.

The Chola Prince Kulokottan brought artisans and granite stones from South India. He built many temples, each with a thousand pillars as seen in the five Eeswaran, the Sivan temples, built in Ceylon. The Swami Rock temple complex had three *gopurams*, a well and a sunken tank built in its vicinity. The water in that well was used for the rituals and rites of worship in the temple especially during its festival time. With its fame spreading far and wide, many pilgrims from India visited this temple and they named it Dakshina Kailasa, the southern abode of Siva. It was the most prestigious temple of its time and was called Koneeswaran temple. The name Koneeswaran was derived from the Sanskrit word for Siva, Gokkaneeswara. In fact, the rock of the temple and the whole place surrounding it, including Trincomalee, was referred to as Gokkana, the name which remained as such till the Portuguese arrived. The anglicized Trincomalee was from the Tamil word Thirukoneeswaramalai, which literally means the holy Koneeswaran hill.

King Gajabahu the Fourth was an ardent worshipper at this temple and endowed it generously. Many Tamil poets sang hymns in praise of the temple and the verses of their hymns were carved on the inner surface of its granite façade. These hymns were later written in books of Tamil poetry.

The facade too had an oracle carved in Tamil that described some physical features of the would-be conquerors of Lanka. They were described as the 'blue eyed' ones, the 'blonde haired' ones, the 'cats-eyed' ones and lastly the 'doe-eyed' ones.

One of the most ardent devotees of this temple was King Segarajasingham who ruled in Jaffna. He obtained the Sanskrit Hindu literature that gave the early history of the temple and translated it to Tamil. It was fortuitous that the Mogul Empire did not extend to southern India or Lanka, as it would have meant the destruction and desecration of these enormous temples, as was done in the north of India. However, the Portuguese arrived, and the king of Portugal ordered the Viceroy de Saa to destroy all temples and mosques in the north. In 1624 on the auspicious day of the Hindu New Year, the Koneeswaran temple was destroyed. The pillars, walls, carvings, oracles and every part of the temple was destroyed. Since the entrance of all Hindu temples faces the east, the great doorway of this temple, with its granite lintels and pillars that were closest to the promontory of the rock were pushed over into the sea.

The fleeing Brahmin priests managed to drop some of the larger bronzes into the well in the vicinity of the temple, but fled with the more beautiful processional bronze statues to a place which later became the village of Thampalakamam, named after the Thampalaeeswaran icon. It was so named as it had a circlet of small copper phalli carved on the bronze icon. The devotees themselves hid some of the icons under the soil of the temple. The Portuguese made use of the huge granite blocks of the temple to build the wall of their fort around the peninsula that included the remains of the temple. The carved poems and oracles disappeared within the wall of the fort.

The Dutch, who conquered Trincomalee after the Portuguese, rebuilt only a part of the wall of the fort destroyed by them and had no inclination to restore the fort or the temple. The Dutch then had to build palisades and smaller fortresses to withstand the British onslaught of a later date. The Dutch refused entry to the Hindus to worship at the promontory of the rock.

The fort was named Fort Frederick by the British, probably in honour of the first governor of Ceylon. They allowed freedom of worship to all religions. The Hindus trekked back to the rock and commenced worship at the place where the original shrine was and later at the temple built there.

It was only in 1950 that the restoration of the temple was done but never to its original grandeur. The bronze icons were remade. Deep sea divers, Arthur C. Clarke and Mike Wilson, recovered some of the large bronzes and the larger granite statues from the seabed below the promontory of the rock. They were brought to the surface and the granite icons placed near the temple. Those bronzes recovered from the sea, the buried smaller bronzes and those that were hidden in the well were retrieved and worshipped again in the temple.

The long walk from the gate of the fort to the promontory of the rock was an act of devotion to the Hindus and a walking exercise to non-Hindus. The Hindus would do this frequently, but more so on Fridays when a string of devotees in colourful attires, *pottus* on their foreheads and flowers in their hair trudged that long and uphill road to attend the evening *pooja*. The *pooja*, at whatever time it was held, had one distinctive feature. In the midst of the *poojas* to the different icons within and without the temple, the Hindu priest stepped down with his acolyte on to the narrow ledge just beneath the promontory. He performed a *pooja* towards the

The Chola Pillar

The pooja – from the ledge to the old temple below

original doorway which was believed to be under the water. While chanting, his prayers he threw fresh flowers, held a lighted lamp with burning camphor on it and swung a brazen censor smoking with incense in the direction of the entrance of the old temple.

A coconut was broken and its halves tipped over into the sea. The devotees remained at a safe distance from the ledge. The other onlookers were groups of monkeys. They were at every pooja awaiting titbits of coconut, banana and cooked rice that were in the hands of the devotees. If not given they snatched them from the devotees hands as they had become quite cheeky after many years of living in the vicinity of the temple. The scenery round the *pooja* was sharp and beautiful at sunset, the colours of the sunset adding to the picture. A small granite pillar, a part of the original temple, was buried upright and kept as a reminder of the ancient past for posterity. This pillar was mistakenly thought to be the spot where the Dutch maiden threw herself into the ocean on seeing her faithless lover sailing away.

The gate of the fort had a large granite icon to god Ganesh. The British occupied this fort for many years. Its courtyard teemed with tame deer which were fed by the residents. Their numbers dwindled after the British left, with loss of their sustenance and poaching. Within this fort stood a colossal banyan tree whose branches had gone to root and gave the impression of many trees standing together. There

Fort Frederick

Banyan Trees in the Fort

were primitive cannons and cannon balls lying around. The walls of the fort had been broken in many places and hardy trees grew in these gaps and leaned over the ocean. Colonial houses were many in that open space, some probably of Dutch origin, with open spaces, columns and large windows within those houses. Many were built by the British for their official use.

The festival of the temple held in the early months of the year lasted eighteen days. As in all other temples, each day had its particular rites and rituals for particular icons. Each family who had been in residence for many years in Trincomalee took pride in conducting the non-Brahmin activities on a particular day of the festival. The ceremony of the immersion of the icons was quite different. The old temple tank had not been rebuilt. The well of the temple was made sacrosanct and was kept covered and locked until festival time. On the auspicious day of immersion of icons, the well was opened, filled with water to the brim and the immersion ceremony took place.

The temple's processional icons were taken out in ornate chariots pulled by the devotees through the main gate of the fort to the main sea beach of the town. More devotees followed it and thronged the beach. The icons were placed in a colourful boat and taken out a little distance into the sea and immersed accompanied by loud salutations from the devotees. Many of the devotees plunged into the sea after the icons were immersed. During

A Colonial building in the Fort

Sivarathri, the processional icons were taken in gaily decorated chariots through equally decorated streets of the town. The chariots stopped at every welcoming home and the icon's blessings were showered on it.

The Chola dynasty that built temples in the north conquered more lands towards the south and made Polonnaruwa its capital, under King Rajendra I. Hindu temples of Chola architecture, mainly Sivan temples, were built in it and the city was first named Jananatha Mangalam and named after the settlers who were Brahmins. The Chola Viceroy Lankesvara ruled as proxy for the king. The province became divided into *nadus* and *urs*, which meant cities and towns in Tamil. The regional name was changed to Jananamapuram and then to Polonnaruwa. The Chola rule went on until 1067, when the Pandyans and the Sinhalese rulers who were the common enemies of the Cholas battled against it. Ultimately King Vijayabahu defeated Kulothungam the Chola ruler. The Chola presence came to an end in 1070. Poets sang praises of many temples they visited. Pulasthavar the poet who sang the praises of the temple was honoured with a granite statue in Polonnaruwa which has escaped the ravages of time.

Vijayabahu and the kings who succeeded him till King Parakramabahu's reign supported Saivism, in addition to safeguarding Buddhism. These kings had wives of the South Indian dynasties, especially of the Pandyan kingdom. Parakramabahu was a grandson of a Pandyan prince. These kings followed non-Buddhist Hindu rituals as well as keeping to the Buddhist texts. Since these Saivite temples were protected by the kings, the ruins were due more to time than by destruction by the armies of conquerors.

Trincomalee was not only beautiful in its harbour area but there was beauty along the North Eastern coastline too. Almost opposite the sea beach was the largest, starkly white, columned building. It was probably built by the Dutch, and the British used it as an Admiralty building, coordinating all their naval activities in that region. Viewed above its retaining walls it looked as if it had no doors or windows, only colonnaded spaces within, with the sea breeze rushing through. It must have been the largest and most impressive official building in the East.

With the departure of the British the building was ravaged by time and neglect. The smooth walls changed from brilliant white to a cracked and discoloured one. The elegant lady seemed to have fallen on difficult times. The coastal rutty gravel roads went past the bedraggled end of town with its small insignificant shops and poor merchandise. At the end of these little shops stood the pretty granite church – the church of Our Lady of Guadalupe. Her name had been transported from Castille of Spain, where her statue was one of three 'Black Madonnas. A Spanish priest while serving here was probably responsible for this name in Ceylon.

Legend said that this statue was carved by Luke, the Apostle of Christ and later Pope Gregory I gave it to the Diocese of Seville. When the Moors overran Seville, a few priests took this statute and buried it near the river Guadalupe in Eritremadura. Later, a shepherd, in the fourteenth century, claimed he saw a vision of this Madonna and persuaded the priests to dig at the site of his vision. They found the statue and built a shrine which later became a great monastery. When King Alfonso the Eleventh defeated the Moors in the fourteenth century he attributed his victory to the help of the Madonna. Then the devotion turned into a cult. Cortes and his followers took the cult of Guadalupe to Mexico and the most number of churches to it were built there. The official crowning of the icon was only in 1928.

The Navy House

Devotion of the worshippers was no less at the church in Trincomalee. It had a black granite and grey mixed appearance. The inner sanctum reminded me of the Madhu church but the latter was small.

The coastline road went past small sleepy villages made picturesque only by the sea and the broad seashore. One of them was Nilaveli. A few small hotels were seen. This village, however, had fertile soil and produced the tastiest onions and vegetables. The women folk in colourful saris sat by the roadside adjacent to their gardens and sold their harvest. The Methodist Mission left its mark in the village with its church, vernacular school and homes for the poorer children of the area. The sea at Nilaveli had a great attraction for visitors, especially Pigeon Island, a few miles away, reached by boat. The sea around was glassy and blue, with sharp corals and fish even quite close to the shore. Covered footwear was needed to wade into the sea. There were a greater number of crows than pigeons on the island with the intrusion of visitors. Pigeon Island was deserted most of the year especially during the harsh monsoon months.

The coastline was not only bleak but hotter, with the direct rays of the sun beating on us. It shimmered with mirages and was interrupted by groves of coconut palms and houses within. The road then met a lagoon with its ferry, which had to be boarded to cross over to the fishing village of Kuchchaveli. The rest house of that village, built exactly like any other rest house, was at the edge of a wide open beach. It was the only one for miles around. The rest of the village and most of the seashore was the domain of the fisher folk. Kuchchaveli was the ideal retreat for a day's picnic and sea bathing.

If a branch road was taken on the way to Kuchchaveli, it would lead to the Buddhist temple at Thiriiyaya. This temple as well as the one at Velgam, close to the Kanniya hot wells, had Hindu Dravidian architectural bases and a white *dagoba* built on it. Velgam *vihara* had in addition a large number of granite stones strewn in its courtyard. The surfaces of these stones were covered with Tamil-lettered sentences. This may have been a sign of conversion of the locals to Buddhism.

The north coast road then ended with a ferry to Pulmoddai. The ferry travelled over a large calm and beautiful lagoon, surrounded by shrubs and trees. The lagoons teemed with fish, crabs and prawns. They were sold very cheap at both ends of the ferry as very few travellers visited this region. The sea sands of Pulmoddai were rich in ilmenite. The beach was noisy with machinery and gangs of workers hauling out this sand for export to Japan, for its manufacture of ceramics. A little further inland there was an uphill gravel path to the Seashore. To reach the beach we traversed a beautiful green glade of shrubs and tall elegant slim trees. Their branches made a canopy for us and shielded us from the hot sun and the humidity of that place. After twenty minutes of walking there was the dazzling sight of the most beautiful and bluest sea that we had ever seen. We had to carefully tread the rocky outcrop that led down to the beach. The grains of sand on that beach was large, almost the size of grains of raw rice. The beach is named '*Arisimalai*', the rice beach. The sand, when poured on the splayed palm of the hand did not trickle out between the fingers. Further on and over a larger hill was another beach named the 'Kurakkan' beach as the sands of the beach was fine. The walk to that beach was considered quite difficult for most people. The coastal road ended at Pulmoddai. There were no motorable roads to Mullaitivu, the next town on the coast, had to be reached through the Vanni.

Trincomalee had not only the main beach in the heart of town, popular and populous every evening, but there were other less visited beaches further south. There was the sea beach at Sandy Cove. The sea was rough here, with huge waves. It was not popular for bathing because a story of it taking a human sacrifice every year was rife. There was a Hindu temple near it and many worshippers came to this beach to perform the final rites for their dead and to visit the temple. Trincomalee had the most number of Hindu temples per square area of land and per population. Every Hindu icon had its own temple.

There was also the Marble Beach. The sea of this beach looked like a calm, leaden and salty lake with hardly a ripple of a wave. It was not popular for the joy of swimming was lost without waves.

Trincomalee was the only town where there was a temple to Saturn. Many would flock to this temple every Saturday of the Hindu month of October. They lit wicks in small clay pots filled with gingelly oil and placed it in front of the temple to placate the god of the planet Saturn to nullify the bad periods in their astrological charts.

It was very much later in life that I visited Arippu, the coastal town that had Hinduism and Roman Catholicism existing side by side. It became famous for its pearl fisheries. When we saw Arippu, its coastal region was truly barren, especially in the region of Condaachi. It was a little village, once green with luscious paddy fields. These fields had been watered by a tank - the water to it probably was brought by a tributary of the Malwatu Oya. The village had lost its initial glamour when the Hindu temple was destroyed by the Portuguese. The temple was always the centre of the lives of villagers, who had lived near it and now had moved further away. The tank was left in ruins. The village and the coastal areas were the dustiest and the most barren of the places we had seen. Condaachi had come to life and became noisy in that season when the Portuguese started the pearl fisheries. There was then the influx of Arabs, Indians and the Tamils to Mannar and Kalpitiya. Condaachi Bay and the further sea had the richest fields of pearl oysters.

Ruins of Governor North's Bungalow

In the midst of all this barrenness stood the still elegant but ruined house of Governor North. The white coral and sand-structured architecture was even seen in the ruins. The Dutch had exhausted the pearl fisheries when the British arrived in 1796. The British were broke, and the pearl fishery seemed to promise a wonderful source of revenue.

John Jarvis, a junior officer of the East India Company, was requested to start the fishery. He neither saw its value nor wanted to run it and backed out. In 1796 a native of Jaffna living in Coromandel leased the fishery from the British and then leased it to another and made a fortune on that transaction after the abundant haul of pearl oysters. In 1797 Candappa Chetty, a native of Jaffna, leased it out and made another fortune on it.

In 1804 Governor North arrived in Ceylon and was determined to revive the fishery. He wanted to personally supervise it and built a house near the sea and on a rocky headland. History related that he designed it himself. He was an admirer of white Doric columns and built his two storeyed house of that design, a few miles from the fishery. Though it was small, it had a splendid appearance and was considered the most beautiful of buildings in the island as it glistened white in the hot sun. The ground floor had bedrooms and the upper floor his large bedroom and a dining room. A small staircase from the upper floor led to the terraced roof from where he saw the entire surrounding land and the sea.

Governor North and his retinue of officials were carried by palanquins which took six days to reach Arippu from Colombo. In addition to the officials there were the sepoys, soldiers and the cannon taken for his protection. Their huts, tents and barracks were built near his house and on the seashore.

The pearl fishery started in the fine weather of late January, which was between the northeast and southwest monsoons, and each fishery lasted for thirty days. Renters of the pearl banks were called for and of all his subordinates only the renters were permitted to sit with the governor and discuss business. The renter in 1804 was from Jaffna.

The successful renter brought his boats and the divers from Jaffna, the coastal villages of the northwest of Ceylon and from the

An artist's impression of the original house of Governor North

Bungalow of Commander – Pearling Station

Coromandel Coast. The divers were the former expert divers of chanks, the conch shells.

There had been one hundred and fifty banks and six thousand divers for the fishing of thirty days. The boats were equipped with everything needed for the fishing of pearl oysters. Fishing rights were sold to the owners of the banks who built their huts on the seashore of Condaachi. They were more like shelters rather than houses. The pearl banks with one species of oysters to be harvested were predetermined the previous month of October, and only a couple of fisheries were worked for one month of harvesting. Ceylon Moors and Tamils were the only communities involved in the pearl fishing.

Fishing started at dawn after the Hindus finished their religious rites and rituals. A pilot boat guided the boats to their appointed fishing areas. The diver in his attire of only a loin cloth would get ready to dive. The tools he used were absolutely primitive. A granite stone of fifty pounds in weight had a strong thick rope passed through a hole bored through the middle of this stone. A loop of this strong rope left on the top of the stone was attached to the oar of the boat. The diver stepped out from the boat onto the stone, put his foot in the loop and balanced himself. A basket, a crude wooden hoop with network suspended by a rope, was thrown after him. He went down holding his nose with one hand and with the other jerked the rope on the stone which was a sign to give a length for him to go down to the bottom. When he had reached the bottom he disengaged his foot and the stone was raised and another diver took his place. Two men worked with the same stone. While at the bottom, on the richly oyster covered soil, the diver collected all the oysters into his basket, filled it and tugged at the rope and came up, usually before the basket did. He would come up earlier if he had a nose bleed. A nose bleed was considered good for the diver to do successive dives. On a good harvest day, he brought out of that sea one hundred and fifty oysters.

Fleet of Pearling Boats

The village of Condaachi had come to be associated with the pearl fishery. The name of this village may have been the name of a Chetti pearl merchant. Condaachi and Ondaachi were merchants who came from Madurai, South India. With the closure of the pearl fishery they migrated south along the western coast. They came under the influence of the Dutch with regard to religion, language and at times by marriage the ending of their names, became like that of the Dutch.

The fishery meant that a large number of hangers-on were around. The shark charmer was assured of his job every day of fishing. He sat, almost naked, on the seashore or in a boat, chanted his *mantrams*, ritual verses till the fishing ceased for the day. He was the *kadalkatti*, the binder of the sharks. The divers wanted to be safe rather than be sorry, though the charmer's effectiveness was suspect.

The boats returned to their allotted places at Condaachi Bay, where the shore became a hive of activity. The oysters were stored in palisades and attached enclosures nearby. A drain ran through these enclosures and picked up any pearls that might have dropped off when the oysters were cleaned. The divers were paid by a quarter of the oysters brought up and cash in Portuguese pagodas.

Diving for Pearls

Of this, a diver had to pay his fellow boatmen, the shark charmer and his servants.

The divers quickly disposed of their share in the market at Condaachi, which was a hub of activity. Since most of those employed at the fishery were Roman Catholics, fishing was not done on Sunday, and the construction of a church was the duty of the governor. The main feast days of the church too were holidays. Women were employed to extract the pearls from decayed oysters. This species of oysters was not edible as it was gummy.

The language of the pearl trade was Tamil, especially for the grading of pearls. The work of sifting and examining the pearls was rented out. Sand was sieved through ten brass sieves. The aperture of each sieve had a different diameter. They were assessed in size from twenty to one thousand. The pearls that fell through the twenty to eighty sieves were called *mell*, the seed pearl. Those that fell through number one hundred to one thousand were called *vadivoo*, meaning beautiful, and again separated and assessed as *anneis*, *annadares* or of other descriptive names. There were eight types of pearls.

The *aanneis* pearls were the best, perfectly round and had the most brilliant lustre. The different descriptions meant different markets. Next came the drilling, again done by drillers who sat on their haunches and used drills made of jak wood. Each drill was fitted with a needle of a particular size. The drill was held by a coconut shell pressed to the forehead of the driller.

With these ready-to-sell pearls the Condaachi market was a hub of bargaining. The sellers spread the pearls on a contrasting bright blue carpet. The Tamils, Muslims and the Chetties bought the pearls. Pearls suitable for a string of pearls were not a great favourite in the north, as pearls never gave the best lustre on a dark skin. The pearls were bought to be inserted in *padakkams*. The Chetties bought them and traded them in the western market but most of the pearls were taken to India. The brokers flourished in this environment of trade. They bought the pearls in lots of the same size. Every night was a carnival night, with gamblers, jugglers, dancers and music. The best had been a female contortionist.

Governor North was disappointed at the poor harvest of pearls that year and did not try again. The only outsiders who made money at the time of the pearl fishery were the fishermen from Negombo, who came to catch fish in demarcated areas away from the pearl banks. They sold their catch to that motley collection of people gathered at Condaachi. With the absence of the pearl fishery, the village went back to bleakness, poverty and to the dusty plains.

My thoughts wander back to Yaalpanam – Jaffna. The name came from the gift given to a musician who played the *yaal*, a basic stringed musical instrument. He won Jaffna as the prize at a competition for musicians. The stringed instrument looked like the mandolin, a musical instrument of the west. The musician who played that *yaal* was probably a minstrel, the song more important than the accompaniment on the plucked strings. The *yaal* was seen by us embossed on stone or in concrete on prominent buildings of Jaffna or seen only in pictures. Nobody played it.

My grandnephew grumbled that there was not only the absence of the *yaal*, but of electric lights itself in Jaffna during the horrible years of the war. A bowl of water topped with a layer of oil with a wick in it burned ever so dimly but longer than a lantern. The students studied by that light. The more ambitious ones sat under the solitary electric light on the road opposite the General Hospital. One read the text, and the others who sat around him heard, learnt and revised their lessons.

The hospital itself was bereft of many medicines during the years of the war. The injectable medicine to stop bleeding from the womb of a woman who had delivered a baby was not available. This was to prevent the Tigers obtaining it too. They should bleed and die from their injuries was the reason.

I long to go to Jaffna, but I am told and don't believe, that there is no train to Jaffna and worse still no railway track on the northern line. I would imagine my niece 'who always received' me at the Jaffna station standing on its platform. It was years before I knew that she had left Jaffna and had left the world too, and I go on.

Violence was unknown in Jaffna in my time. A murder in the peninsula would have been the topic on everyone's lips for six months at least. It all changed with the war. Murder and violence was the stamp of both the army and the LTTE.

My memory always drifts back to my grandfather. As noted earlier he was striking in his physique and personality. His American Mission school education gave him status and respect among the villagers. He was the welcome arbiter in the affairs of the village and sent for when a quarrel started.

Emergency or not, he would still dress in a spotless white *verti*, shirt, and shawl over his shoulder, striding across the sandy lane wearing *chappals*, the slippers, on his feet and holding his silver-knobbed walking stick. He did not wear his turban as it was an unofficial matter. As he approached and spoke to the quarrelling parties, they stopped arguing, smiled sheepishly and dispersed. He had such a winsome and persuasive manner.

The villagers liked him as he was impartial and kind towards all. Quarrels among relatives were rare as relationships were symbiotic. They were dependent on each other for cooperative help in their agrarian activities. Each household was within shouting distance, and when someone was needed or looked for, a shout of "Hoo" was shouted across the compound and someone answered it!

Grandfather's presence was a source of pride to me. However, as I grew older, I realized how matriarchal our households were. My grandfather towering in height above his petite wife was rather afraid of her tongue. Once, his sister's son came to him for financial help. Grandmother was around. Grandfather raised his voice and rebuked his nephew and told him that money didn't grow on trees and that he hadn't any at that moment. In a little lower voice, he said something aside to his nephew. Grandfather seemed to have disappeared for a few minutes. He sneaked back to the house after meeting his nephew in a lane and had given him the money The entire performance was to make his wife believe that he did not help his relatives! Many of the men in that compound would be bossed around and forced to listen to their wives' views too. They did do mostly what their wives requested of them.

The lanes branching off the main road and the one closest to us had a fine layer of sea sand. When it was cool in the evenings, the older male villagers would congregate and sit on a side of the white sand. My grandfather was the presiding villager, giving them all the second-hand news he got from his sons, grandsons, nephews and from whoever dropped in from Jaffna town. Later, I would smile at this memory and thought he must have been the one-eyed man in the land of the blind.

With his robust health he outlived his wife. My father had requested a transfer to a Karainagar school. We were truly surprised when he took over the supervision of grandfather's house. When grandfather took ill and was sadly bedridden he bathed him and fed him with the help of the domestics of the Koviyar caste. We were astonished that father was capable of all this as he was rather selfish and demanding in his ways. He remained in the village till grandfather died. Saddened by his death, the villagers and we keenly felt the loss and openly wept for him.

From early times the Tamils were under the supervision of the Hindu priests. They were present after a newborn's arrival, at puberty, marriage and death. They conducted all the ceremonial rituals and rites of these events. As soon as grandfather died, the *Saiva Kurukkal*, the non-Brahmin priest, was sent for. News of his death was spread verbally. Since grandfather was much revered, respected and was so involved with the local temple and the Sivan temple near Casuarina beach, the villagers wanted to cremate him in a sitting position. This was usually done for a deceased male of the Pandaram caste who worked and cooked for the temple. The first indication of the funeral house was the appearance of an uprooted pair of plantain trees, bearing unripe green fruits, planted at the sides of the front gate.

As soon as grandfather died he was kept in a sitting position by tying his body to a stout pestle. This cannot be done after the body stiffens with time. The washerman and barber were the first to be called, with the drummer. The barber had to shave and give a close hair cut to the eldest son, who had to perform certain rituals of the ceremony with the priest. The washerman made the wooden framework decorated with young coconut leaves which would surround the bier.

As a teenage Christian, I was all agog looking at these ceremonies. A householder brought in so many ingredients, like turmeric, gingelly oil, betel, mango and plantain leaves. There was incense and sandal wood perfume and many other items that I cannot remember now.

The corpse had been washed, dressed and laid on a makeshift bed of planks kept on the cemented platform on a side of the inner courtyard. An uncle had referred to the Hindu calendar and found an auspicious day, barring a Tuesday and a Friday, for the cremation. A brass vessel of water was kept at the head end of the body, but there was no ceremonial brass pot that held a coconut and mango leaves.

Relatives and close family friends sat on mats which were laid round the inner courtyard. The official mourners came along. They were either close female relatives or official paid mourners. They sat or stood in a circle close to the body, put their arms round each other's shoulders and in a keening, loud, high-pitched voice moaned. In their loud moaning the episodes of grandfather's life, what he was and did, especially that he gave generously and was kind to all, was intoned. The mourners gathered at six in the morning and six in the evening to mourn loudly again. I was told that noise and the mourning at a funeral kept evil spirits away.

No fire was lit in the kitchen; food and coffee were brought by family members and relatives, while the body was in the house.

The Pandaram, a member of the middle-level caste, came and sang Hindu lyrics continuously, till the main ceremony started. The *Saiva Kurukkal* arrived and the funeral ceremony started. The body was taken outside and put on a makeshift wooden structure. A mixture of herbal *siyakai* pods and sesame oil was placed on the body. This ritual was done by every male member of the family. Then the same males washed the body, each pouring a vessel full of water on it .The body was dried and dressed in a silk *verti*, shirt and shawl, just as he would have dressed on a happy occasion. As the body was upright, I saw it was more difficult to dress it. The body was kept with the head towards the south.

The priest started the ceremonies. At first he made a small fire in a pot by burning nine kinds of wood, one of which was sandalwood. Then my uncle was asked to pound with a pestle some herbs and rice that were in the mortar, while Sanskrit verses were recited by the priest, who was seated in front of a fire kept aglow with wood shavings, ghee and herbs. At the end of the ceremony all of us grandchildren stood round the body with lighted tapers of coconut fronds, while the priest chanted again. If my grandmother had been alive, it would have been sad to see her dressed in white without the red *pottu*, removing her *thalikodi*, and placing it on his body. It would never be worn again by her. I was truly saddened that very soon his body would be removed for cremation.

The son who did the ceremonies (my father being the eldest was a Christian and was not expected to do the rituals) prostrated himself before his father and took the small pot of fire. The relatives then put grains of rice and silver coins on the mouth of the body probably to wish him a prosperous rebirth. The Koviyar caste of the household touched the bier in respect. Though they were next in caste to the Vellala, they could not take part in the funeral rituals. The bier was then lifted by the Koviyars and taken to the door and on to the road with the older females and the children weeping loudly.

Since grandfather was very active in temple matters, a Brahmin priest did the same ceremony in another part of the compound. Camphor was burnt at regular intervals in various parts of the *valavu* too. The son with the pot of fire led the funeral procession outside the house treading the *pavadai*, the white cloth laid by the washerman. The males of the Koviyar caste carried the bier to the cemetery. The funeral drum beaters of the *Parayar* caste (and only some of that sect did so) accompanied the procession, lit the loud fire crackers and threw a handful of sea sand at regular intervals at the tail end of the procession. This was quite non-religious. In the past, cremations were done within the nearest forest. The mounds of sand indicated the way home from that forest. The children and the females never went to a cremation. Grandfather was taken seated upright to the cremation ground. Flowers and money were thrown on the bier by the villagers.

There was much to do before the males returned. The house was washed, sprinkled with water mixed with saffron. Everything used in the ceremony was discarded. The washerman took away all the clothes used for grandfather after his death. The clay pots were broken, including the kitchen ones. All of us had to bathe ourselves and wash all the clothes we wore before we entered our homes. I was told that the son who did the ceremonies had carried a pot of water on his head and walked round the bier thrice. The pot was pierced by a knife at the end of each circumambulation, signifying life being poured out. Then he had walked backwards to the pyre which he lit. Grandfather had been laid on a sandalwood pyre. Thereafter the lowest caste people had been involved with the cremation till the body was burnt completely.

The house was considered ritually ready when my uncle returned from the cremation ground and his wife poured a vessel of water on him as he entered the house. The first meal cooked in grandfather's home after his death was served to the family and the relatives.

The ashes were collected the next day in a clay pot and kept in an unused part of the house. For the next thirty-one days a constantly lit lamp, an umbrella, a clay pot of water with his tumbler and a pair of sandals were kept in his room. The belief was that he needed these on his way to his next birth, and it was envisaged that the path travelled was similar to that of hot and humid Jaffna. Hinduism was a karmic religion and even the caste born into at any birth was an endowment of karma. It was hoped that each birth brought one's soul closer to God till it merged with the divine. After thirty-one days, similar rituals of a funeral were done by a Brahmin priest and my uncle who did the funeral rites. The priest was given cash, provisions of food and a *verti*. For those thirty-one days, the household was considered an 'untouchable caste.' The householders do not visit nor do others visit them to avoid drinking and eating with them. Temple was taboo for a month if they did so. Meals were vegetarian for the family.

The son who did the rituals and other male members of the family went to the Keerimalai beach with the pot of ash. After some more rituals, the son had waded into the water, with the pot of ash on his shoulder. When he was waist deep he made a gash in the pot with a knife and watched the pot sink.

This particular ceremony at home was repeated on every anniversary of his death. We didn't attend them. We missed grandfather very much. These rituals after death meant nothing to us as Christians. The funeral service for a Christian was so simple.

Prayers were said, lyrics were sung and the dead was always buried. The Roman Catholics in town hired a carriage too to take the dead to the cemetery. The mourners were accompanied by the music of western dirges played on a trumpet and a drum. It was such a mournful procession.

On those rare occasions when we travelled to the south, it was delightful to see streams, lakes and waterfalls, whatever their size; they broke the monotony of the green land. It was not so in the north. Apart from the irrigation tanks, there were no running streams or rivers, leave alone a collection of water. Ponds and pools appeared after the monsoonal deluge and lasted till the sun came with its hot, water-evaporating heat.

Lakes in the east coast were not natural phenomena. They were estuary formations. The Arabs called them the 'Golbs of Serendib.' The water of each lake was prevented from entering the sea by sand bars and deltaic lands of its own making. These formed an indented network of waterways over a distance of almost fifty miles. It stretched from Kinniya in the north to Samanthurai on the south of the east coast.

It was with joy and much anticipation that during the Easter holidays we crossed the seven waterways by ferry when we travelled from Trinco to Batticaloa. There was no proper road to Batticaloa, most of them were rutty and some non-existent. The coastal distance by ferries would be about sixty miles, but the leisurely travel took almost seven hours, as long as by road.

We passed by the largest collection of water, the Allai tank. Allai had been the name of a female chief who ruled that region probably centuries ago. Teals were numerous and flew in swarms over the water and it was renamed Seruvila. King Kavantissa built a *dagoba* at Seruvila but it had gone into disrepair twice over.

These journeys done almost annually became part travel, part picnic, and a leisurely time to stand and stare at every change in scenery and skyline from the ferry, which went over running or still waters. The trip always started at the crack of dawn to catch its coolness, and Batticaloa was reached at the zenith of the day. Everything was packed into the old Plymouth car, a breakfast of sandwiches and coffee was always the menu. The children would see that it went into the car first! The first ferry to Kinniya took half an hour to arrive. Ferry service started only at six in the morning. Kinniya was a small sleepy village of Muslim farmers and poultry keepers. Activity in the village would have started at five and a few men would be waiting for the ferry to Trinco.

We were the first to be ferried for that day. The ferry man would be late at times. He would bolt out of his house with a few shouts. Once, however, he could not be roused. My husband, who always carried his .22 gun since army days, shot into the air and woke the ferry man. He bounded out, dishevelled and bleary eyed, probably so after imbibing his evening toddy of yesterday.

The ferry with its sloping, movable end would be at the water's edge, with the guiding strong iron chain just below the water. It was like a broad platform, a wooden structure which looked sturdy and practical. We got on avoiding the water and jumping on after the car was safely driven onto it. The ferry was guided by the chain together with the ferry man, who guided it with a long bamboo pole, using it as an oar. He was so dexterous with it, turning and rotating the pole to keep it on course and taking us safely across.

The water of the Kinniya over which the ferry went was a large expanse formed by one of the terminal tributaries of the Mahaweli River. The water was usually brown in colour at dawn, a mixture of river and seawater, but still a beautiful scene. There were no plants in it but plenty of water birds skimmed over. Cormorants were plentiful and the grey was interrupted by the purple herons on the shores. The gulls swooped and dived without fatigue.

Too soon for us the crossing by ferry was over. There was a clash of wood and the iron chain noisily scraped the shore. The platform was lowered and the car driven across it. On disembarking, the ferry hire was paid, the ferry man tipped and on we went by those rough roads to the next ferry. It had taken thirty minutes from home and to be ferried across Kinniya. The duration of the trip depended on which side the ferry man was. We would be delayed quite a bit if the ferry was on the other side or in the middle of the water. Patience was a great virtue if a ferry trip was anticipated.

I would look out for Ibrahim, who for years brought eggs and chicken from Kinniya to sell at our doorstep. He was squat, dark skinned and had a brilliant smile that lit up his face. He would take a bus after the ferry ride and walk all over town with a basketful of eggs in one hand and a small circular cage of plaited coir with a few chickens on the other. One week's supply was bought by me, so sure that he would be there in a week's time. He grew richer, and then came on a bicycle with a large wooden box tied to the pillion with eggs and chickens in it. With greater prosperity he came on a motorcycle with more eggs and chickens. He never lost his simplicity over almost twenty years, after which I lost track of him. Probably he had become a big-time poultry farmer. Muslim villagers had a great talent for poultry farming. One unforgettable routine when buying eggs was to immerse the eggs in a basin of water. The good eggs lay flat in the water while the bad ones stood upright. Ibrahim would, with a smile, replace the bad eggs.

We drove on to the next waterway and ferry called Upparu, which meant salty river. The water was brackish with the sea mixed with water from another tributary of the Mahaweli. Unlike Kinniya it seemed fast moving. The ferry man manoeuvred with great finesse to the shore. A few people, and fewer bullock carts, were seen on the opposite shore. Our car was a thing of wonder to them! The road was full of ruts and potholes which slowed progress, but we arrived at the next ferry Raalkuli, which meant the prawn hole. Prawn fishing was the livelihood of that village. There was nobody around; probably the catch of the previous evening would have been sold. The Raalkuli ferry crossed another tributary of the Mahaweli River.

The ferries were replicas of each other and the ferry men seemed similar – tall, lanky and weather beaten. If one ventured into the village, prawns would have been plentiful and selling fast, but it had no interest for us as we knew that a seafood banquet would await us in Batticaloa.

The next ferry was to Muthur. It led us into the large, rich farming village of Muthur, and a part of it had become a town. The village near the ferry was a typical Muslim one. The Muslims in these coastal villages were converts of Tamil Hindus. They were dark skinned, sharp featured, wearing much jewellery, including nose studs. In their culture, they retained the *thalikodi* as a decorative necklace, which was also given at marriage. The dowry system was similar, with the daughter bringing a dowry with her in marriage. This was so unlike the Arabs who had brought Islam to the East, where males in their country had to provide the dowry. The language spoken was as in the north if they had been schooled there or colloquial with every word ending with a prolonged 'ae' sound. The Muthur ferry trip was the longest. The water we crossed was the largest tributary of the Mahaweli River. The Mahaweli ultimately fell, freely and at with great force into the sea at Kottiyar Bay. The ferry man once more cleverly negotiated the ferry over this fast flowing water. The Muthur village we arrived at was sandy, dusty, but shady under the huge tamarind and satinwood trees in the vicinity of the water. It was almost half past ten. The Muthur ferry was always the busiest, as the agrarian society of Muthur had to take its grain and poultry by ferry to Trinco to get a better price for them.

We had a late breakfast. The village urchins never saw much motor traffic there, so they gathered round the old Plymouth, a rarity there, touched it and were bemused by those large tyres. The mothers of these urchins would come by. Their sari was worn differently. They would drape a longer length of the end of the sari over the right and not the left shoulder. This end of the sari would be brought in front and tucked into the waist. These demure conservative females would take the loose fall at the back and modestly cover their heads when they came out of their houses or saw a male. They never covered their faces.

It became hot and humid. We were midway to Batticaloa. However, we had time to visit the spot where Robert Knox landed and the site was marked by a tamarind tree, with no wall round it but a plaque near it. It was here that he was taken prisoner by the Kandyan soldiers and incarcerated in Kandy for many years. It took several years for travel to be made easier to Muthur. A motor launch took passengers from the Trinco harbour and sped through the outer harbour to reach Muthur.

A few miles of travel by road and we arrived at the Kilivetti ferry, which crossed the smaller and probably the final tributary of the Mahaweli River. Crossing that waterway was easy and we arrived at a small modest village. We hardly glanced at it or stopped there as the ground and roads shimmered in the heat. We drove on and arrived at the Verugal ferry, which crossed the fast flowing Verugal River. This being a fresh waterway, the scene from the ferry was very pretty indeed. The birds were more varied and the weeds and plants by the shores were greener. Kingfishers darted across and made a splash of colour among the white and purple herons that stood in the green weeds and the water hens swam passed them in a great hurry. A few further miles by car and we were at the Kathiraveli ferry. Its name meant sheaves of paddy in open spaces. We were nearing the granary of the east. Kathiraveli was a placid and beautiful lake which formed a tributary of the Verugal River. The lake was made even more attractive by the appearance of lotus and hyacinth blooms bobbing on the water, adding to the beauty and peace of the waterway. Birds and butterflies skimmed over the water. Flocks of teal flew across and the cormorants sat like sentinels on rocks drying their wings - which were not waterproof, and herons were in plenty. It was the most pleasant experience we had when we went across the water to the village, which was modest in size but green with paddy within which parakeets screeched.

A few more miles on the road and we came to the last ferry, the Panchenkerni ferry. The place was bustling with small-time

"White Man's Tree"

traders as the shore next to the ferry was covered with seafood and the buyers' purchase of the seafood seemed never to stop. The lagoon formed by the Verugal river was crossed with ease and quickly too. That was the last of the seven ferries. It was long past noon when we entered the town of Batticaloa, a bustling place with waterways, lagoons and long bridges. My husband's niece, as generous as my sister-in-law, had laid out every type of seafood on the table. The giant prawns of Batticaloa did look the most gorgeous of the dishes. Every meal had some new preparation of seafood. The cuttlefish in Trinco were tastier as they were smaller, cut into little rings and then cooked.

We spent a few days and returned, taking the same ferries back home but more tired than when we had set out, which had been in anticipation of a holiday.

I am eighty-six years old. My siblings are no more, so too my close friends of years gone by. I am left with memories that become sharper with time. It seems that their lives, their laughter and their smiles touched me in so many ways. I see familiar places too. I was lucky to have seen many beautiful places in the northeast and regrettably less in the south.

Landscapes of Jaffna opened up as soon as we passed over the lagoon and the salterns spread out at Elephant Pass. The place means where the elephants went through to Jaffna to be shipped from Elephant quay, Kayts. Elephant Pass had a picturesque rest house where we would break journey for a meal or stay overnight. The rest house was so different to the humble dwellings scattered sparsely in that wide space. It was originally a Dutch fort but smaller than the other Dutch forts, probably only a station for the Dutch soldiers who travelled on horseback to or from Jaffna. They would have travelled on the narrow bridle paths, bordered with shrubs, to stop and have their repast at this small fort. We reached the rest house after traversing the bridge common to both motor and rail traffic and taking a sharp turn onto a gravel road that led to a white two-storeyed building. It stood white and stark and bordered the lagoon, breaking the monotony of solitary space and the dry or absent vegetation. A margosa tree had struggled and grown close to the building. The rest house was quaint in its appearance, but still had the Dutch colonnaded and arched

Elephant Pass Rest House

architecture. As a fort it was inconspicuous when compared to the Jaffna fort, the Citadel.

The cemented ground floor with its dining and kitchen rooms led to a wood-floored upper storey reached by an old wooden stairway. The stairway went straight up and abruptly took a right turn in the middle of it, with further steps up. The upper floor had the bedrooms, each large and airy. These rooms always reminded me of my childhood and the Dutch house we lived in Jaffna. There was a corridor running along the length of the upper storey and each room opened onto it. It was sparse in structure and furniture. The amiable rest house keeper, like all his kind, wore the same uniform – the white sarong, the gold-buttoned tunic and slippers on his feet.

If on an overnight stay, we would be up at the crack of dawn, take a hurried breakfast and try to cover a good distance of the road in the cool of the morning. We would pass the salterns and each saltern looked like a bunded paddy field, brilliant white in colour instead of green. The salt pans glistened with salt crystals, and as the morning light fell on them they sparkled and dazzled the eyes if they were looked at for too long.

The 'A9' road was a monotonous straight one. In no time we arrived at Murunkan. No driver of any vehicle or of any religious faith proceeded to Jaffna without stopping and stepping out. It was a sign of respect to the shrine of god Ganesh & Skanda. The Hindus would pray, break a coconut and everyone dropped a few coins into the cash till. The familiar roads, villages and towns with their old unchanged names passed by. As a salve to tired eyes that only saw the arid earth, Pallai would rise up brown and green, with its coconut groves and vegetable plots. We then passed Chavakachcheri, once a village of the Malays and then Navatkuli, dotted with their Calvinist churches, temples and modest homes among open spaces. The churches were originally Dutch and reminded me of the stories we heard about the Dutch, especially of two of them who became a part of the social life of Jaffna. There was Christopheel Wooly, a tradesman, who lived a greater part of his life in Jaffna. He spoke Tamil like a native, and this in itself, and his trade, made him one with the Jaffna people in their social life, and a confidante in their private lives.

Then there was Baldeus, the Dutch pastor who spent eight years in Jaffna. He preached not only in the Calvinist churches, but wherever and whenever there was a crowd gathered at a public place. He would not hesitate to do so standing under a spreading shady tree. Pastor Baldeus travelled much and wrote of the places seen and heard of, both in Jaffna, the east and further south.

Shrine of God Ganesh & Skanda at Murunkan

When travelling to and from the East, the most familiar and frequent stopover was at the Habarana rest house. There seemed to be no variety in the architecture of rest houses. They all had the same long verandah into which the rooms opened. The garden of this rest house was vast, and looked a part of the jungle that surrounded it. A breakfast break, a typical English one, was always looked forward to by us.

Christian missionaries to us meant that we remembered Elizabeth and Mary. They were sent by their mother missions from abroad after being trained more in teaching and less in preaching. Mary had been an Oxford graduate. They came beautifully groomed in pretty, fashionable dresses with beribboned hats and high-heeled shoes. They found out, early in their life, that teaching young ladies was not their vocation. They requested a life of social service wherever it was needed and in any corner of Ceylon.

They were sent to the north. Elizabeth of the Methodist Mission was sent to work at *Navajeevanam* in Paranthan, and Mary a little later was sent to *Karunaillayam* at Kilinochchi. Their silks became dresses of dull coloured printed cotton. They discarded their high-heeled shoes and they slipped their feet into locally

Habarana Rest House

made slippers. They even went barefoot like the northerners and felt more comfortable walking on the cool cemented floors. Like the locals their footwear was always kept neatly on the front verandah of their homes and worn when they left their homes, to tread the hot earth and roads.

Elizabeth and Mary were in charge of the homes of the orphans and destitute. They received their stipends from abroad, which were sent through the main post office in Jaffna. They diligently credited their money to their savings books and would be thrifty in their spending. Very soon though their stipends were wholly taken out in cash and spent on the children and the homes which had little money. They themselves became selfless. At first they taught and preached to win souls for Christ, but later they were keen to bring up the young people in a Christian environment rather than to make them nominal Christians. They taught the girls the rudiments of housework, cooking and sewing and hoped that they would marry into their local community. They even acted as marriage brokers and gave a little cash and jewellery as dowry to the girls.

Mary was very industrious in earning more money for the home. She would get the young girls in the home to make cloth dusters, brooms and to weave baskets from palmyrah fronds. The train to Colombo stopped for her at an unscheduled spot, almost a jungle, near the home to help her load her things and get on board.

In Colombo she would take a rickshaw, which was packed with all the products and herself, and went to every Anglican school to sell them. These schools did buy them to help her home in spite of having had dozens of dusters and brooms in their school closets. Generosity of the south too maintained these homes.

The bicycle was the mode of transport for the missionaries. Mary did not think twice about tying a bag of cement to the pillion of her cycle and riding along lonely rural and jungle roads while she sang loudly and lustily the Tamil Christian lyrics which she knew so well. Her singing probably kept the wild animals away. Mary and Elizabeth hardly went home on leave. Their savings books and passports gathered dust. Passports were never renewed and probably the representatives of the Crown did not know that these British women were in the Jaffna peninsula and had been there for years. These missionaries would probably die in Jaffna, known and loved by the people of the north.

All these missionaries with their idiosyncrasies had with love and enthusiasm preached the gospel whenever an opportunity came by. The people of the north were tolerant of such preaching of their God, as the Hindus themselves believed in a Supreme being, though their way to him more circuitous. The missionaries' audiences always listened to their sermons, and we always wondered whether they did so because they may have thought that listening to them was good for the missionaries' souls! They were the last of the missionary Mohicans. In spite of their zeal some of the converts faced a lot of difficulty from their families. This was seen mostly at Vaddukodai with conversions at the American Mission. The new converts had not only to stand against the opposition of their parents, but, worse, were driven out of their homes. They would then be allowed to live in the mission compound and a sponsor looked for in Boston to finance their education. Invariably at their baptisms, they were given their sponsors' names.

I ate the pulp of the jak fruit yesterday and I instantly remembered the compound of our home in faraway Karainagar. There was a solitary jak tree in the midst of the mango trees of many varieties. The jak tree had larger spreading branches than the mango. Its large leaves had to compete for sunlight. The dry leaves fell fast and regularly. The ground beneath the tree looked untidy with these leaves but Kunchi would be glad to pick and spread them in the compost pit. The fruits appeared on the trunk of the tree and seemed to cling to it. If ripe and ready for plucking, I would see my aunts get ahead of the bats and squirrels who relished the fruits. The aunts smelt the fruit for its ripeness or gently tapped the fruit with their knuckles to hear the sound of a ripened fruit. Over the years they became experts at smelling and tapping these fruits before plucking them. The fruits were cut into segments and distributed to the relatives who looked forward to receive them. Each segment with its individual small fruits would be relished. Its sweetness on the tongue was so different to that of the mango.

More than us grandfather enjoyed eating the fruit with *puttu*, which was crumbled rice flour and scraped coconut flower steamed in a cylindrical, wooden, bamboo-shaped cooking vessel. The coconut was added after each handful of rice flour, and the whole looked pretty when the steamed *puttu* was pushed out of the bamboo.

Old events and people of the past make frequent appearances in my mind, unlike the people met yesterday. Grandfather made the greatest impression, as did David much later. I met David when I lived on the east coast. He was the son of an English priest, Rev. Paynter and a Sinhalese mother. David was a quiet, charming man. He was not a missionary but had a missionary zeal for the home founded by his family. This Paynter Home was the refuge of the unwanted and illegitimate children of the planters, mostly English or Scottish, and the local Indian labourers in the tea estates of the central hills. David had a wonderful artistic talent. He painted beautiful portraits of people he knew. He hardly painted scenery, but if he did so painted them only as a background to the portrait. He was a self-effacing young man when I first met him. He sold his paintings to friends and acquaintances. He sold them for much less money than he would have got for them at an exhibition of his paintings. Not a single painting had his signature. We had a couple of his paintings for many years.

His art was his life work and the money he earned was selflessly given to the home and the welfare of these waifs. David had a voracious appetite for reading, and the titles of the books included every type of reading material. I would be the happy borrower of his books. He would lend gladly, and I too would get lost in these books.

The children of the Paynter Home on reaching adulthood would be sent to a place in north India, almost at the foot of the Himalayas. The land was given years ago by the British who ruled India and a colony of these young adults set up home there. They were given Indian citizenship too. They married within or out of this colony and set up their own homes there. The Indian government later stopped further immigration of these orphans. This did not deter David from finding an alternative place for the school-leavers of the Paynter Home. David loved the east coast and its sea and he enjoyed it more as he was a good swimmer. He persuaded the government to give a few acres along the north coast road a few miles from Trincomalee. He built a home and started a farm with the help of the boys. A few chalets were built for their use and to be rented to tourists, whose money would help to maintain them. They were enterprising and struggled to grow vegetables, which became commercially viable. Unfortunately the civil war saw an end to their homes and their stay there.

I had left my home by then and lost touch with David, and much later came to know of his death. To me he was a most wonderful, true, selfless and kind man.

Now, much older, I still remember the old relatives and friends considered old by me when I was not. One of them, Chellacca, was an old and loved relative who was a regular visitor to our home, and when she did visit she would be persuaded and was willing to stay with us for a couple of months. She was never stuck for words, which were interrupted by bouts of hearty laughter. We had this gramophone, an HMV, with the emblem of a dog embossed on the trumpet of the player. This was our earliest record player. It had to be wound by hand and had a long, curved stainless steel arm with a sharp replaceable needle at its end. This arm had to be turned over and the needle placed and kept on the groove of the outer part of the record placed on the turntable, which then started to revolve and the music came to life. To us it was so modern. The records were mostly of Bing Crosby's songs. When not minded, my young son would start the player and, instead of placing a record on the turntable, kept his plastic horses and other animals on it and enjoyed seeing the toys go round till the machine unwound. Chellacca enjoyed this with him, she being at her age very childlike and childish.

From that simple machine we bought a large boxlike structure, the Radiogram, which held seven records on a steel rod that went through and above the turntable. The records were dropped gently and singly onto the turntable. Every manoeuvre was electrically operated. There was no more picking up of a needle from a flat orange-coloured metal box which contained more needles. This box of needles always came with the HMV record player.

Then there were the extremely old female acquaintances who would drop in for a little monetary help. A ten rupee note went a long way in those days. They would make it a monthly visit to collect this money and invariably brought with them, as a gift, a couple of mangoes or a quarter of a jak fruit from their gardens. I think of them with nostalgia and happiness as I do with my memories of my father-in-law, a mudaliyar in the *kachcheri* of the British. He too met David many times and held conversations with him in impeccable English and was very proud of his grasp of that language. My father-in-law, like my grandfather, was always dressed in an immaculate white *verti*, its shirt and shawl. My grandfather was physically more well-built and lighter skinned than he, but did not know English, not having had the opportunity to learn it. He was erudite in Tamil.

My grandfather was fastidious and took a long time to eat his meals, especially his midday lunch. I can still visualize him seated at the solid square table near the inner courtyard with his shiny brass plate and his beaked, water-filled brass tumbler set before him. The rice and curries were also in brass utensils. His way of eating lunch was typical of most northerners who had the time and leisure to do so.

He would start by savouring a mouthful of rice with one curry. This would be repeated with every non-gravy curry and there would be five of them if it was a vegetarian lunch, including the lentil dhal curry soaked in clarified butter. Rice and curries would be then mixed and eaten followed by rice eaten with a hot gravy curry. This was not all. He would eat the rice with *rasam*, the pepper water. Curds were always there for lunch. He would eat curds with rice, but since he had such a sweet tooth, he would also add sugar or jaggery to it. I was amazed at the amount of rice he ate! He topped it all with the perennial banana and told me that the banana was like a king. 'Everyone made room for him, even if the room of the stomach was over crowded.' He loved the mango and jak in their seasons. I would stay near him during lunch and was given tidbits from his plate.

He had the habit of talking of history, usually of the ancient past, and this would make time at table so much longer. Grandfather told me that the rock edicts of King Asoka mentioned the kingdoms of Chola, Pandya, Keralaputa and Tambapanni. The people of Salem and Coimbatore were described as tribes. In early AD, South India was divided into Chera, Chola and Pandyan kingdoms. Their language was Brahmi, a mixture of Tamil and Sanskrit. It was the Sangam period of two hundred years before Christ. The kingdoms lasted for three hundred years. The proximity of these kingdoms to Tambapanni, later called Lanka, made a great impact on Ceylon, especially on the northern regions.

The greatest and the most profitable exchange of people and goods was between Chera, the Malabar coast kingdom, and the Jaffna kingdom carved out of the former Tambapanni. The Chera king had a palmyrah fibre in his crown. Trade was brisk with cardamoms, Calicut tiles and bananas named *kappal*, which in Tamil meant it came by boat, and these were exchanged in Ceylon for cinnamon, tobacco, cloves and cloth. The attire of the cloth and jacket came from Chera and was worn by the young females for comfort and convenience. For the sake of modesty a piece of cloth was thrown over the left shoulder and to keep the right arm free. The females however were not allowed to leave their homes dressed like this. It was quickly replaced in the north by the sari, probably from the Chola kingdom, which was regarded as the more modest attire.

The commonest link, recalled my grandfather, was the cuisine. Rice was common to both, but the Cheras introduced the other meals like *puttu*, stringhoppers and hoppers, all of them made of rice flour. They needed moulds, steamers and pans. In Jaffna, coconut milk was added to the hopper while cooking and this speciality, called a milk hopper, and was usually eaten with jaggery. The use of coconut milk in making a variety of vegetable curries was a speciality of the Cheras. However, the greatest difference was the red chillie and its powder added to the curries in the northern peninsula. Chillies were not indigenous to the Malabar Coast. The Portuguese introduced it from South America to India and Ceylon. The Ceylonese relished it and made the curries hot and hotter.

The *kool* was a culinary speciality of the north and east. It was a convenient way of eating fish and vegetables together rather than separately in curries. It was really a broth of fish, fish heads and all varieties of shell fish, cooked in a large pot of water. Palmyrah yam flour was used instead of rice to thicken it. For nutrients and to be tastier, beans, jak seeds and leaves of the drumstick tree were added to the broth. Saffron was the preferred spice, used in greater quantity than other spices in the broth. Most loved eating the broth but a few disliked it. It was considered tastier if it was eaten seated round the pot under a mango tree and from a cup made from a part of large palmyrah frond. The other types of food came from other parts of India and very much later. Another favourite food was the fish dish *theeyal*, which literally meant cooking the fish with plenty of tamarind over a low fire for a longer time. This was a Chera speciality.

Though the Chola, also named Pallava, and the Pandya kingdoms had their seaports, the Chera had most of the foreign trade. Wrought iron lamps and wine were brought to her port by the *yavanas*, the foreigners of Rome and Greece.

The Pandyan kingdom had a great influence on the jewels we wore. The *padakkams* were of their workmanship. The Pandyan kingdom had contact not only with the north, but with the southern Kandyan kingdom as well. The Chola kingdom was always at war with the other kingdoms, especially the Pandyan kingdom. The kingdoms of Lanka always joined hands with the Pandyans and never with the Cholas. With the war treaties there were many marriages between the royal families of the Pandyan kingdom and those of the Kandyan kingdom. This saw the appearance of the Pandyan jewels, especially the *padakkams* among the Kandyans. They were usually worn by royalty on a gold chain or on a baser metal chain if worn by a commoner. Pearl chains were rare.

When the Pandyan king Chakravarthi ruled Jaffna he built the first temple at Nallur. Nallur was the name of a town in his homeland. A palace was built within the temple premises and later used by king Sangili, but he destroyed it before the Portuguese could when he fled from them.

The Cholas were always warmongering, but at the same time introduced the different types of attire and the exquisite Hindu architecture to the temples of the north and south of Ceylon. Tanjavur was the cultural centre of the Chola kingdom. The Cholas were great seafarers and took Hinduism and their temple architecture to the east as far as Bali via Bangkok. Hinduism was later replaced by Buddhism and then by Islam except in Bali. All three South Indian Kingdoms fought each other but never allowed Jainism or Buddhism to take firm root in South India or north Ceylon.

So said grandfather, as I too had lunch with him. The lunch seemed to have taken ages. Then, on another day, he told me that in spite of the three Hindu kingdoms, the Portuguese made a dent in the Hindu religious beliefs of the locals and introduced Christianity.

My memory takes me back to the *valavu* of our village and the gathering of the young unmarried females prior to any celebratory event. They may have been dressed in a variety of attire but a constant feature was the black *pottu* on their foreheads. Each household had its own cleaned half shell of a coconut layered inside with a black glistening hard thick surface. This was made of burnt and then boiled sago, which then became a thick mess that was poured to line the shell. It hardened immediately. When a *pottu*, the black round mark was required, a little water was rubbed on to that hard surface and the thick liquid was put on the forehead. The perfect round *pottu* was made with the ball of the forefinger. This black *pottu* was seen on infants of both sexes and thereafter on the young females till marriage. With marriage the mark became red with *kumkumam*, a red powder, and an additional red *pottu* was made on the parting of the hair above the forehead. The men came back from the temple with a sandalwood or *kumkumam pottu*. Grandfather said that a *pottu* on any infant's forehead deflected the gaze of a visitor from the infant's face and with it removed the effects of an admiring 'evil eye.' In the adult the *pottu* should remind both, the person putting on herself and anyone looking at it, of the spiritual eye within us that makes us discern between good and evil. This he said was more important than the physical eyes; this inner eye was referred to as the third eye of god Siva.

I remember the many hymns we sang in church and at home. They became so familiar that they were impressed on my memory. One of many favourite hymns was:

Thy will be done
My God my father while I pray
Far from my home on life's rough way
O teach me to from my heart to pray
Thy will be done.

Though dark my path and sad my lot
Let me be still and murmur not
O breathe the prayer divinely taught
Thy will be done.

What though in lonely grief I sigh
For friends beloved no longer nigh
Submissive would I still reply
Thy will be done.

If thou shouldst call me to resign
What most I prize, it was never mine.
I only give thee what is thine,
Thy will be done.

****

Bibliography

Abeyasinghe, Tikiri, *Jaffna Under the Portuguese*, a Stamford Lake Publication, Colombo, 2005.

Arumugan, Thiru, *Nineteenth Century American Medical in Missionaries in Jaffna Ceylon*, MR Publications, South Asian Studies Centre, Sydney, 2009.

Baldeus, Phillipus, *True and Exact Description of the Grand Island of Ceylon*, Janossonius Waesberge, 1672.

Brohier, R.L., *Seeing Ceylon*, Sooriya Publications, Colombo, 1965.

Cave, H.W., *The Book of Ceylon*, Cassell and Company Ltd., London, 1908.

Cave, H.W., *Ceylon along Railway Tracks*, Visidura Publications, 2003.

de Silva, C.R., *Ceylon under the British Occupation*, Vol. I-III, Colombo Apothecaries Co. Ltd., Colombo, 1942.

de Silva, K.M., *A History Sri Lanka*, (Vijitha Yapa Publications), Penguin Books, India, 2005.

de Silva, R.K., Beumer, W.G.M., *Photographs of Paintings from the Illustrations and Views of Dutch Ceylon*, Serendib Publications, London, 1988.

Holmes, Dr. W. Robert, *Jaffna*, Christian Institute for the Study of Religion and Society, 1978-1980.

Indrapala, K., *The Evolution of an Ethnic Identity*, Vijitha Yapa Publications, Colombo.

Nelson, W.A., The Dutch Forts of Sri Lanka, Canongate Publicity ltd., Scotland, 1984.

Peebles, Prof. Patrick, *The History of Sri Lanka*, Greenwood Press, West Port CT USA, 2006.

Steuart, James, *An Account of the Pearl Fisheries of Ceylon*, Church Mission Press, 1843.

Printed in Great Britain
by Amazon